People of **COAL TOWN**

BY HERMAN R. LANTZ

WITH THE ASSISTANCE OF

J. S. MCCRARY

Southern Illinois University Press
Carbondale and Edwardsville

Feffer & Simons, Inc.
London and Amsterdam

COPYRIGHT © 1958, 1971 *by* Herman R. Lantz
All rights reserved
Reprinted by arrangement with Herman R. Lantz
Arcturus Books edition October 1971
This edition printed by offset lithography
  in the United States of America
International Standard Book Number 0-8093-0531-3

To Judy

for her effort and faith

PREFACE TO THIS EDITION

WHEN *People of Coal Town* was published in 1958 several questions were asked by reviewers. The questions raised implications of life in a local community for the larger society. Some reviewers felt that discussions of violence during the history of the community were interesting but of little relevance to the present. Other reviewers asserted that covert community tensions in the racial and ethnic area were of local interest only. Still other reviewers commented that community life in America was happier and more peaceful than the Coal Town experience would suggest. As one sociologist remarked, "America is no longer a violent society." Violence, it was noted, was characteristic of a prior period, the by-products of economic tensions, earlier movements of blacks into our cities, and the introduction of Europeans from earlier decades. One need hardly stress that these views about the nature of American society were incorrect, and one must ask why some sociologists found it difficult to accept the potentiality for discontent and for racial and ethnic disturbances, phenomena that now are of such great concern to Americans. Moreover, one may ask why so few sociologists were able to anticipate the violence that ensued in the next decade? The question has many answers, but two are of special interest to the writer.

Such misperceptions are likely to arise in a context in which the dominating sociological concerns center on the study of processes leading to order, adjustment, stability, equilibrium. This orientation is furthered when sociologists see their role as one whose main objective is to assist society with ways of achieving accommodation and order. Impetus was given to this perspective when sociologists became self-conscious about the scientific status of their discipline in the post-World War II period, a period when we moved rapidly into programs in which quantitative measures of sociological analysis became significant in the training of graduate students. My remarks here are not intended as any general criticism of quantitative methods in sociology, a subject which has been debated ad nauseam. It goes without saying that such training is essential. Moreover, many leaders and exponents of quantitative methods are not only aware of the limitations of quantitative training, but they are also sensitive to the varying ways in which sociological data may be obtained and processed. But intended or not, sociologists may have paid a price. Large numbers of them looked upon nonquantitative studies as being something less than studies employing quantification. Such a view had the effect of encouraging the kind of research amenable to statistical manipulation, while discouraging other types. Given both an ideological orientation concerned with accommodation restricted to particular research techniques available, the net effect was to gather data which may not have been sufficiently sensitive to the ethos of community life. Note, for example, our failure to go beyond the significant contributions of the "Chicago School" in the 1930s, which was responsible for some of the richest and most insightful material sociology has produced. The works dealing with the City, the Homeless Man, the Marginal Man, the Gang, the Taxi Dance Hall, and the Prostitute remain classics, and continue to be the theoretical bases of further work.

Both the sociologist and public funding agencies have contributed to the neglect of studies sensitive to the conditions of life in these periods. Public funding agencies, which have a managerial view of society, saw in the sociologist both skill and perspective consistent with a managerial orientation. They were thus able to tap needs of sociologists and their departments — needs that were also related to the sociologists' insecurities and anxieties in an academic discipline. It is improbable that an investigator who suggested that he wanted to do an in-depth study about the tensions in the community without appropriate devices for quantitative measurement would have received much support from public funding agencies in the 1950s. It is ironic that these very public agencies, pragmatically oriented, emphasizing demonstration projects looking for particular patterns of research designs, were unaware of how their requirements might result in data lacking in sensitivity sufficient to understand the problems of community life. What took place is also a reflection of the involvement of the sociologist and the granting agencies in which perhaps neither were really free, each controlling the other, the one with funds and the other with research techniques. It is, of course, naive to assert that our insensitivity to the impending violence of the 1960s would have been remedied if only our research had been different. But one can always wonder.

The tensions that one may observe in many small community contexts, such as Coal Town, are in some ways a reflection of problems in the broader society, albeit that the problems of generalization are complex. The isolation of the community a century ago has disappeared; thus many of the elements of conflict in the broader society may be more readily felt at the local level. Yet there is every reason to believe that sociological concerns and writings dealing with the small community are decreasing. There has been a shift of sociological effort directed toward facilitating change and adjustment of groups to the massive problems of urban living. While there are occasional radical proposals for change, the overwhelming majority of proposals are those which seek changes within the scope and aims of contemporary bureaucratic, structural arrangements. But we are still in a stage in which we know relatively little about the dynamics of social change or about variables to change, and we are insufficiently informed about the consequences of change. The lessons from societies involved in large scale social planning, both in western and eastern Europe, testify to the many unresolved problems that remain.

In view of this state of affairs, it is all the more interesting that many social scientists plunged themselves into a change effort in the last decade. To raise the question of a need for change in view of the many social afflictions of our society and age is the responsibility of us all, and certainly to conceive and initiate possibilities of change is essential. But it may be time that some of us stopped running around behaving as though answers for some of the most complex questions of change rested simply on obtaining more financial support. Unless we do, we may be in danger of adding to the despair which now exists. For example, while espousing the significance and dominance of cultural and social patterns in explaining the life style of groups we have rejected the implications of such knowledge for underprivileged blacks and whites. Either sociologists do not seriously believe the data regarding the persistence of culture patterns and life style or they have somehow chosen to exclude large sections of our population.

Sociologists generally view poverty in terms of defects in the social structure, but some of us have failed to appreciate the full implications of culture patterns at two levels, the social and the personal. If the life experiences of people are associated with failure, is it not probable that the personality will protect itself by developing a perspective that encourages an orientation of acceptance and noninvolvement? Might such experiences be related to a social and cultural orientation in which resistances to change predominate? Moreover, how is a reversal of these patterns to be achieved, particularly when the classical model of the so-called "economic man" responding to opportunity may have little reality? Our inability to deal with this question may be a result of a value commitment in which many, especially the young generation of sociologists, have gone through a redefinition of role and see their role as implicated not in advocating change but a role in which change is precipitated through confrontation. Other sociologists may shy away from facing the complexities of change for fear of becoming labeled conservative.

And there is always the question of the funding agency, which usually operates with political considerations. Some years ago the writer heard an official declare that his agency had five years to learn how to eradicate poverty. What is the impact of such a policy on the kind of research that takes place? Coal Town represents a community which has suffered both socially and economically and has components of resignation—a phenomenon quite understandable given its history. The phenomena is noted in the writings of several people, although it is not always conceptualized as resignation.[1] Resignation represents a response to prolonged failure. In *People of Coal Town*, I was unable to delineate a theoretical perspective except in the most general and limited way; indeed, the concept of resignation itself needed and continues to receive much clarification.

[1] While the phenomenon of resignation may have a long history under other labels, there are several people who have had a significant role in its theoretical development. From a sociological perspective, the following works should be noted. *The Unemployed Workers of Marienthal* by Marie-Jahoda Lazersfeld and Hans Zeisel (Vienna: Socio-Economic Institute, 1933) is a significant landmark in identifying and delineating the concept of resignation. More recent efforts include: Elmora Matthews, *Neighbor and Kin in a Tennessee Ridge Community* (Nashville, Tennessee: Vanderbilt University Press, 1966); Harry Caudill, *Night Comes to the Cumberlands* (New York: Little Brown, 1963); Oscar Lewis, *Five Families: Mexican Case Studies in the Culture of Poverty* (New York: Basic Books, 1959); Carl Bridenbaugh, *Myths and Realities* (Baton Rouge, Louisiana: Louisiana State University Press, 1952): Charles C. Hughes, *et al., People of Cove and Woodlot* (New York: Basic Books, 1960 [Chapter V]); Jack E. Weller, *Yesterday's People* (Lexington, Kentucky: University of Kentucky Press, 1965); Michael Harrington, *The Other America* (New York: McMillan, 1962). Each of these books is important because each deals with the phenomenon of resignation in a different cultural context. All of these suggest an association between the development of resignation and socio-economic failure.

At least two psychoanalysts have contributed significantly to our understanding of resignation at the intrapsychic level, Karen Horney and Ralph Harris. Karen Horney was important in the formulation of the concept; she also suggested an outline of the dynamics of resignation. Ralph Harris, as a practicing psychoanalyst, has extended the meaning and utility of resignation. Horney's views on resignation may be found in *Neuroses and Human Growth* (New York: W. W. Norton, 1950, Chapter XI). Harris' views may be found in talks before the American Institute for Psychoanalysts in New York. Unfortunately, this gifted theoretician and practitioner has not been concerned with publishing his insights.

xii   PREFACE TO THIS EDITION

My current research on resignation is being conducted in co-operation with Ernest Alix. Our effort is centered around developing analytic distinctions between resignation and other possibly related concepts such as anomie and alienation. We are also studying the relationship of resignation both as a general concept with implication for the change process and resignation in relation to specific areas of life, education, and work. One major investigation involving the development of a scale to measure resignation to predict performance on job retraining has been completed, but further work remains. Our work has proceeded along four dimensions of resignation which appear consistent in the accounts of people with resigned patterns. These include detachment from others, lack of commitment, aversion to work, and restriction of hopes. A fuller discussion of the resigned syndrome may be found in a chapter prepared by the author in *Blue-Collar World,* edited by Arthur Shostack and William Gomberg (Prentice-Hall, 1964, pp. 258–70), and in a forthcoming volume, *A Community in Search of Itself* (Southern Illinois University Press, 1971).

The theoretical and applied significance of resignation as a socially-induced resistance to social change is perhaps best seen in the significant pockets of chronic unemployment and areas of chronic poverty. These areas have always existed in America. Note, for example, that in data compiled by the Area Development Administration of the U.S. Department of Commerce in the 1960s there is an analytic picture of areas designated as having "continuous substantial unemployment." Under this category one finds substantial areas of Maine, New York, Pennsylvania, West Virginia, Ohio, Tennessee, Illinois, Indiana, Michigan, Wisconsin, Minnesota, Idaho, Washington, Arizona, New Mexico, Texas, Louisiana, Mississippi, Georgia, Alabama, South Carolina, Oklahoma, Arkansas, and Missouri.[2] Poverty among substantial sections of our population has been so continuous that it is no longer simply an economic matter. Equally

[2] U.S. Economic Development Administration, "Qualified Areas," July 1, 1966, in Washington, D.C.

important are the social and psychological resistances to change, resistances based on fears and uncertainties of the future. These remarks should not be construed to mean that people prefer to remain poor. It does mean that they may be caught in social and psychological patterns which are obstacles in their efforts to change economic status.

No effort was made to restudy Coal Town in any systematic fashion in preparation for this paperback edition of the book. I have talked with many residents over the years, and have felt that there is no reason to believe that the themes and ideologies noted at the end of this book have changed substantially. A good many of the youth have been able to transcend life in the community, others have remained and accepted life as it is. What has happened to these people during the last decade? First, like many other communities in America, they have been unable to produce changes which would have made life very different. They remain peripheral to the economy, and they are among the first to feel economic decline. Moreover, they have been unable to cope with the pace of change; therefore they may be receding into the past at an accelerated rate. The problem is neither that of intelligence in the abstract nor that of motivation in any simple way. Efforts to produce change in a context in which the community's future is controlled by economic forces beyond its control is excessively difficult, although the very existence of any resignation complicates the process of change. I am much less convinced today than I was when this book originally appeared that communities who are peripheral to the economy can recover without some massive and systematic intervention on the part of the state or federal government. Efforts far greater than those we have at present are needed. But this process involves not only basic changes in political and economic ideology; it also requires considerable political effort. Unfortunately, these communities who are peripheral to the economy are also those who have never developed politically and, hence, are lacking in significant power. The nature of a competitive and changing economy inevitably carries with it a

"fall out." The results are communities with an outmoded
economic base, unable to change and compete with the rest of
the society. These become our pockets of chronic unemployment
and poverty.

Some sociologists have suggested that the more recent economic concentration of wealth and technology in the large urban
community has aggravated the difficulties of the small community. The notion that the dominance of the small community
by the large community is a recent development is, in my judgment, not correct. I believe that a re-examination of the history
of the last century may indicate that such factors as local prices
bore a significant relationship to price setting in the larger urban
community. The accounts in nineteenth-century newspapers are
replete with complaints of shopkeepers about citizens who
did not patronize the local community and complaints from
local citizens about high prices in the local community which
forced them to shop in the nearby urban community. Changes
in the production of goods in the urban community of the nineteenth century probably had a significant effect on the smaller
communities of the period.

There has always been a problem of differential rates of development both within a society and between societies. Such
differential development within a society has resulted in the
less successful sections of a country becoming a burden on the
successful. The answer has invariably been some form of social
planning, although we in America vacillate more than most
industrialized nations on this point. Yet the nature of a dynamic
economy is such that differential growth is inevitable. The
typical economic plight of the small community has often been
one of avoiding a large capital investment in the production of
commodities which were soon to become obsolete because of
changes at the broader economic level. In Coal Town and the
surrounding region we have a good illustration of an area which
has seldom been fully linked with the larger economy. For some
years the production of coal produced such a link, but new fuels
emerged, and technological displacement of men created serious

difficulties. In this sense one can speak of rejection from the economy. One finds such rejection expressed through chronic unemployment and all of the social-psychological by-products. Such by-products have been cumulative, and are especially important in understanding the responses of area residents to the disturbances at Southern Illinois University in the spring of 1970.

The rapid expansion and development of Southern Illinois University since 1948 represented an effort to produce social change in an area that was depressed, economically and culturally. It was anticipated that over an extended period of time the University would have an effect on the economic and social development of the region. While many persons from the area were ambivalent about the role and significance of the University, there was tremendous pride in its growth, since it was compensatory for the many shortcomings that were felt. In the spring of 1970 the University was closed because of student disturbances. Sentiment in the area ran deep, and there were rumors of counter-reactions from some groups of citizens. While resentment was directed toward several elements of the University, most of the resentment was directed toward students. There may be several interesting reasons. First, as is the case in other sections of America, student rioting was seen as a rejection of the older generation, but such rejection may have provoked greater resentment from a population which had already experienced considerable economic and social rejection by the larger society. The fact that students may have reacted in part to our involvement in Vietnam really did not help, since the native probably saw this as an attack on his patriotism.

If students at the University justified their actions on the basis of frustration and the absence of legitimate channels for the expression of their discontent, the citizens of the area may have felt their own frustrations based on their economic and social history in which few in the larger society have listened or cared. The resentment of area residents was aggravated by a tendency to view students as coming from economically secure homes, in contrast to their own more underprivileged children. Thus, one suspects that native resentment focused on a situation which for them symbolized rejection at several levels: the age level, the economical level, and the social and cultural level. If one examines this theme in broader perspective one basis for the so-called "silent majority" in America may emerge. These communities which we have created and for which we are responsible are the products and the price we have had to pay for the very success of our society in broader economic and social terms. Yet they represent also the results of inevitable inequities, which cannot be measured solely in economic terms. They have to be seen in terms of our response to them. By not listening to the problems expressed or by not taking them seriously we often show our disdain for what appears to be, in intellectual terms, "a lack of development."

If these rather large and substantial sections of our country cannot identify economically, socially, or culturally they will search for those values with which they can identify. In this context, ideologies embedded in "Americanism" and "patriotism" become important. Identification with them is not dependent on the amount of education, social class, and wealth; identification is open to all. These values become a sustaining link to the larger society in a context in which other sustaining ties, economic and social, become increasingly fragmented. Given provocation, there may be a harsh response to those perceived as threatening "patriotism." Communities, like individuals, will not endure indefinitely a state of "not belonging," but will move toward a resolution. In a society in which many people feel they have no place because they have not been able to keep pace with the changing economic and cultural shifts, there may be a move to those values not already usurped by others. In some circles concerned with political ideology, fears about moves to the political right are too often explained in simplistic terms: the result of isolation and poor education. But in some ultimate sense the problem is one of how the larger society can remain in touch with its rejected sub-sections. The

1960s have provided us with illustrations of complexities and dilemmas that are involved. These regions and communities are often treated like the poor relative who comes knocking at the door; gradually he realizes that he is not really welcome. Sometimes the poor relative stops knocking and remains at home; the tragedy is restricted to the family. But he may also go knocking on other doors, sometimes even on the wrong doors, and this may lead to more encompassing tragedy.

I am grateful to colleagues, friends, and many students from the area for their helpful comments and appreciation of *People of Coal Town* in the period since the original publication of this book in 1958. In this connection, I should like to mention Ralph Harris, Charles Snyder, Walter Taylor, Charles Lange, Oscar Handlin, Wilson Record, Al Clarke, Mel Tumin, Arthur Vidich, Dave Pittman, Ernest Alix, Frank Nall, Sid Aronson, Dan Piper, August Hollingshead, and the late Clyde Kluckholn. None of these people are in any sense responsible for the problems and limitations of this manuscript.

H. R. L.

Southern Illinois University
March 1, 1971

CONTENTS

People of COAL TOWN

CHRONOLOGY OF EVENTS FOR COAL TOWN

1804	First settlement in area near MacTrela
1900	Work begun on sinking Coal Town Mine Number One
1904	Workers pour into the coal camp
1904–1914	The coal camp era
1904–1922	Period of lawlessness
1908	Strike started in the spring
1908–1910	The two-year strike
1910	Swift Mining Company takes charge of Coal Town Mine Number One under a royalty agreement
1914	Coal Town incorporated
1918	First organized religious services
1918	Swift Mining Company opened Coal Town Mine Number Two
1918	Private property could be purchased in Coal Town
1918–1925	Formative period of separate threefold class system for native and immigrant
1922–1931	Period of intermittent lawlessness
1925	Initial signs of economic decline
1940	The World War II boom
1948	Rapid economic decline
1948	Coal Town Mine Number One closed
1956	Coal Town Mine Number Two closed

CHAPTER 1

INTRODUCTION

THE need for basic research in the natural sciences has long been recognized. Of equal significance if social science is to develop is the need for basic research into the personal and social processes of human existence. This need is recognized by social scientists and its recognition is manifest in their orientation and conception of social research. The study reported here is in line with this development; in the pages to follow a description and an analysis of life, past and present, in a coal-mining community will be offered.

The particular form of this analysis, the community study, represents a type of research which has had considerable appeal both for the professional social scientist and for the layman. For the professional the possibilities of the richness afforded by seeing life in a total setting are intriguing. For the layman these studies possess a vitality and zest which make their characters come to life and unfold a quality which is moving and real. Further, the community study, quite apart from any professional merits, is a potent way of communicating basic social science insights, and it takes what may normally be for the untrained observer a dull scheme of jargon and integrates this into a dynamic system providing insights into living people. Throughout the development of this study we have been conscious of the potentialities for the fullest realization of our data and we have tried to communicate our findings in a way which would be meaningful to our colleagues as well as to the layman.

It is difficult to tell when any particular study crystallizes in the mind of the investigator. For some social scientists the many pressures to pursue research create a need consciously to seek out problem areas for study. Such a need in so far as we can tell does not underlie the present study. Instead the interest was an emergent one which developed with our observations of life in coal-mining communities over a number of years. Here were communities which had been thriving industrial towns, with hope and a future, with a vast melting pot of persons possessing different nationalities and creeds. Here there had been a history of people who had initiated efforts at developing a way of life. Today much of this has disappeared. The economic base has been removed and where once the soil which nourished hope was present there are only the ashes and dust of time-spent years and the memories of the past embodied in those who remain. Here, we might say, was a chapter in American history which needed recording, and so like the artist exhilarated by the undertaking of a new painting, we projected a plan and started its implementation.[1]

THE PROBLEM

In a formal sense we might say that the present study is an analysis of a coal-mining community which is typical of an area with respect to economic base, the ethnic origins of settlements, and the way of life that emerged. It is a study in the rise of social organization and subsequent developments of such organization including the following:

a. The patterns of economics, law, government, religion, family, education, and recreation.

b. The values that emerged out of the framework listed above.

c. The quality of interpersonal life which characterized the community and the resultant personality configurations present during prosperity and decline.[2]

[1] This project was sponsored and completely supported by the Graduate School, Southern Illinois University. The total expenditure including salaries of various kinds was approximately $8,000. The research team included two professional social scientists, one professional newspaperman, and four graduate assistants, working over a period of four years.

[2] In all research, whether concerned with social man or the nature of the physical world, demands are increasingly made for practical applications. These

Throughout the analysis an attempt was made to relate life in Coal Town with life in the larger society and to observe, as well as record, the common ethos which appeared. We were to learn that although Coal Town possessed certain features unique to its development, many of the more basic processes and developments were and are characteristic of American society. We shall pursue this central theme throughout our analysis.

SELECTION OF THE COMMUNITY

We surveyed a number of different communities prior to our selection of Coal Town. Our search was dictated by a set of four requirements we had established, and Coal Town was selected because it met all of these.

1. It was a community that has gone through a period of rapid expansion, prosperity, and decline and has, during its history, experienced social and economic changes typical of coal-mining communities in the region.

2. The community of Coal Town is of recent origin (incorporation date 1914). Thus its social history and subsequent analysis could be constructed with a high degree of accuracy. Further source materials in the form of newspaper documents, census figures, statistics of births, deaths, marriages, and divorces were readily available for examination.

3. The total population is sufficiently small (population 2,300) so that the community could be studied intensively. Further, mem-

---

demands have been so persistent in recent years that many scientists have turned away from the study of basic life processes and redirected their energies toward the study of specific problem areas and their amelioration. At the outset of this project our attention was focused on basic community processes without concern for the question of application. Nevertheless, as our data unfolded, considerable knowledge emerged regarding the problems of social change and rehabilitation for one-industry communities. Knowledge, for example, which pointed to problems in producing changes and insights pointing to the direction of change appeared. Thus we observed that the development of a set of basic data was in reality the most expeditious way of understanding the nature of certain community problems.

4 INTRODUCTION

bers of many of the families who lived through the rise and decline
of the community were living and available for interview.

4. The ethnic make-up of the community included groups typical
of coal-mining communities in the region.

THE SETTING

The community of Coal Town is located in the southeastern section of Marshall County in a state known for its coal production.
(See Figure 1.) It is thirty miles from the county seat of Hartdale.
Five miles southeast one finds Nobility, twelve miles north one finds
New America, six miles north is Frenchtown. The nearest metropolitan community, Riverview, is two hundred miles northeast and
is the important marketing center in the region. The principal industry in the immediate vicinity is coal mining.

Streets in Coal Town are generally wide and well paved. The
homes are modest and have been given good care. Considerable
pride is taken in small flower and vegetable gardens. Most homes
are wooden frame, many possess an imitation brick siding in
vogue some twenty years ago. This community, similar to other
coal-mining communities, has been in a state of economic decline
for the past twenty-five years. The present population of 2,300 has
a disproportionate number of older people, with young persons
moving away for greater opportunities. Business and trade, except
in one or two instances, have been declining for many years with
the most devastating reduction occurring since 1948.

THE METHOD

The methods we employed in order to pursue our interests included the techniques usually found in social science endeavors of
this type. We studied newspapers,[3] court records, mental hospital
statistics, and other indices of community life.[4] We developed
schedules for collecting data and employed I.B.M. cards to record

[3] See Appendix A for a critical evaluation of newspaper files.
[4] See Public Records section of Appendix A.

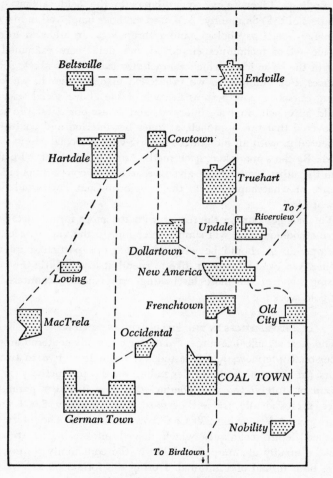

FIGURE 1. MARSHALL COUNTY

the findings. Likewise we spent hours in the field talking with members of the community.[5] We used methods employed in history, sociology, social psychology, and anthropology. In addition to any specific set of techniques employed, our data were examined in light of the basic ideas which characterize each of the above social sciences. For example, as we proceeded in our research, we kept asking ourselves how persons in each of the above social sciences would approach, analyze, interpret, and assess our data. We soon discovered that this approach, at times bewildering and confusing, presented us with an integrated, holistic view of social life in Coal Town. By the same token, each method and point of view isolated from the other would have given us at best a compartmentalized picture of what happened to the people of Coal Town and their way of life.[6]

We shall not burden the reader with the more formal details of our methodology but will simply refer him to the various sections of Appendix A should he wish to pursue this particular interest further. We would, however, like to spend at least a little time discussing some of the more fascinating experiences encountered in our field work.

OUR EXPERIENCES IN THE FIELD—THE INTERVIEW

The most significant source of data for our study centered around a personal interview, which lasted anywhere from two to twenty hours (at different periods) depending on the productivity of the informant. Interviews were conducted over a two-year period by three professionally trained persons. Approximately 2,000 hours were spent interviewing 250 Coal Town residents.[7] The interviews entailed depth techniques which delved into feelings, attitudes, and the quality of interpersonal life in the community. Interviews were both formal and informal. During the formal interviews one of the members of the interviewing team initiated the discussion

[5] Prior to the writing of each chapter the writer developed an outline of the dominant themes uncovered in these interviews. Inevitably such a process led to a filtering out of some themes which were part of life in the community. We believe that no essential patterns were lost in this process.

[6] See Frames of Reference section of Appendix A.

[7] See Appendix A for a description of the sample interviewed.

while the other member recorded responses verbatim. Informal interviews were largely the result of conversations with community residents which stemmed from casual meetings. Material derived from such conversations was later formally organized and written up.[8]

We were able to contact interviewees by initially getting in touch with well-known leaders in the community and by explaining to them the purposes of our research. They in turn suggested other persons whom we might contact. In addition to this procedure, two other persons, possessing rapport with certain sections of the community, were put on the payroll. They were sent out to contact members of the community in order to explain to them the purposes of our research. One name led to another and in each instance the interviewee knew about our research and our interest in obtaining an interview prior to our arrival. We found that, whenever possible, placing natives on the payroll increased our rapport with members in the community. It signified that money was being brought into the community and this was interpreted as a sign of our interest in them. The training of each member of the interviewing team was crucial. All our efforts could prove meaningless without proper personnel. In part this was a problem of professional training in human behavior science, but more significant than formal training were the sensitivities of each investigator to the informant, without which the interview could become worthless. For example, in many instances responses from informants were direct and obvious as to meaning. At other times, however, it was necessary to "listen with the third ear" in order to capture the essence and significance of the

[8] All material derived from formal and informal interviews was checked, cross-checked, and rechecked in succeeding interviews. Conversation centered around the following topics: age, marital status, religion, nativity, occupation, years of employment, working conditions, occupational attitudes, occupational hazards, fears, occupational backgrounds of parents, nativity of parents, years of residence in community, community life at time of arrival, lawlessness, bootlegging, gambling, vice, prostitution, fraud, corruption, mechanics of local government and problems, economic disputes, history of churches and religious activity, family life, family rule, family patterns, interpersonal relations in community, community values, education, curriculum, ethnic groups, interaction of ethnic groups, food habits, marriages, intermarriages, divorce, social activities, clubs, general social structure, social organization, social values, and social change.

informant's remarks. Often this procedure enabled us to arrive at new leads and insights and to move our understandings to newer and deeper levels of community life. For example, as the interviewing proceeded, we wondered whether the question of mining safety was tied to the irresponsibility of the miner. This moved us to ask specific questions about safety in the mine. We discovered that both management and labor shared responsibility for accidents. One miner had this to say:

The miner is supposed to follow safety rules but you couldn't get any damn work done if you followed those safety rules. Besides, if you did follow them, the boss would fire you and there is no regard for safety at all. For instance, you're not supposed to smoke down in the mine but I always took two packs of cigarettes every day and then four or five extras and I would smoke any time I got ready to. But what some of those jackasses would do would be to sneak off in some abandoned room and smoke and if you smoke there, there would be apt to be gas and you'd get blowed up. If they would be brave about it and smoke out in the open there wouldn't be danger, but those bastards would always go back in there and smoke in one of those abandoned rooms and that would cause trouble.

Many times chance or inadvertent remarks provided clues. At other times, hunches derived from the general trend of a conversation suggested new leads. We discovered that allowing the informant to follow his own associations frequently afforded us a community material to which the particular informant was sensitive. The inner resources of the informant presented us with an opportunity to explore insights which were in one sense part of his unique perceptions. We believed that from such a process the quality of our material would be enriched and the boundaries of our knowledge extended. All of this made it necessary to maintain a flexible schedule capable of shifts as dictated by our empirical experiences with informants and data.

OUR PROBLEMS IN THE FIELD

The research team attempted informally to immerse themselves into segments of community life and into the patterns of interaction. For example, we soon found ourselves exchanging gifts with some of the residents and on some occasions received dinner invitations. We hoped that out of such interaction we might develop an appreciation for the feeling tones that pervaded human relationships in Coal Town. Nevertheless, we discovered that among certain groups a failure to maintain our identity as university researchers almost resulted in a loss of rapport with our informants.

For example, one of the common patterns of interaction among community members centered around the ability to "take a joke" and to "return a joke." Often many of these jokes possessed destructive, sadistic undertones, a problem to be discussed more completely in other sections. During one of our informal interactions with a group in the community one of the informants kept kidding the interviewing team. He remarked that teachers are lazy, have nothing to do, and are essentially impractical. Soon a stillness came over the group as this informant pressed for advantage, which in this instance would have meant humiliation for the research team. At a crucial point in the interaction the informant blurted out, "You fellows are probably overpaid, how much do you bastards make, anyway?"

"That's none of your business," replied one of the researchers.

The informant stated, "Well, that's no way to talk to a taxpayer, now is it?"

The reply was, "That's the way to talk to you."

The researchers immediately sensed a positive change in the feeling tone of the group. A smile came over the members as they looked at the aggressive informant. Had the researcher not responded as he did, the team might well have lost rapport with that particular group. Subsequent interactions confirmed our hunch that we had gained the respect of the group. We discovered later that we were able to maintain our rapport by effectively counteracting the informants' attempt to be derisive. By so doing we maintained our identity as academicians able to defend ourselves.

The role of self-effacement in community rapport. As we proceeded with our research we were struck by the attitudes of self-effacement and self-contempt which many residents of Coal Town displayed. This became manifest in their tendency to belittle themselves, to speak in disparaging terms about themselves, their neighbors, and their local institutions. Thus for certain sections of Coal Town citizenry any attempt on the part of the researcher to identify with local patterns brought with it initially an impersonal familiarity followed by a lowering of prestige, and finally contempt. Put colloquially, "If one could be like them, he couldn't be much." We soon learned that what was necessary for real rapport was not a wholehearted immersion into the values and patterns of community life but instead marginal participation which involved understanding about when and when not to identify with group values. Throughout the range of interviewing experience we preserved a tenuous balance between identification with community life and the maintenance of our personal identities as human beings. Needless to say, rapport was difficult to establish, and such difficulty was rooted in the basic apprehension of these people regarding interpersonal involvements. Our analysis of this community has led us to the belief that a native of the community would have had equal difficulty breaking through the psychological barriers which the residents of Coal Town possessed.

The role of suspiciousness in community rapport. The response of the community as a whole was cautious but friendly. Many were suspicious of our motives, purposes, intent. With the assurance that personal names would not be identified and the locale of the community would remain a secret, acceptance became more manifest. Nevertheless, an undertone of suspiciousness pervaded a good many of our interviews. In some instances it was marked and overt, in others covert and subdued. It constituted for us the most serious obstacle and made it exceedingly difficult to penetrate the surface of community life. The following illustration will point out the nature of the difficulty we encountered. One merchant who had welcomed us at the outset became increasingly suspicious about our activities over a period of time. He confronted us with his feelings and suggested that others in the community felt the same way. He stated that for grown men, our research activity did not constitute real work; it seemed childish; we could certainly discover all there was to know about Coal Town by talking to any six people at random. Since, however, we were spending so much time at this project there must be some sinister motive behind our activity. Put bluntly, our research activity was a cover-up for something else, possibly a business swindle. Since we were driving cars bearing the University name, we asked whether this was not sufficient proof of our affiliation and our intent. The answer, "How do I know you fellows didn't paint the name of a university on the car yourself?" We offered to show University identification cards. The answer, "How do I know you didn't have them printed yourself?" As the discussion proceeded our informant revealed a pervasive suspiciousness regarding the motives and intent of various persons and national groups. Such suspiciousness extended to persons holding top govermental positions as well as their subordinates. Our informant had acquired a vague rumor regarding the bribing of FBI agents, and he was eager to use this rumor as justification that trusted government employees could be bribed.

Relationships with some community members were often tenuous and difficult to predict; moods seemed to fluctuate. At times informants, previously friendly and productive, would "clam up" and behave sullenly; only to become friendly again at some later date. Some were afraid that the community might be hurt. Others were simply fearful of digging up old scandals in which they were involved. In some cases informants whom the researchers tried to befriend turned against them and became destructive. An illustration of this is to be found in the case of Mrs. X, a widow living by herself who received public assistance.

One of the researchers became personally interested and concerned for the welfare of Mrs. X, whose personal history revealed her to be a lonely, unhappy individual with poor familial relationships. He took a few minutes each day to visit with her. Mrs. X reacted overtly with considerable pleasure whenever these visits occurred. She offered refreshments and always insisted that the researcher remain longer than originally planned. After a few such visits, however, it was discovered that Mrs. X was spreading destructive gossip about the researcher and the purpose of the research. She told neighbors that the researcher imposed on her time and was engaged in the practice of asking foolish questions about irrelevant matters.

The psychological motivations for Mrs. X's behavior are open to interpretation. It is certainly clear, however, that she was unable to accept the constructive efforts which were offered and had to distort the motives of the researcher.

Although suspiciousness constituted an obstacle in our interviews, it soon became a vital datum itself and opened up new leads of inquiry for us. This moved us to observe suspiciousness with a view toward understanding what in the personal and social life of the community had produced it. We were later to discover that suspiciousness was woven into the fabric of social life in Coal Town.[9]

And so we pursued our inquiry. Each confrontation was for the moment thwarting and frustrating. But with time each obstacle gave birth to new insights and avenues of direction. Finally each lead, each road which at some point dangled without form or unity, emerged into a whole—the story of the People of Coal Town.

[9] See Appendix A for typology of informants.

CHAPTER **2**

PREINDUSTRIAL SURROUNDINGS

AN understanding of the change that took place in Coal Town is rooted in the sociocultural history of the area prior to industrialization. Patterns and traditions already present foreshadowed consequences still to come. With these we will deal in the present chapter, as we outline the major historical factors pertinent to our study. The data cover the period 1800–1900 and were derived from historical documents and autobiographies, as well as selected interviews.

The majority of migrants who moved into Marshall County, prior to the discovery of coal, came from the hill country of the South.[1] The first settlement was established in 1804 about two and one-half miles southeast of MacTrela. The second settlement was organized in Old City in 1811. The county seat of Hartdale was founded in 1841. The majority of settlers were Old American of Scotch, Irish, and English mixture, representing the poor white element who had left a rocky, unproductive soil that was unable to afford them even a subsistence livelihood. Others from the more fertile southern areas were retreating under pressure from Negro slave labor. Still others were small farmers who refused to adapt to the plantation system, whether or not they owned slaves. An eighty-seven-year-old resident, speaking about her father's reasons for settling in this region prior to the Civil War, stated:

Our people came from Tennessee. They felt they had to get out of them rocks. It was so rocky, it was good for nuthin'. They got up here and they knew that they ought to have gone farther north, but this looked so good to them. Mister, this was no good for farming either.

[1] For a discussion of the small, economically secure group that settled in the area see Appendix B.

THE CULTURAL ORIENTATION

Life for the vast majority of these people was characterized by three major themes: resignation, violence, and superstition.

RESIGNATION

The settlements during most of the nineteenth century consisted of people who were devoid of any deep interest in large-scale agriculture and who made few demands on life. They enjoyed a casual, simple existence unhampered by pressures to accumulate wealth or property. The original settlers were attracted to the county because it possessed prairie land which could be inexpensively purchased and could immediately be settled without the difficult task of large-scale land clearing. It is not altogether clear why they failed to seek out an area which would be more conducive to personal subsistence. Many, however, have suggested that these people were easily threatened by a cultural milieu which necessitated change in their personal habits and mode of living. More ambitious farmers, with greater agricultural knowledge, refused to settle in this country and quickly moved on when the inadequacy of the land became apparent. Thus, the area was never really favored by the substantial, more stable farmer class, who settled in the southern and eastern sections of the state. Although Marshall County was one of the earliest sections to be settled in the state, it remained one of the most isolated and backward. Social changes have been slow, hampered by cultural inertia and resistance. Life is still very much the same for many of the descendants of the original settlers.

The economy of nineteenth-century agriculture. The tendency to be satisfied with little was not only an important motivational factor determining where these people settled but it also pervaded the economy. People made a submarginal living by raising grain, castor beans, hogs, and horses, the last of which were found in the wild state. Industry was practically nonexistent until the discovery of coal. An old settler stated:

Well, we raised corn and some wheat, not too much wheat and oats. Oh, if you had a little corn you could get fifteen cents a bushel for it, if someone would buy it. There wasn't much corn sold. Nobody didn't keep more stock than what they had to. They kept plenty of hogs. Back then a family never run without meat and lard hardly. They had plenty of meat and lard in the fall of the year to do them till the next fall. I have seen my Dad kill as high as fifteen hogs. Of course, they wouldn't be real big hogs like they are now. We would kill them when they was still small. They was about a year old but they didn't weigh over 150.

The creek bottoms surrounding the prairies were fine hunting grounds. One informant stated:

In the old days there weren't any stock laws. The country was plum full of cattle and wild game that just run out. We had turkey, squirrel, fish, quail, hog meat, beef, and some mutton. They liked pork better. We could have turkey. The wild turkey was thicker than quails are now. Just a lot of fish, buffalo and catfish. Me and my brother used to net quail. We would drive them around. In them days they didn't have any shot-guns. They shot rifles mostly. We would set a net there twenty-five feet long. It was eighteen inches high. We would start off here with a wing fifty by twenty-five feet long. We would set one end of it at the mouth of the net and get on a horse with a bell on the horse and the birds wouldn't fly. We would ride around them and they would get down to one of these wings and run right into the barrel we had there. All you had to do was jump down off your horse and twist the net over them. Then when you get them all killed you would just open your net and dump them out.

Farming was primitive; the soils were generally deficient; and techniques were poor with little understanding of crop rotation. A ninety-two-year-old farmer said:

My father moved up here after the Civil War. I can remember that my grandfather said that he bought this land for 75 cents an acre from the railroad. Of course, that wasn't much money in those days but the land wasn't too good either.

Everything by hand. You didn't have no plows of no kind that was any good. You had an old turning plow to turn the dirt over. It was made of wood. I don't know how they fixed it but they twisted it some way. I don't know what kind of timber it was. It had a steel point, but what turned the dirt over, it was made of wood. You just shoved the dirt across the field. In those days you done farming by walking all the time instead of riding. We had teams of oxen. I learned how to drive oxen. We had to break our ground by walking a ten- or twelve-inch plow.

Farms were small, averaging from forty to eighty acres. As time went on the soils became increasingly worse owing to improper cultivation and erosion. With limited control over the geographical environment and little interest in innovation on the part of the farmers, the general economy remained unchanged and failed to improve. One of our informants described the economic life in the latter part of the nineteenth century as follows:

She was just pretty poor going. I can remember when lots of fellows would come around and want a day's work. They wanted something to eat. They would work all day just for something to eat.

Farm labor was cheap and frequently the less fortunate farmers found it necessary to work for others. An eighty-year-old resident reports his experiences while employed by a wealthy landholder:

These farmers lived on an average of forty to eighty acres of land. Now one or two of them had some money but that was an exception. I can remember one man, though, who had 200 acres of land between here and Nobility. He used to whip the niggers when they wouldn't work. Well, he treated us workers poorly, and I don't think that to him it was any different between the way that he used to treat the niggers and us. I can remember that when we ate, we didn't get to sit at the table with the food before us, but we would pass our plates and he would put on our plates what he wanted us to have. It was that sort of thing that made me remember him.

The diet. The tendency to avoid ventures which were new or risky was manifest in the animals raised for meat as well as the subsequent diet. Almost no beef was raised since it required greater care and involved more risk than pork. Pork was considered simpler to raise, and animals were left to run on their own. The diet during the nineteenth century for persons in this county consisted largely of boiled, fresh, and smoked pork, biscuits, gravy; this was supplemented by wild game, venison, vegetables.[2] Those who possessed some financial security ate the choicest cuts of pork, and this was known as "eating high off the hog." Less fortunate persons "ate low off the hog." A native couple, eighty-seven and eighty-five years old,

[2] For a treatment of Southern food habits, see Margaret Cussler and Mary De L. Give, *Twixt the Cup and the Lip* (New York, Twayne Publishers, 1952).

reported the dietary patterns which characterized the entire population of the area:

We used to eat hog and hominy. We are pork eaters. People from here are pork eaters. We used to have sixteen or eighteen hams hanging in the smokehouse. Everybody that came knew what they would get. I helped my father bring a carload out of the bottoms off the range. Two hundred pound hogs. We smoked our own meat with hickory. We had many farmers that sold hogs for meat. For breakfast we had homemade bacon and eggs. We had biscuits and thickened gravy. On Saturday some one of the girls of the family would make for supper Saturday night half-moon pies fried with fruit in it. We always had coffee. Every fall we had a lot of sorghum made. That with a big lot of lard and the smokehouse hanging full of ham and bacon. We had dried fruit and canned fruit. Pumpkin was hung on sticks and dried. That was good.

We had our big meal at noon. We had boiled dinner. We had pork with greens. We always had potatoes. For our evening meal we had what was left warmed up. We had corn bread for dinner. That was put in the oven and patted down. Mother had two Dutch ovens. She had them full of sweet potatoes in it when we came home from school. We had lots of milk and butter. We made homemade cheese, not like that they make now. We had corn bread and sweet milk. We would crumb up the corn bread in the sweet milk and we called it "crumb-up." We laid cheese up and had dried cheese. We let beef hang up and dry too. We would take a piece of dried beef and an onion and the beef would be raw and we would take some corn bread and eat it like that.

Food habits, like other phases of the basic culture pattern, have not undergone a great deal of modification for certain sections of the native population.

VIOLENCE

Violence, a second theme which emerges out of our analysis of these people, was manifest in problems of law and order, the recreational practices of the group, as well as family rule and the interpersonal relations of the people.

A lack of political order and maturity characterized the county during the nineteenth century. Differences were often settled outside the legal framework and were characterized by violence. When court was in session the room was crowded with adults desiring to be entertained. Personal behavior during court trials up until the twentieth century often had an undisciplined quality. For example, an autobiography reveals:

During a trial, the opposing attorneys became involved in an exchange of hot words. One of the attorneys drew a pistol from his holster and fired at the opposing attorney. He failed to hit the attorney, however, and outsiders intervened to stop the fight.

The failure of institutions to deal with violations against person and property often left popular justice as almost the sole preserver of public peace. Citizens were frequently terrified by gangs of horse thieves, robbers, murderers, and counterfeiters.

Recreational practices. The patterns of violence described above permeated many recreational practices in the county during the nineteenth century. The fact that persons were almost always armed facilitated this pattern. Heavy drinking was common and fights frequently ensued. For example, one sixty-five-year-old informant:

Back then purt near everybody had whiskey. It wasn't over ten cents a gallon. My Dad used to drive oxen to —— and haul castor beans and stuff, and he would buy him a fifty-gallon barrel of whiskey over there. They just had an old smokehouse and they would put it in there, just a pick in the door. That is all the lock they had. Fifty gallons of whiskey in there. They come all hours of the night and he would sell them a quart of whiskey for a dime. My uncle did that, too. They would sell it for ten cents a quart. Forty cents a gallon. My, you wouldn't get to smell of a bottle for forty cents now.
Every time they had a shooting match or horse race, there were certain men here who would get drunk and fight. One man lived in our place got in a fight with another man who lived close. He got his finger in this fella's mouth and it was chewed off.

A merchant describing storekeeping in the 1860s had this to say in his autobiography:

What I did not like about storekeeping was the liquor-selling part of it. Frequently several of the imbibers became helpless and had to be taken care of until they sobered up. It would not do to turn them outdoors so I often watched over them in the store at night. They were generally good, honest farmers from the country who worked hard when at home, but liked to dram when in town and didn't know when to quit. Saturday was the time such characters usually selected to meet in town and have a good time and to get drunk together at a bit's expense to each. Sometimes a quarrel would spring up or an old grudge be rasped open, to settle with a fist fight. The belligerents, stripped to the skin above the waist, would enter a ring formed by comrades to insure fair play and fight it out. No weapons were used except such as nature had furnished, and when one of the combatants got enough, he so announced and the other fellow quit and the fight was over.

Practical joking which possessed a destructive component was commonplace among the populace. It was often the practice to string piano wire across someone's yard, and then observe the un-suspecting individual trip and fall. On other occasions friends might agree to steal a neighbor's livestock at a particular time. One friend, out of sport, would inform on the other and then watch gleefully as the farmer unloaded buckshot (usually small pieces of hard bacon rind) on his original partner. An autobiography reveals this practical joke:

One day some people sponsoring a fair felt that things were getting dull. They decided for the sake of humor to announce from the grand-stand that prisoners from a nearby penitentiary had broken out. Much to the announcer's chagrin, however, about half the people left hurriedly for home, either to guard their premises or to be there to welcome possible arriving relatives.

Marriage and the family. Patterns of violence found their expres-sion in family feuding, in father-son relationships, in the develop-ment of mother-centered patterns, and in certain pranks which fol-lowed the wedding ceremony.

Family life possessed patterns which were father-centered and mother-centered. The father-centered family was described as rigidly organized around the personal whims of the male who had license to do as he pleased. In many of these families the male enjoyed his whiskey and would become unmanageable when intoxicated. A seventy-eight-year-old male described his father:

My Dad always had a jug of whiskey. If he run out, he would go and get some and come home too full. This happened one time in particular, I was a grown, young man. I weighed about 180. We weighed our hay. My Dad stayed in town and bought some fruit trees. Instead of shipping them to our home the fella shipped them elsewhere by mistake. My Dad thought this fellow cheated him. He run on to the man that he bought them from and they was both drunk. He wanted to whittle him up with a little knife that he always carried. He was fussing and cussing with that man and the sheriff was just watching him. I told the sheriff I would take care of my father. We got the wagons weighed and I gathered the old man up and put him on my wagon. Then he got mad at me and told me that he was going to give me a good beating. We got home and he was still pretty full. The old man picked up a hoophole and struck at me. He hit the basket instead of me. I hit him right in the forehead with a big ear of corn. I told my stepmother that night that if he started upstairs to wake me up. I didn't aim for him to get upstairs. He didn't try to get up there, though. The next morning he asked me who was going to be the boss. I said, "I guess both of us part of the time!" I told him that if I needed a whipping to give it to me, but to never try that again. I told him that if he wanted me to pack my clothes I was ready. I had left once before and he had to hire a hired hand. He told me to go on out and get to work. That was typical of how the men treated the sons.

The patterns of feuding, fighting, and drinking often made the life and behavior of the male unpredictable and tenuous. At times serious injury and death followed the carousing activities of the male. Thus among some elements in the population, family life was integrated around the mother whose behavior was the most predictable in the home. We shall deal with this development in greater detail in Chapter 8.

In a lighter vein we note that the "charivari" was characteristic and was an expression of amusement or disapproval on the part of some people in the neighborhood at what they considered an unsuitable marriage. A party of men and boys would collect at night near the house where the newly wedded couple were living, carrying bells, tin horns, and anything else that would make a noise, sometimes even shotguns. They would stay around the house, making all the hideous noises possible until they became tired or the groom called a truce and suggested a treat for the crowd inside the house. Occasionally the groom or his friends would become angry and sally forth and a small battle would take place. Even here it was not uncommon to hear of someone being shot.

SUPERSTITION

The culture of the country was replete with superstition during the nineteenth century, a by-product of the social isolation which characterized the area. Such superstition was manifest in several areas of the cultural milieu, but appeared particularly in relation to medical care, attitudes toward education, and certain religious practices.

Medical knowledge.[3] Medical knowledge, even in comparison to what little was known in other sections of the country, was exceedingly primitive in this area for most of the nineteenth century. Laymen resorted to folk remedies, while physicians (usually without formal medical training) often did the same. Bleeding of persons and animals was not uncommon. An eighty-seven-year-old resident reports:

My mother was bled. Her father would bleed her when she had fever. She said that was his way of doctoring. Mother had little white places in her veins from being bled. They used to bleed horses around here. I have helped bleed horses. You would lance him in the neck and bleed him and then pin that up.

Medicines designed to make the child vomit were used repeatedly without regard to the severity of their therapy.

My father was a herb doctor. He was mighty wise on that. I never used that too much on my family. I nearly killed my cousin's boy on that. He had eat too many persimmons and he had cholic. I was trying to vomit him. I had doctored my kids that way and didn't kill any of them. I was raised on tincture of Epecoc. You would just give a child a spoonful of that to make him throw up. It would make him throw up right now. That was the way we got our kids over the croup.

In the excerpt below the reader will note a description of medical insight and treatment. Professional medical knowledge was scanty and physicians appeared to manifest hopelessness when confronted by serious illness. An old settler stated:

They used roots for the chills. Back then there was a lot of chills. They would take horse roots [horseradish] and it was really bitter. Quinine wasn't as bad as horse roots was. Then they would get white walnut bark and cherry bark and make a syrup out of it and pour a little whiskey in it and drink that for the blood. They used to give the kids medicine every

[3] The writer is indebted to Professor Harold M. Kaplan, Chairman, Physiology Department, Southern Illinois University, for his assistance in dealing with material in this section.

spring and fall. You purt near had to. There wasn't no water in the
country. They would use creek water and like that. They would haul
water for a mile or two sometimes. That water was full of malaria, you
know. Of course, they didn't know how to boil it and treat it like they
do these days. If you was working in the field and a creek run through
you would just lay down and drink out of it. They would just use it as
it come out of the creek or pond. They would give them stuff to work
them and clean their bowels and so on. When you was taking that if you
ate one thing with a drop of grease in it, boy, what a sore mouth you
would have. Doctors give that, too, along. I forget what they called that.
You wasn't allowed to eat one drop of grease while you was taking that.
You would give them a round of that every spring and in the fall you
would doctor them for the chills and keep the malaria chills off of them.
You would take malaria fever and get down to nothing but skin and
bones. There used to be quite a bit of that. Pneumonia fever if you took
that, just about nine out of ten you just as well take an axe and knock
you in the head because you was gone. They didn't know how to doctor
it and it would kill about nine out of ten. There was a right smart of
typhoid fever, too. Just starve to death with it. The doctors wouldn't
let you eat anything. If you ate anything, it would kill you and if you
didn't eat anything, you would die anyhow. There wasn't much hope
for you. An old man down there he is dead now, and back when he was
a young man, of course, he had a family, but he took typhoid fever and
they wouldn't let him eat anything. He got to where he was getting a
little bit better and could eat. They would just get him a little bit of
certain things. The woman cooked a mess of dried beans. They was the
best smelling stuff he ever smelled in his life. "How am I going to get to
those beans to get some of them to eat?" he said. He had one or two
kids. The old lady took the kids and went to the barn to do up the night
work. He managed to crawl over to where the beans was and he cleaned
up that bowl of beans while she was out at the barn. He couldn't get
back on the bed he was so weak. They was old corded bedsteads. I expect that is the kind of bed he had. This woman come in and there he
was. She said, "How come you are up here?" She got him back in bed. He
said, "If you look at that bowl of beans you will know what I was up
for." She called the doctor. He came and said, "There ain't a thing I can
do. If you live three hours you might get over it." He just went and left
him. In just a short time he was up and going. He said, "I believe I
would have died if I hadn't got hold of that bowl of beans; they cured
me."

In still another account we learned of the use of a folk remedy
which confused the physician:

There was a man down there, his name was ——. They had three different doctors with him that day. He had typhoid fever. All three of them
said, "He will not be alive by morning. There is no chance for him at all."
After they left, this fellow said, "Let me doctor him tonight with my
home remedy." The wife said, "What are you going to do?" He said, "I
am going to the woods and get me some bark and make me some stuff."
He said, "I will set right here and rub that on him all night and he will
be better by morning." She said, "He is going to die anyway, I don't guess
you will kill him any quicker." He set right there and he changed them
all night just ever little bit. Next morning he was a hundred percent
better, seemed to be. That went on and he doctored him all day. When
the doctor came back he wouldn't doctor him any more because they let
the fella use that home remedy. The man got well and lived several years
after that. The doctors weren't too good in those days. They never went
to school any. They was just like us. They just took it on themselves.
This one doctor he had never went to a doctor school one minute in his
life.

Education. Separation and isolation from outsiders was traditionally valued. Strangers with different patterns of behavior were
viewed with suspicion and feared as potential disrupters of the
existent culture. Resistance to innovation was always marked and
up until industrialization attitudes toward formal education vac-
illated from ambivalence to overt hostility.

In spite of the high rate of illiteracy prevalent, persons in this
area were from the first generally reluctant to foster education.
Federal census takers in the 1850s reported that five-eighths of the
illiteracy in the state was located in this general region. The opposition to education, public or private, was based on the fear and superstition that school attendance would "corrupt the mind of the child."
Opposition to the public schools was based on unwillingness to pay
taxes for their support. All of this made it difficult for any system
of education to become well entrenched.

The teachers of the early days were limited in education; this
necessitated a system whereby they would contract with parents
to teach only the first three years of spelling, reading, writing, and
arithmetic. Thus, early schools were termed "subscription schools."
The early books employed were the traditional Webster Spelling
Book and McGuffey's First and Second Readers. A series of bills

passed during the years 1841 to 1870 established free schools. In addition, a denominational college, established in 1874, lasted until the early 1900s.

Public schools at the outset were crude with respect to curriculum and physical structure. Discipline, bordering on violence, was in vogue and liberally applied. A former schoolteacher describes discipline in the 1880s:

I was a schoolteacher. I was twenty-six years old. I taught at the Delta School southeast of here. I taught eight years. We just had the school and the people sent the children to school. We taught all grades. The teacher made the children mind. If they didn't mind they gave them a thrashing and that is what lots of them needs now. You turn a bunch of kids loose and they know you ain't going to punish them and they will do a lot. I remember one day a boy took out his knife and commenced whittling on his desk. I said, "No, you are not going to cut any more on that desk." I got a pointer and gave him a few licks across the back and he said, "I won't quit," and I wore that hickory out on him. He told me before I quit that he would stop cutting on that seat. He is living today. He told me after he was grown that he had needed that and was glad that I had done it.

Religion. Although religiosity was never very pronounced in this county, during the nineteenth century it was dominated by Protestantism of the extreme fundamentalist variety. The early settlers brought with them ministers who were generally ignorant and bigoted. When competent ministers entered the area they soon became discouraged because of the general state of ignorance, superstition, and apathy which characterized the populace.

Church buildings were constructed in a haphazard way and services were interrupted by various disturbances. An early church at Old City had this to contend with:

The church house was built on a hillside. Hogs would run under the church house and they would make a bed under there. You could barely hear the preacher above the hogs. Fleas came up through the floor. Hogs died under there once in a while, and man, would that stink!

Religious revivals for indefinite periods of time were common. Emotionalism, accompanied by the "jerks," was associated with tent meetings. Such patterns of behavior are still prevalent among some religious groups in the county.

An excerpt from an autobiography describing a revival of the 1870s reveals the following:

After revival meetings the baptizing of the converts was performed in the open air in a pond or creek. Following a short service the minister walked out in the water. The dresses of the girls ballooned in the water unless there was shot in the hem. Then their skirts went down gracefully into the water. At one baptizing the minister took a young widow out to the stake. The water was very cold and when it came around her, she yelped, sprang partly out, grabbed the astonished minister around the neck, hooked her heels around him, and held tight. He tried to quiet her, but to no avail, and he had to carry her out unbaptized to the delight of some of the onlooking sinners.

Religious fundamentalism was manifest in a literal interpretation of biblical teaching at prayer meetings. A religious meeting in the 1880s went like this:

They would have preaching and prayers. They never call a mourner. They ain't got no mourner's bench, like they call mourners up some places and they come up. They believe in praying for you and so on just like others, but if you was there setting back there in the seat and you wanted somebody to pray for you they would go back to your bench and kneel down there and everybody in the house would kneel and pray for you. After the prayer they would go back to their seats and so on, but they didn't have no mourner's bench to call you up to. They believed in eating the bread and drinking the wine and washing your feet. It didn't make any difference how many different denominations was there, they would go there and eat the bread and drink the wine. One thing we would do, I would take and pull off your shoes and your socks. I have a big white towel and I would wash your feet and put your shoes and socks back on. Then you would do me the same way. They would hand it over to two more. The women does the same thing. They wash one another's feet, the women does. When they get one done the other one that washes the feet that time would just turn right over and get her feet washed. If there was very many they had several pans of water and towels. If there happened to be an odd one the preacher would wash his feet because he ain't got no mate to do that. Of course, somebody has already washed his feet. Women don't wash men's feet. If they don't belong to the church, nothing doing. Then after they get through washing the feet they eat the bread and drink the wine.

Religious orientations of the nonfundamentalist variety have never been able to establish themselves in this general area. In a later chapter, concerned with religious institutions, we assess in greater detail the origin and function of religious behavior as it developed during industrialization.

This, then, represented the general social setting when coal was discovered in the county. Almost at once, an industrialized economy implemented by thousands of foreign-born immigrants and native migrants with diverse culture beliefs was superimposed on what may generally be characterized as an isolated, resigned, provincial, and superstitious settlement. Patterns of violence underlay the social structure. The end product of such interaction and the social products which emerged will concern us throughout the remaining sections of our study.

CHAPTER 3

A COAL CAMP

COAL TOWN was initially conceived in 1900 as a privately owned, unincorporated camp, dominated and controlled by the six Basil brothers who had pooled their individual resources in order to speculate in coal.[1] The most dynamic figure of the six was Victor Basil, spokesman for the group. His ability to influence his brothers in the establishment of mining policy made him an important figure during the early days in Coal Town. The records suggest that Victor Basil derived considerable satisfaction from impressing others with his wealth and power. He visualized himself as a great benefactor of the coal miner and entertained visions of setting up a self-sufficient coal camp, which would be organized according to his wishes and

[1] Coal mining and the existence of coal mines was discussed by travelers passing through the region early in the nineteenth century. Such mining, however, was initiated by individuals either alone or in small groups using extremely crude implements. Up until 1870 the mining of coal was not particularly profitable since machinery for the mass extraction of coal was limited and industry had failed to reach a point where coal as a fuel was feasible and practical. By the 1890s the coal industry was well on its way toward development in the general area. In 1900 six brothers from West Virginia hired a geologist to explore the possibility of sinking a mine in the vicinity of Coal Town. His report was favorable and the brothers purchased several thousand acres of land. The land was purchased inexpensively since the farmers were unable to comprehend the economic possibilities of coal mining. One farmer stated: "Yes, sir, they bought up all this old land for coal. They got it cheap, for about ten dollars an acre. In some cases they paid more. They got it for just a little or nothing. The farmers, they thought it was a gift. They said, 'Why, my Lord, that coal will never do me any good.' The money was good money at that time. The people that bought the land knew what it was worth but they always try to keep the farmers as ignorant as they can." In 1900 work was begun on the sinking of Coal Town Mine Number One; by 1904 operations started and miners began to pour into the coal camp from all sections of the United States and Europe.

demands. He saw himself as a lord of the manor, the responsibility for which was implemented by his own police force and system of law. One of Victor's assistants gave this description:

Victor was 5 feet 2 inches, fat and robust, a free-hearted fellow, and when he once made up his mind, he stuck to it. Victor was not interested in the miner as a person but in making money and control. The people were controlled completely by him. They were little more than slaves. I can remember that Victor broke up a play at the theater just because he got bored. He was a strong man and he wrecked the place. I mean he really tore it up.

Victor possessed a flair for the dramatic and the unusual:

One day in the streets of Hartdale, Victor drove up in a tallyho with horses and he had his servants, they were all dressed in livery, all of them had proper colors. There were two men and two women in the tallyho. Well, everyone in Hartdale crowded around to see what in the world was taking place, and sure enough, here stepped out Victor Basil himself, went into the little state bank there, that a fellow and his father ran, and he walked in. He said, "I'm Victor Basil and I want to deposit and open an account here. I own a coal mine over here in the other side of the county and I would like to put some money in the bank." Well, this fellow said okay and pushed the deposit slip over to him, and Basil took a roll from his pocket which was the largest roll of money that the teller had seen in a long time. And he opened an account. Basil said, "Well, I've got a little bit of money here that I want to open this account with." He plunked down $40,000. That was the most money that was ever deposited in one bank in one day here in this entire region. The teller almost fell over. Well, that was Basil, he liked to show off.

From the very beginning Victor Basil and his brothers were beset by serious social and economic difficulties. With the opening of Mine Number One in 1904 the miners demanded an appropriate wage and union recognition. Basil and his brothers refused to meet their demands and claimed that with the high degree of mechanization the miners would easily earn enough to meet their wage requests and that further guaranties were unnecessary. The Basil brothers claimed that this was a free country and the union could not tell them how to operate their business. On the other side, however, were several thousand well-organized miners of the area who were willing to back the strikers of Coal Town. Original issues at

Coal Town were confused and highly controversial. What started as a disagreement about wages and union recognition soon developed into a struggle for power between the Basil brothers and the union representatives.

Victor, with a background of rugged individualism, found it difficult to conceive of working conditions dictated by the union. On the other hand the union, with a long history of conflict in its struggle for recognition, found it difficult to trust Victor. This conflict was symptomatic of similar conflicts all over the country. For the people of Coal Town basic patterns of distrust regarding labor-management relations came out into the open and spread to other areas of human interaction. An informant familiar with the controversy reported as follows:

Victor was not against paying good wages but he objected to being told how to run his coal mine. You see, it was his plan and his property. It was his wages and his conditions and they were comparable to other mines. He wanted to prove that he could beat the union.

A self-educated miner, who developed a deep interest in this controversy, suggested that the union representatives were predominantly concerned with the implications of letting a coal mine operate without the union:

Victor was bound and determined to fight the union to the last ditch. Money was no object. He did not want to be told what to do. It wasn't the money, it was the fact of principle. In a sense he was right. That is, at the time in which the unions were organized, unions were a conspiracy. Now the conditions he offered were not bad, considering the period. The union felt, however, that without some organization that a bad precedent would be set for other coal towns and the miner would be in a position to be exploited.

The union men walked out in the spring of 1908, setting off a strike and a period of hostility and violence which plagued the Basil brothers and the people of Coal Town for the next two years. Since all of the property belonged to the Basil brothers they retaliated with eviction notices for all miners out on strike.

The organized miners from other camps and union officials came to the aid of the evicted miners, most of whom were housed in an emergency tent colony east of New America. The emergency camp was used as a base of operations to discourage strikebreakers. The fact that many of the strikebreakers were Negroes made the problem more acute for the natives from this region. Trains going to Coal Town were often stopped and examined by strikers. Many miners, discovering they had become strikebreakers, frequently left, making the entire enterprise exceedingly costly to the Basil brothers.

Meanwhile the Basil brothers' coal camp was fenced in. Careful check was made of those entering or leaving the stockade. Passes were required of all. The stockade was described as follows by a miner who remembered the early days:

When I first came here, why the stockade was all around. There were machine guns and searchlights posted. The Company felt the guns were necessary because they were afraid that they would have trouble from the men from the other communities who were union men. You see, Victor was afraid of union organizers and he was afraid that someone would come on and try to blow up the mine. They had searchlights and Gatlin guns in the office and on the tipple. Over there in New America the darker the night the lighter it was. I have seen it light there when it was dark as a dungeon. They kept the big searchlight moving. They was watching for these miners to come in. They spied a mule down there and thought it was a bunch of men and they turned that Gatlin gun loose on that mule and killed him. Next day they found out what it was and it belonged to a fellow by the name of Jones in Birdtown. His mule had got out that night and they come back to the office and told them what they had done and Victor wrote him a check for $250 and sent it over there to him.

During the two-year strike period Coal Town was a fortress besieged. Battles raged intermittently. Few were reported killed but many were wounded and the general unrest intensified the chaos and hostility on both sides. The production of coal was markedly disrupted. To make matters worse several mining explosions, which cost the lives of many mining personnel, occurred during the two-year strike.

At the end of two hectic years the Basil brothers were faced with financial bankruptcy and a hostile mining element. They were able to prevail on Victor to turn the mining operations over to another company. In 1910 the Swift Mining Company took charge of mining under a royalty arrangement with the Basil brothers. A contract with the miners' union was negotiated and the strikebreakers were "sent away."

THE AFTERMATH

It was difficult for Victor to accept defeat even though his brothers had recognized for some time that the end was near. The loss of the strike was a blow to his personal prestige and position in the community. He continued to make efforts to demonstrate to others that he was a good fellow and that union recognition was a mistake. Since the brothers still owned most of the property in the community Victor prevailed on them to allow him to pursue some of his plans. One miner said this:

Victor's idea was that each miner should have at least five acres of land. Then Victor would lease the land to him for ninety-nine years. He wanted to lease it at a very reasonable price because he wanted to do something for the people to show them that he was right, and that they didn't have to join the union, and that he was going to do alright by his people.

Further, Victor envisioned an agricultural system that would provide for the members of the community, but his motives for this were misunderstood and his immaturity was responsible for a lack of efficiency and planning. A merchant recalled:

I was nine years old when Victor was here and my Dad was sold on Victor's idea of the ideal community. Victor did put out a great deal of money to make this dream come true. Why, he built a forty or fifty thousand dollar barn here. He started a dairy and started a farm. The reason for his failure was mismanagement. Mismanagement was really tremendous. I can give you one example. A mine engineer was hired to run an orchard and it was really a lovely orchard. He asked my Dad how to spray the orchards since he didn't know anything about agriculture, and my Dad gave him the formula and since he was supposed to spray the trees three times a year, he figures that if he made it three times as strong, that he would only have to do it once and so he sprayed the trees and killed every tree in the orchard. Well, it was mismanagement like this that ruined Victor and turned him against the men. Victor wanted an agricultural place here so that stuff could be sold to the miners. He used to bring in, I remember, trainloads of Herefords here because somebody had given him the bum steer that Herefords were the type of cows to be used for dairy herds. There were the chief herdsmen appointed and many other people under him who were in charge of this herd, but they knew· very little about it. The people here didn't understand Victor's idea and they used to butcher his cattle. They killed them and shot them down like birds. Well, that gives you some idea of why Victor got tired of this community. It is also a good picture of the type of people here and the fact that they had little respect for law and order.

Shortly after Coal Town was incorporated (1914) Victor employed an architect to develop a plan for improving the living conditions of the miner.[2] In spite of the elaborate plans developed, Victor found it difficult to maintain consistent attitudes toward his plans, as is evidenced in this quotation from Victor's builder:

The foreigners were being kept in the Flats which were those long building in the north side of town near the mine, and Victor sent for me since I had had some experience in building homes and said that he wanted some mining homes built. Some homes for the miners, without basements, and he would give me any amount of money that I wanted to build them.

[2] The early life was typically crude and the physical surroundings were characteristic of coal camps of the period. One of the early miners reported, for example: "When I moved to Coal Town, my impression of the community was, 'Heavens! Do I have to stay here?' We hadn't a single paved street. It was the dirtiest hole when I came here. The streets were full of holes. It was the last place in the world, so to speak. In them days if it rained a little you was marooned. It got so bad from here to New America that we assessed ourselves a dollar apiece to put coal cinders on it so we could get out. It was terrible. I remember that the first thing I bought my wife when she came here was a pair of hip boots. You sure did need those hip boots when you walked along the streets in Coal Town, especially in the winter time." Health problems during the early days were prevalent. A sixty-five-year-old woman: "My brother came to Coal Town but he didn't stay here but just a few months because the water was so bad he got dysentery. Just mud used to come through the faucets many times." Living quarters were crowded, many lived in tents, while others moved into the Company flats which resembled a military barracks. The barracks were divided into apartments. Although inadequate, the apartments, along with the houses available, were improvements over the shacks common to other mining camps of that period. A description of living quarters by a native miner: "The Flat was built when they started sinking that shaft. They had two-story, frame buildings. There were ten apartments in the bottom and ten in the top. These were mostly for single men who came from other parts of the country and other parts of the world. The toilets were outside these Flats but there was running water inside and they were heated by coal. Electricity and water came from the mine."

I asked him how he wanted them built. He told me, he said, "Alex, you build those homes just one degree removed from a pigpen, that's alright with me." I told him that I didn't do business that way. So he saw that he couldn't control me, so he said, "Alright, you do it whatever way you want to and I'll give you the money." "Well," I said, "I guess I needed about $40,000," so all he did was press a buzzer on his desk, in came a secretary, and he said, "Write this man out a check for $40,000." That's the way he operated.

In spite of Victor's attempts to maintain power in the community, he was singularly unsuccessful. In 1914 the community became incorporated and organized a local government. Hostility toward Victor Basil was entrenched and became manifest in the reactions of many Coal Town citizens. By the time Victor's building plans were implemented, a city council had been organized and it was necessary to receive approval for building sites. In the excerpt below we learn of the composition of the City Council and its attitudes toward Victor and city development. Victor's assistant reported as follows:

Now I can remember one interesting incident and this was when Victor's secretary came down here and presented to the City Council the plans for the additions for the city of Coal Town. This secretary was a very fine man, a religious man. He used no profane language whatsoever and was all dressed up. He went into the City Council one day and presented the plans to the City Council for their approval, and he went through the explanation stating that he had to have the Flat approved by the city and then they would be filed in Hartdale, etc. Well, the City Council, which was composed of the Mayor and certain councilmen, paid no attention to him. They were a rough lot, dirty, unshaven, they were sitting there playing cards and smoking. They were natives and most of them, well all but one, couldn't even read or write. They were really tough guys. The Mayor got up when the secretary finished and just cursed him up one side and down the other and told him that they weren't about to approve Victor's addition to the city of Coal Town. They would approve it only on one condition, and that was that Victor would give each member a new suit, all the whiskey he could drink, a free trip—transportation paid —to New York for one week with all expenses paid for them to do anything they wanted. Well, that really caused the secretary to explode. He just stomped out of that council meeting and came to me. Well, I said I would take care of it, so I went around and saw each of the City Council members separately and this was how I put it to them because I knew that I couldn't put it to them on any moral grounds. I sai 1, "Men, if you don't approve that addition to the city there won't be much graft here in Coal Town, but if you approve it that will mean that more people will come in, and the more people that are here that means more graft that you will get." I put it to them on this basis and I bought each man about two drinks of whiskey. Well, by the time of the second drink, I had blown the picture up so that he figured that he would make thousands of dollars off the new population that would come in here. Well, this is how it went over. The City Council finally approved it, you see.

In addition to the difficulties from the City Council, Victor had problems with citizens. The son of a builder reported:

Victor meant well but he often lost his temper. One example of this was when he was showing my Dad a new house that had been finished and it was all cleaned up and ready for somebody to move in but some bastard had come in and had crapped right on the floor and it was things like this that sort of destroyed his faith in the miner.

Victor possessed many threads and currents which ran counter to each other. On the one hand, many who purportedly knew him spoke of his generosity and friendliness. There is no reason to doubt that this was true. On the other hand, such constructive gestures seemed frequently to be dependent on others following his edicts and demands. He grew up in an era of rugged individualism and found it difficult to accommodate his personal wishes to the demands of a highly organized, intelligent, and physically aggressive group of labor leaders. These leaders controlled a large mass of persons who were sometimes easily led, and who were uncritical of the purposes of organized labor.

Victor initiated changes which suggested his interest in the miner but his general manner was ambivalent and governed by his personal whims of the moment. Thus he became a victim of his inconsistencies and of a mining element which neither understood nor trusted his motives. With persistent failure in his efforts to convince the community of his good intentions, he became disillusioned.

In 1918 Swift Mining Company put Coal Town Mine Number Two into production under a royalty arrangement similar to the one previously arranged with the Basil brothers, who were by this time fatigued with the experience, the struggle, and the result. The Basil brothers commenced selling non-mine property to individual citizens. A vision for an empire had collapsed, but the patterns of violence, distrust, and suspicion which emerged from the actions of both labor and management during this early era continued to plague the citizens of Coal Town.

CHAPTER 4

THE NATIVE LOOKS AT COAL TOWN

IN considering the attitudes of natives toward Coal Town and its population, we are considering the reactions of at least four categories of persons: the natives who remained in agriculture, the natives who shifted to mining, which constituted the largest group, the natives from the South who migrated about 1920, and the natives who became merchants.[1] Each of these groups was ambivalent about industrialization and each held the Negro and the immigrant miner in contempt.[2] Although there were those who welcomed certain economic features of coal mining, the majority of natives resented the new way of life precipitated by the development of mining and the speed with which it was ushered in. There were objections to the reverberations of the new industrial economy: the growth of cities, the industrial smoke, the increased tempo of living, the work routine, and the Negro and immigrant groups which became symbolic of all these changes.[3] As previously suggested in Chapter 2, the natives of the region were isolated and provincial. They were satisfied with little and were generally content with subsistence farming. Their way of life was well entrenched and inflexible. These were people who had always lived on the outskirts of organized group life, with a history of unsuccessful attempts to compete with industrialization and the forces of cheap labor. Their adjustment was always marginal and characterized by mobility

[1] A small group of these merchants were outsiders with different cultural practices.

[2] For an additional discussion of the attitudes of the native toward mining see Appendix C.

[3] Cf. Malcolm Ross, *Machine Age in the Hills* (New York, Macmillan Co., 1933), pp. 33–125.

whenever things became difficult. The culture, or way of life, of the area was not in any sense a dynamic one, and prior to industrialization it was a culture that had remained relatively intact and without change for some time. The development of coal mining inflicted a type of change for which there had been no preparation. From the point of view of the natives all those things ushered in by coal mining were antagonistic to their way of life. The industrial economy with a substantial economic investment demanded high production and a good profit. This created a demand for persons who could accept and follow an industrial routine and whose working efforts would be serious and dependable. The natives who wished to engage in mining were totally unequipped to deal with such innovations in terms of their background. Absenteeism resulted from their general indifference to steady employment and production schedules and from the fact that in mining they could earn as much in two days as they formerly did in a couple of weeks on the farm. Further, the native's interest in the pleasurable pursuits of hunting and fishing accounted for much absenteeism. A retired miner:

Bird-hunting was a pleasurable pursuit in this community and I believe that it contributed much to labor disputes. For instance, when someone would want to go bird-hunting, why he would either not show up on the job or else he was looking for something so that he could get out of work and was more apt to pick a fight or look for some grievance that could be brought against the Company. It was said here that a man would give his wife anything except his bird dog. The bird dogs were much more important than the wives and there were many dogs here. I'll tell you that.

The natives were indifferent to the values of industry, frugality, and productive efforts.[4] Instead, as we shall see later, it was the immigrant who held to these values. Those natives who wished to change wanted to do it slowly, in their own way, at their own pace,

[4] The natives in our study constituted an exception to the general thesis that Protestantism and the values of thrift, industry, and frugality appear together. For a complete discussion of this problem see Max Weber, *Protestant Ethic and the Spirit of Capitalism*, translated by Talcott Parsons (London, George Allen and Unwin, Ltd., 1931). See also C. Wright Mills and Hans Gerth, *From Max Weber* (New York, Oxford University Press, 1946).

and under their own control. Such an adjustment was incompatible with the demands of the coal industry and it was at this point that both Negro and foreign miners were introduced into the area. Although the Negro lasted only a short time, the immigrant remained. The immigrant generally was a hard worker, steady, predictable, and easily controlled. These were the traits to which the management in the mine was attracted and these were examples held up for the natives to follow. Because of this, considerable hostility on the part of the natives toward the immigrant developed. There is no doubt that many natives refused to adjust to the industrial order, but even for those who wished change, there was an undertone of inferiority and hopelessness about ever making an adequate adjustment. Such feelings stemmed from the inadequate adjustments these people had made in the South.

Thus a combination of factors including the economic threat of the Negro and immigrant, the drastic social changes, plus the native's hopelessness about understanding and adjusting to these factors made the natives behave as an "oppressed minority," in spite of their control of the existent social institutions. The natives compensated by becoming sensitive and defensive about their way of life and by developing intense hostility toward the immigrant and the way of life which he characterized.

In our conversations with the natives, we encountered various reasons for their antagonism toward the immigrant. We were always impressed with the contradictory and superficial nature of these reasons. For example, many of the natives complained about the "foreigner's drinking habits," and yet drinking was part and parcel of the native pattern. Or they would speak of not being able to trust the immigrant, and yet in the early days it was the native who took advantage of the immigrant. We were forced to conclude that the stated reasons for dislike of the outsider were essentially superficial and symptomatic of the deeper causes previously mentioned.

For many natives who remained on the farm there was envy, envy of the money the immigrant was earning, and yet there was also the hopelessness and fear about engaging in coal mining. For the native miner from the region and the South there was the hostility based on the need to compete with these people, if they were to keep their jobs. The native miner resented having to work harder and longer than he felt necessary.

In the quotes to follow the reader will note the pronounced reaction to the immigrant described to us by natives of the area. A native woman:

We thought the world was coming to an end when the mining camps came in. We thought that the coal towns were dirty. They ruined the towns by bringing in foreigners. Them foreigners would just as soon kill you as not.

A farmer:

The character of the foreigners changed the country. Nine out of ten of them was no good. We would have been a heap better off if they had never been brought here. They couldn't get others. They could get the foreign people. They mined well and they just suited the mining people. The old people hated it when they brought in the foreigners because they were so different. I know my father did. He said it was a sad day when they found coal here. Their way of living was different.

Another native woman:

I can remember when they first brought the Eyetalians in 1902 for them to work on that bridge across the Black River. I was a little seven-year-old girl at that time. Why, they brought them Eyetalians in by the carloads. My father told me to take a good look at that because he said, "Daughter, that's the worse thing that could have happened to this country." Well, it scared me half to death to see them strange Eyetalians. One time just me and my brother were at the house and they came over from the railroad to ask for some water. We couldn't understand them and we were frightened and we didn't know what to do. By sign language he made it known that he wanted water and we told him where the well was. Well, after that they came over for water every day.

The attitudes of suspicion and fear which were felt in relation to the immigrant kept the native isolated and destroyed the possibility of meaningful interaction. Social isolation was facilitated by the native's preoccupation with and hostility toward the cultural differences in language, food, religion, and work habits. The cultural differences emerged as social barriers. Once constructed the barriers appeared to perpetuate themselves, evolving into a cultural pattern of discrimination. Stereotypes and distortions regarding immigrants emerged which are still present.

An interesting question to contemplate centers around the necessity of the native to focus on the differences which he saw between himself and the immigrant. We recognize that isolated people may be so imbued with the essential correctness of their way of life that they simply reject all others. But in this case we believe that for these particular natives, the cultural differences were disturbing because they so acutely became symbolic of impending social changes. It was under these circumstances that their way of life became more rigid and resistance was invoked to minimize and destroy the industrial culture. The question of the extent of sucess which the native culture had in destroying the industrial culture is an interesting one to contemplate and will be discussed later.[5]

The first large group considered undesirable by the natives of the area were Negroes brought in to break the strike of the natives in 1908. The patterns of Negro-white relations prevalent in the area prior to industrialization were carry-overs from Southern traditions. Many of the natives from the region historically had fled from Negro competition in the South; the fact that Negroes were imported to force the wage scale down and break the union precipitated considerable resentment. The Negro was envisioned as a strikebreaker of organized labor by both native and immigrant. A German immigrant exemplifies this belief:

When I come here from Germany it was tough. Then nigger he was all scab. In Mipquip County they put up this sign, "No Nigger Allowed in Here—Nigger Get Out." Those mine operators try to ship niggers to break the strike—in boxcars—the strikers they shoot in the boxcars with

[5] At this point, however, it may be well to suggest certain implications for the understanding of anti-intellectualism as a fabric in the cultural pattern of these natives. If the spirit of anti-intellectualism is one which is anti-change and against the rational consideration of new patterns of living, then a society such as we have described has within its make-up the essential ingredients of the anti-intellectual ideology. The anti-intellectual climate becomes one which is, at the most basic level, a means of coping with social change by setting up resistance to any examination of new patterns.

rifle till the blood run out from the cars. They never know how many they kill. The driver-engineer put his head down an' back the train away, my brother tell me. Nigger, he was all scab, every place.

Some of the Negroes denied that they were anti-union and reported they were simply unemployed people looking for work who were unaware of the labor-management conflicts in Coal Town.

They say we come here to scab an' break conditions. 'Tain't so. When they was no work here, some white men went to Kentuck to scab against colored, too. Like any kind of poor people we go where der is work, we know nothin' 'bout union fight.

The evidence would suggest that the Negro was brought in to fight the union, although he may not have been told so at the time. It is likewise clear that the Basil brothers felt that Negroes could be more easily controlled than the natives. Many of the Negroes employed by the brothers reported pleasant experiences. Victor invited them to picnics and dances. Wages were relatively good for what Negroes could get elsewhere.

Underneath it all, however, was a tenuous calm, which could burst into violence at any time. In the quotes to follow we find the familiar patterns of antagonism about the Negro not knowing his place and manipulation of the Negro for the benefit of the white. A white native miner:

The niggers lived over on Candy Street way out there in that part of town and there was one or two that was killed every week or so. They used to get a carload from the South and when they first came, they were good niggers. Then they got bold after a while and when they first came they called you Mister and then about a week or so they didn't call you Mister and you weren't a Mister to them any more. That's how they changed and it was all for the worse, of course.

There was a considerable tendency for the white native political leaders to attempt to control Negro voting behavior. In the following statement the political ethics of white politicians are revealed.

Yes, in one race I ran and there was a fellow who was boss over the farm here and he always did take an interest in politics and he would get us fellows together, that is when I run for town clerk, and he said, "Boy, them colored people aren't going to vote Democratic if we don't get together and get them a little beer and stuff." I went my part on the beer and we come in and we went to a place and them niggers I don't know how many there was there. This one place I remember, they had about drunk up all the free beer and finally one young nigger he got up and said, "By God, I wouldn't vote for a Democrat no way in the world." I said, "Well, that learned me a lesson. You couldn't trust them."

Many of the attitudes expressed had hostile undertones. Lynchings were always a potential danger, although few occurred. A retired white miner reported the following:

I remember one time that when I was a miner, a group of us walked into the shower and who should be there but a black nigger. He was taking a bath and the miners yelled and threatened him. The nigger then told them that he had taken a bath in there a long time before they did. Why, they almost lynched him. I had to talk to them a great deal to keep them from stringing that nigger up.

The natives have never allowed Negroes to settle permanently in Coal Town and contemporary attitudes toward the Negro have not changed. In spite of mass unemployment many natives would reject new industry if it meant bringing in Negroes. The Negro is viewed as being categorically inferior; to the native he constitutes a potential economic threat which may not be controlled if the Negro is allowed to settle in large numbers. A barber:

I don't think that they would let any Negroes live here today, even if a new industry came in and said they would settle here if they could hire Negroes. I don't think that we would let them. That is as bad as we need industry, if it meant bringing in Negroes, we would not want it. We don't allow any Negroes here now. Why, we seldom see one of them when they even pass through here. We would not like for them to come through here or to come in the community.

As mining developed, labor from Europe increased greatly. The natives who considered themselves trustees of the area soon felt that the immigrant was taking over and reaping the profit. This the native resented and such resentment has persisted. A merchant in the community:

There was a great deal of envy here. When the immigrant came here he was one of the have nots and the natives were the haves. Later the situation was reversed. There was hard feelings against foreigners who came and made money in the mine.

The immigrant groups attracted to Coal Town were predominantly from Central and Southern Europe: Polish, French, Russian, Austrian, Hungarian, Croatian, Montenegrin, Rumanian, Bulgarian, Greek, Italian, and Syrian. The immigrants from Northern Europe included Lithuanians, Estonians, English, and Irish.

Persons from the English-speaking countries, England, Scotland, Wales, and Ireland, found it relatively easy to assimilate when they so desired. Nevertheless, the natives felt that these English-speaking immigrants remained aloof from both native Americans and non-English-speaking immigrants. In issues between native Americans and immigrants the English identified themselves with and were loyal to the natives. But in issues between native Americans and the English-speaking group the Old World loyalties held. In their conversations with the research team the English-speaking group spoke of "us," meaning themselves and the research team, as over and against "those foreigners." Never did we have the impression that these people considered themselves to be outsiders, and yet their history in Coal Town suggests that they remained aloof and isolated from Americans as well as from non-English-speaking Europeans. From the point of view of the interviewer, they were the most difficult to deal with of all the ethnic groups. Although exceedingly polite and friendly, they appeared never to commit themselves about issues, to minimize difficulties, to deny the most obvious occurrences, and in general to give an exceedingly favorable picture of community life. They denied any feeling of prejudice or ill-will on the part of other groups toward them, even when hard feelings were clearly discernible to the untrained observer. The feeling of the natives and the non-English-speaking immigrants was that the "Johnny Bulls" (a derogatory name in this setting) were opinionated, arrogant, and considered themselves better than others. Much of this resentment was based on the favorable economic position of the English miner. These persons often had extensive mining knowledge and experience acquired elsewhere, which enabled them to occupy semiexecutive positions in the mining industry. One native informant put it this way:

The English would have better jobs in the mine because they had studied gas and mining conditions in England, and they came here to study mining conditions in America. Now the miners usually called the English such things as Johnny Bulls and different other things. Some of the best mine examiners were English people. You see, they knew gas and they knew mining from experience.

The vast majority of the natives were not disposed to such kind remarks, however. What inferiority the natives possessed was often intensified by a feeling that English miners looked down on them. Some, although not the majority, disliked the English-speaking immigrant more than the non-English-speaking. The following illustrative statements reveal characteristic attitudes of the white native miner toward the English-speaking immigrant group:

Most of the English people had the good jobs. They were the most hated of all the immigrants. They were hated because of their disposition and because of their position here.

We have people here who think that they are better than you are, I can tell you that. The English seem to think that they were better than anyone else. They will stick together all the time. They would be much more apt to stick together than the foreigners would. Why, you see the English today even sticking together. They seem to always back each other up. They are just like the Germans used to be during World War II. They think they are higher-class people than the rest of us are.

I worked with the English. They are hard to work with, I can tell you. They always want to get a safety lamp or to be a boss. There's not too much hard labor as far as they are concerned. They are more for bossing.

The English always had a dominating attitude. They wanted to be ruler more than anybody else. The Englishman would push you around, too. You have to really watch them in the mine. Many of them are sucks in the mine. You see, they know it all and they can always tell you something but you can't tell them anything. They got the mine examiners' jobs. Those crooked lazy bastards want to be first in everything—get the best—won't work, just suck around.

There is an old expression that "You can tell a Johnny Bull as far as you can see him but when you see him, you can't tell him anything." They really put it over on the officials and they got most of the good jobs. They did not know any more about coal mining than some of the natives did but the officials were always impressed when they asked for a job and usually they would give them the best jobs.

Those damn Johnny Bulls were into everything. Wanted to be big shots—either boss in the mine or officers in local unions. They think they are better than anyone else—even Americans. Give 'em a little authority and they go hog wild.

The Englishman was a braggy sort of fellow. He didn't go over very big. Most of the people stayed away from him and he stayed away from other people.

Resentment toward non-English-speaking Europeans was more intense. The majority of informants openly expressed contempt for them and their way of life. Resentments during the early history of the community were bitter, and although attitudes have changed the term "those damn hunkies" is still frequently heard. A native businessman made the following observation:

There was a tremendous amount of jealousy and envy for those who lived better than the natives did. You see, the natives would call the foreigners "hunkie." The man who did not speak English was a "hunkie" unless he was your friend, but if he was your friend, then an exception was made. If he wasn't a friend, then he was just a good-for-nothing "hunkie."

Many who claimed to be unbiased revealed their latent attitudes toward the immigrant this way:

We had good people in the mines, why even the foreigners, many of them were good.

Before the union trouble I had many good friends here and some of them you couldn't beat even if they were foreigners.

The man next door is a nice person, even though he is a foreigner.

I have had people tell me that lives here, that my neighbors are foreigners, but even so, they are as fine a people as I ever lived by.

Although the native was hostile toward the way of life of the non-English-speaking European immigrant in general, it became most manifest in relation to *observable differences. Upon these they focused.*

Native Attitudes toward Language Differences

Social distance between the native and immigrant was facilitated by the fact that the immigrants spoke their native languages. The immigrant relied on the use of his language not only as a means of communication to other immigrants but also as a means of maintaining his cultural values. The native could never really understand or appreciate such behavior. The native was annoyed and insisted that the foreigner cease and desist from engaging in that "damn hunkie talk" and "start talking American." It was not simply the difficulty in understanding the immigrant but also the difference in gestures which seemed strange and peculiar. This made the barriers of communication and interaction exceedingly formidable. Considerable misunderstanding kept the native from fully gaining entry into the immigrants' way of life and patterns of thinking. Reactions to language differences appeared in working relationships. A native miner:

When Swift Mining Company opened up that is all there was here [foreigners]. Well, I will tell you, man, the foreigners would just gather in here and they would hire them. Well, the foreigners are different. I can't understand the foreigners. That is all I have against the foreigners, I can't understand them. I went out one day at the mine and the boss gave me a foreigner for help. He had to hand me what I would call for. I told him to give me one of them one and one-half inch bolts laying there. He give me a three-quarter inch one and that made me mad. I said, "Buddy, you can stay here if you want, but I'm quitting." The boss said, "Where are you going?" I said, "If you can't give me anybody to work with besides a goddamn foreigner, I am going home." It was hard if you worked with a foreigner because you couldn't tell him nothing.

Speaking in a foreign tongue was defined as a refusal to assimilate by the native of Coal Town. Native miners had this to say:

You see, they were for the fatherland. They used to bring up something about the Old Country and this used to make us mad. We used to tell them that if they liked their goddamn country so much, why in the hell didn't they get their ass back there. That was how we felt about it and that was the quickest way in which you could get an argument from a native, would be for some foreigner to spout off in his native language or else talk about his Old Country in English and say how good it was.

We had a Russian population here too and it really used to burn the Americans up when they would use their old language in the presence of Americans. Why, you didn't even know what they were saying.

It was just like a gang of geese in the washroom. All them different languages. You should read that sign up over the viaduct. It says, "This is America, if you don't like it, move." That was back in the thirties. When that went up there wasn't a word of foreign language spoken. They would get a job over anybody. Big ship companies brought them in, I guess. They would say, "Me work in a mine, me work in a mine in the Old Country." When he went to work it didn't take long to find out that he hadn't. They bought jobs and everything else in the world.

These foreigners were a lot different. Us Americans, we like to never got to where we could understand them. Some of them come here when they couldn't talk.

The differences in language which the natives were unable to understand created suspicion and fear. In some instances Negroes were preferred to whites. The wife of a miner:

You couldn't understand the language of the foreigners. Why, I would just as soon live alongside a nigger family as some of these foreigners. I think that the niggers are whiter than the foreigners are because at least they speak your own language. Why, if you lived next door to a foreigner, they would be sitting and talking about you right in front of you. They might be plotting to kill you and you wouldn't even know it. At least you can understand the nigger's language. They remind me of these old-time people back in the Bible. The women would have a shawl of some kind on their head, you know. They had a different look from us. They couldn't talk our language.

Another native woman stated:

I met my first foreigner when I was about seventeen or eighteen years old, but I'd heard a lot about them but I had never seen any of them so I was curious. Well, the thing that I remember was that you couldn't understand their language and that to me was very funny that they would speak another language rather than the American language.

The native's resentment of the immigrant coupled with the immigrant's language difficulties made the immigrant easy prey for exploitative farmers and merchants. A native farmer:

I had another neighbor up here on the farm that made lots of money there in Coal Town peddling. He would sell things at ten cents apiece or two for a quarter. The foreigners would take two. There was a lot of that around these foreigners. They don't understand. They wasn't used to our money here. It was different.

A few of our native informants expressed sympathy at the plight of the immigrant. One miner said:

I can remember that I was sixteen or seventeen when I first saw a foreigner. I sort of felt sorry for him because he couldn't talk our language. It was sort of a mystery to me, and the foreigner never seemed to understand what was going on. They never did mix too much with the Americans and they did not trust the Americans.

The barriers of language made it difficult to break down misunderstandings regarding the invasion of another's private property for hunting, fishing, and picking fruit. The natives felt great resentment at the immigrant's tendency to invade their property without permission and there is considerable evidence to show that some of the immigrants had distorted notions of personal freedom. A retired native farmer made this comment:

The foreigner said everything was free in this country. You see, they had that understanding and they didn't have any knowledge of the law. Well, when they came over here, they thought that if there was anything they wanted, then they could just go ahead and take it. Well, it wasn't as free a country as they thought it was, you see, so that got them into trouble with the natives that were here who understood the laws. Those foreigners used to hunt anywhere and they would run out and catch chickens right in front of your face. It sort of made you feel funny, you know, and I've heard about the time in which a man was feeding his pigs and a foreigner came along and he decided that he wanted a pig so he climbed over the pigpen and caught a pig and went on home. Well, it was things like that that caused trouble, you see, mainly because the foreigners didn't have any sense.

A merchant reported this:

Freedom more than anything else was what the foreigners wanted. They wanted the right to do as they pleased and the right to prosper. A lot of them had a misunderstanding when they came to this country. They had been taught that this was a free country. They would get out and pick your berries or do anything. They would pick your fruit and seine your pond. They were not too much worse than some of the white trash in this, though. They thought that this stuff was all free. They didn't mean to do wrong. Now they don't do it. They are very nice, but you used to have to watch them in the early days.

NATIVE ATTITUDES TOWARD THE WORKING HABITS OF THE IMMIGRANTS

The conception of work held by the native differed markedly from the conception held by the immigrant. Such misunderstanding became another focal point of resentment and alienation. Natives accused immigrant miners of being overly ambitious, of desiring more work than was necessary, and of making general working conditions difficult for natives. The vast majority of our native informants indicated that the immigrant was hoggish, never knew when to stop, and set a terrific pace in the mine that was difficult for the native to maintain. Such ambition threatened the native, who could neither understand it nor cope with it. One native miner preoccupied with the subject of the immigrant's work habits made the following definition:

I'll tell you what I mean by hard work. Buddy, when an American shovels coal and has to take a piss, he quits for a while. When a foreigner is shoveling coal and has to take a piss, he pisses down his leg and goes right on shoveling coal. That's what I mean by workin' hard. Now these foreigners are really bulls, they work like dogs.

Although many of the natives had mixed feelings about hard work, there were others who were industrious. Even these, however, felt it unnecessary to endanger their lives in risky mining operations. The immigrant felt no free choice in this matter and was likely to incur many risks in order to maintain his job. Many of the natives felt that if the immigrant could have been kept out, they might have had things their own way in the mining industry. The wife of a miner had this reaction:

You see, the foreign element came in here and they just kept coming in and taking jobs away from the Americans. I don't think that is a good idea, do you? I think there would be more jobs here for the American people if so many of these foreigners hadn't been here. You see, these foreigners didn't know when to stop working and this made it hard on the Americans.

A miner:

There were some hard feelings against the immigrant here. You see, the foreign people are very easy to control and they started certain conditions that were very hard to break because the immigrant made it so hard for the average person. This would mean that the boss in the mine would ask you to keep up with the immigrants and what you would have to do would be to almost kill yourself in order to keep up.

During the early hand-loading days, miners were paid by the amount of coal they loaded. Thus each miner was in a sense his own boss. The immigrants enjoyed this and worked as long as possible. The son of an immigrant miner said:

The foreigners, I guess, were the hardest workers. They stayed till quitting time and the Americans would load a car or two and then maybe they feel like going home and take off, but the foreigners stayed all day because they wanted to make all they could.

Many native miners attributed the immigrant's work habits to his plight in Europe. A native miner reacted this way:

The foreigners had been depressed so long that they tried to overdo themselves when they got to this country. They didn't know what a day's work was. They were greedy. After they got more Americanized, they knew that there was another day's work coming but most of them didn't realize at first that there was any future so they worked like hell every day. After they became Americanized they knuckled down. The natives did not try to keep up with them because if they did they would kill themselves. No American would work as hard as they did because the foreigners didn't have any sense. Americans would have more sense than to work that hard.

Native Attitudes toward the Thrift and Ambition of the Immigrants

The immigrant was inclined toward frugality. He generally tried to save his money and spend it sparingly. This infuriated the natives, many of whom felt envious and yet were unwilling themselves to save. A retired native miner:

The foreigners here really knew how to save that money. Here they got ahead of the Americans, I think. You see, the Americans blowed in their money, and I guess that's why I don't have any today myself.

A native merchant reported that immigrants were reliable in payment of debts:

The foreign element will save money and pay a great deal. My biggest job in collecting is with the American people. They live beyond their means. There is not a foreigner in my accounts now who is behind on his payments but the Americans want to stretch out their payments as long as possible.

Another native merchant commented on the immigrants' ambition:

The immigrant group was the most ambitious group. They were much more ambitious than the native white-collar workers even, because the immigrants climbed up from their positions, whereas it seems to me that the white-collar workers were content with what they had in that they did own property and hold local positions. After a while, a few years, they would go down. They would not go up. The immigrant on the other hand would go up.

Some of the natives were resentful of the financial aid sent to Europe. A native miner had this to say:

They did work like dogs and they worked in old clothes. Why, whenever their clothes would have a tear on them, they would come to work the next morning with it all sewed up. The American miner would buy him a new pair of pants or something, but not the immigrant. They used to come to work in rags and they would have their shoes all nailed or wired up. They would do anything in order to have money. Now a lot of them sent money back to the Old Country and this used to make us mad.

Natives were hostile toward immigrants who were successful in business. A native woman:

One good example that I could give you would be Mr. K—— who is in a grocery store here. He got his start by selling beer. He used to buy beer at the Company store then take it down and peddle it by the drink. No American would work that way. Well, eventually he worked himself up to where he owned a tavern and now I guess he has about a block or half a block that he owns, property that belongs to him. Well, that's the way he got his start, you see.

Native Attitudes toward the Mine Official's Control of the Immigrant

The native wished to control the working behavior of the immigrant, but this he was unable to do. He tended nevertheless to view the immigrant's conformity to management as a sign of subservience and weakness. The immigrant was accused of being easily controlled and intimidated, and such control resulted in working conditions which disturbed the native.

Our data suggest that some immigrants were more easily controlled than the natives. The immigrants had left their cultural base to come to a strange land where they were confronted by barriers of custom and language. There appeared to be always the fear of loss of economic security and undoubtedly many of them tried to adjust by following rigidly the orders of management. Thus they could readily be exploited by unscrupulous bosses, and some immigrants became opportunists willing to do anything for financial and personal security, including the betrayal of other immigrants as well as the natives. Courting favor and winning management's approval was not unusual or undesirable for many immigrants. They had come from villages where the large landholder demanded subservience and the knowing person developed techniques for getting along.

Native miners felt that many of the mining bosses degraded the miner by hurling obscene insults when they were dissatisfied with the work. Native miners reported that while the native rebelled against this, the immigrant "took it." This was a sign of weakness. A native miner:

In the old days there was a good deal of cussing and obscene language in the mines, especially the foreigners would take it. You see, the bosses could eat them out and they would just stand there and take it but the Americans wouldn't.

The native miner complained that the immigrant frequently ran to the mine bosses with tales.

The foreigners were more scared of their jobs than the Americans were. I have known them to offer the boss from fifty dollars to seventy dollars for a job. Now, no American would do that. They try to suck around and get a better job. Many of them were sucks who would run to the boss and tell all. You see, you weren't allowed to smoke down in the mine and what they would do would be to run and tell the boss that you were smoking. A few of them never got a good job though despite all this running around. Some of them made bosses but the men wouldn't get the coal out for them and the Company had to replace them. That was sort of interesting. It seemed as if the Company, if they wanted to get rid

of a foreigner, they would make him boss and then after a while the men
wouldn't work under him so then they had to replace him.

A face boss in the mine:

The foreigners were easy to control. You see, one mine manager used to
sell jobs for about two dollars a job and the immigrant miners always
paid for these jobs. When the native miners found out about it, it made
them sore. Some of the foreigners would snitch on the other man for
favors. I never had anybody come and snitch to me on the men. I told
them that I wouldn't stand for any of that crap and I meant it.

When a mine boss wanted to increase production he could play
one immigrant off against another. A native miner pointed this out:

They would get one "hunkie" over in one end of the mine working on a
cutting machine and another "hunkie" over in the other end of the mine.
Then they would go to the first man and say, "The other fellow over
there said that he could cut more coal than you did." Then he would go
and tell the other fellow the same thing. Well, you had men working
against each other here and this really made it tough for all.

Immigrants were reported to be more willing to take risks than
natives.

These foreigners would jump in to any place there was, no matter how
dangerous it was. If the boss told him to stick his head in, why, he would
stick his head in or he might stick his whole body in. They would do
just that sort of thing, you see. If you knew that you were right, you
could hold the boss up. That is, tell the boss that you're not going to do
something like that. These foreigners wouldn't.

Some of the native miners resented the immigrant's conduct although they understood it.

The foreign element are used to looking up to somebody and they are
apt to look up to people like the boss. You see, these foreigners humble
themselves and they won't say a word against the top man. In fact, they
sort of worship him. This, I think, comes from the Old Country. Why, I
can remember that even today some of these foreigners attend union
meetings and then immediately after union meetings are over, they run
out and tell the superintendent all that went on so that the next morning
he would know everything. If you were a little out or caused some dis-
turbance or said something that was against the Company, the superintendent called you on the carpet the next morning. The immigrants felt

that they had to do these things in order to stay in and to keep their jobs. I can understand this but it's a hell of a way to live.

Native Attitudes toward the Immigrant's Food Patterns

The native constructed social barriers, not only on the bases of differences in language, work habits, and control, but also on the basis of food patterns. From the very first the writer was impressed by the difficulty which the native had in understanding or appreciating the specialized food habits of the Europeans in general, and the Central and Southern European immigrants specifically. Implicit in the remarks of our informants was the tendency to devalue and berate the food patterns of the immigrant, and consequently to belittle him personally. Food customs were never viewed as the practices of people with different traditions but were conceived as habits of inferior persons who knew no better. A definition of salami by a merchant in the community:

You fellas know what that salami is that foreigners eat? That's meat that has spoiled, fixed with garlic to disguise the taste.

One native farmer reported the following experience:

That fall the foreign people put up their sausage and dried it and smoked it. They wanted to be friendly so they brought us some but we didn't eat it. We threw it out because we knew that the sausage they make is usually rotten and spoiled. The little girl asked us how we liked it and we said it was fine.

A native farmer selling pigs said:

She come out with the durn beer barrel and she said, "Just stick the pig. I want to make blood pudding." I stuck the hog and let him bleed to death. After it got done bleeding, they drug it out in the back yard. We had to come downtown to get something and then came back. She had that pudding all made up and there was a bunch of them wops standing around eating that durn stuff.

A merchant reported this experience:

The Lithuanians also had some strange food habits. They used to fix fish heads in soup. Now, I know that one time I went over to eat at their house and I noticed some bits of things floating in the soup and after I finished I asked them about the soup and they said they had some fish heads. Well, I didn't say anything but I didn't feel too good.

Among the many foreign food patterns difficult for the native to understand or accept were the eating of garlic and heavily spiced foods and the use of olive oil. Of all the resentments encountered these were most consistently reported. In almost 90 percent of our interviews with natives considerable resentment of the *garlic habit was expressed*. Such resentment from persons accustomed to a bland diet was understandable. Nevertheless, the consumption of garlic was synonymous with inferiority, and natives who ate garlic or used olive oil lost prestige with their friends. A merchant had this to say:

I guess you have really heard a lot about the garlic eaters in this community. We used to have quite a few foreign people who ate garlic. I can remember that my family used to have olive oil in our salads and the natives here thought that we were foreigners because of this; this hurt us.

A miner said:

The foreigners are great garlic eaters. They say it's good for high blood pressure and I've heard the story that garlic is good for mad dogs, too. What you do is close the mad dogs up in the barn with the garlic for a while, and that cures them. Now, of course, I don't know if this is true or not but I've heard it a lot of times.

The following Montenegrin recipe was particularly resented. A merchant stated:

I can remember the foreigners used to fix jerked meat. The Montenegrins were most avid in this and they had what we called "Montenegrin jerk" that was meat soaked in brine, garlic was added, black pepper, then they smoked it. They pickled a lot of the meat. Now, this really was terrible stuff when you used to chew on it and I know that I took some home one time and my wife was having company and everybody ran out of the house when this stuff was put on to cook because it smelled so horrible.

A native businessman reported this:

We had a foreign fellow here from France. I can remember how he used to like to drink wine and eat garlic. When he would tell you a joke, he would get right up in your face and tell it and it was really terrific. Well, it was this sort of thing that was really terrible.

Teachers in the school system resented the use of garlic among immigrant children.

I used to have a lot of kids who ate garlic. I think that they are going away from that. The Americans never came into contact with garlic until the foreigners came over. Used to when you got on the train, by the time you got ten miles down the road, you just couldn't take it.

A native housewife:

Two of our daughters went to teaching. They had to teach foreign children and smell that garlic. The only thing worse than garlic is second-hand garlic, nine out of ten of them foreigners eat garlic. They are what we call "garlic snappers." [The interviewer recording this statement had previously eaten a garlic pickle. He was ten feet away from the informant, writing with one hand and covering his mouth with the other.]

Much antagonism on the job emerged between the native and the immigrant on the garlic issue. One native miner reported the following difficulty:

I can remember one fellow in the mines. He was a big bastard, too. He used to eat too much garlic, and he really did smell. Oh, it was really terrible having to work next to him. We finally had to ask the boss for him to be moved. The boss told him that he would either have to quit eating that garlic or he would have to move him off the machine because the men couldn't work with him. I never smelled anybody that smelled as nasty as he did.

NATIVE ATTITUDES TOWARD INTERMARRIAGE

The barriers imposed by the native's view of the immigrant might have disappeared earlier had his attitude toward intermarriage been favorable. The attitudes the natives had toward intermarriage with immigrants made assimilation difficult. Native children were discouraged from interacting with immigrant children and any serious boy-girl involvement was generally discouraged. Needless to say, such marriages took place over the years, but with considerable misgivings on the part of the adults and usually with forebodings of dire things to occur. An examination of the marriage records suggests that the rate of intermarriage was never high in Coal

Town.[6] The native conceived of the foreigner as being biologically and racially inferior and viewed amalgamation as something to be avoided. Thus many natives looked down upon intermarriage and felt that it cost them prestige. A native woman stated:

There was not much intermarriage between the foreigners and natives when we first came, but there is now. Whenever a marriage would take place, we would always say, "Well, he is marrying a 'hunkie' and that wasn't good."

A merchant told of this situation:

There was one example that I can give you and that was a girl who was born of an Italian mother. This Italian mother was very superstitious. She used to go into trances and do all sorts of things and she believed that she could communicate with the spirits. Well, a native boy fell in love with this Italian girl and his family broke it up. Not because they really cared so much for the children but because they were ashamed to have anybody in the family who had a mother like that.

A native mother:

My son who turned Catholic, well, I don't expect him to live right because he married a Catholic girl. The other boy married a Catholic, too. This was bad. I never did say anything and my husband—it almost killed him. He hated it worse than I did. You see, my husband was so good to the boys.

The son of an immigrant stated:

There was a great deal of resentment against intermarriage between natives and immigrants. Both groups were really against it. My father was against my marriage. My wife is Irish and English and I am Croatian.

Much of the natives' resentment was based on their reaction to Catholicism, as exemplified in the following quotations:

[6] Such a conclusion was reached by first examining the records dealing with name changes with a view toward observing any pattern which might be found. It was discovered that name changes were not frequently made and were almost never made in order to hide the European identity of the person. Instead, we discovered that either the first name was changed or certain letters in the last name were changed to facilitate spelling or pronunciation. For example, the name Harrllampes Boudakis was changed to Harry Boudakis, or Djuro Cergan was changed to George Cergan. Having discovered this pattern, we checked marriage records for marriages of persons with old English names and persons who came from other sections of Europe.

I was reared in the section of the country that had no Catholics. I had never seen any but I had heard a lot about them and I thought that they were some sort of animal. I never saw a Catholic until I came here, and here there is such a mixture it is just like scrambled eggs. I just thought that any person in order to be a Catholic would be rather foolish. I would look at a fellow whenever I would hear someone else say, "Well, there goes a Catholic down the street." I was sort of afraid of them. There was something mysterious about them.

Well, I don't know, it was always claimed that the Catholics was trying to rule the country. That is what they always claimed. You don't know much about them. We don't like Catholics. But now you don't notice much about them. They have had a priest here for the last twenty-five or thirty years who was really a nice man. Fellow by the name of Jones.

The majority of natives were rigidly anti-Catholic and rumors of strange religious ceremonies and the power of the priest were quite pronounced. The three R's, Rum, Romanism, and Ruin, were all intimately related in the thinking of the native, and this anti-Catholic attitude became periodically manifest in the activity of the Ku Klux Klan. A native woman made this observation:

The feeling was strong against intermarriage among the Americans. I think that they just preferred our own breed of people. Mostly it was religious differences. Their religion was the main factor there, I think. There was more consistency among the natives than among the foreign group. We tried to live a good life through the week, not just on Sunday. We didn't want our kids to become like them.

Intermarriage is more prevalent today but there are still those who resent such practices. A native woman reported this:

Now they marry each other and you can't really tell which is which. They're all mixed up. I don't think that parents now care for their children marrying foreigners, but they can't do much about it. I would say that there is more intermarriage between the natives and the foreigners today than there was in the olden time. You see, today there soon won't be any true American because they marry up with these foreigners.

SOCIAL INTERACTION BETWEEN NATIVES AND IMMIGRANTS

This chapter has been concerned with the native's view of Coal Town. Much of what he saw was colored by his attitudes toward social change and toward the Negro and the immigrant, both of whom were intimately tied to these changes. A distinct pattern of human relationships emerged, characterized by impersonality and alienation. The native viewed the immigrant in light of the social barriers he constructed. The associations which did occur between native and immigrant were characterized by formality. They would meet, for example, at union meetings and weddings, but social distance was pronounced. Efforts of immigrants to gain entree into native fraternal orders usually met with discrimination. The interaction which occurred seldom implied an association of equals. For the most part the native reflected the superiority in which he held himself. These patterns of interaction enabled the native to cling to his aloofness and to keep from knowing or understanding the immigrant.

These, of course, were the dominant patterns of interaction but there were those natives who could remove themselves from the vested interests of the moment and see the immigrant in a broader view, as an alien in a strange cultural milieu. A school teacher:

I was in school at the poorest part of the town. I taught at Coal Town School down by Church Street. One year I had forty-eight first graders. At least thirty-five were foreigners. Their parents were just as nice to deal with as anybody. I never had any trouble with any foreign parents.

A native farmer:

These furriners is all good people—hard workin'—honest—do anythin' fer ye if yuh treat 'em half right. I git along with all of 'em. I don't care who knows it—I never did abuse one—even back in the union trouble when they was so hard with 'em. Yuh know, Ol' Pete is like that—don't trust anyone. He trusts me, though. Anything I tell 'im is right, an' he b'lieves me. Lotsa times he'll come an' ask me 'bout things. Yuh know, they give Ol' Pete a bad time, too. But he knows I never had nothin' to do with it.

THE NATIVE'S VIEW OF OTHER NATIVES OF COAL TOWN

The general pattern of interpersonal alienation between the native and the immigrant was also present in the native's attitude toward other natives. The farmers, for example, looked down on native merchants because of their commercial practices and their interest in accumulating wealth. The merchants looked down on the farmer and viewed him as a "hillbilly" who hadn't kept pace with the times. The native coal miner from the region looked down on the farmer who had not made the transition to mining, as well as on merchants whom he did not trust. The natives from the region regardless of occupation looked down on the migrant from the South who had come to mine; and the migrant from the South resented the native from the area.

Each of these groups set up its own walls of suspicion and discrimination; each evolved a set of well-constructed social barriers which time has not completely eroded. The isolation which was maintained between all of these groups enabled them to develop and perpetuate distorted perceptions of each other and to pass them on to succeeding generations.

CHAPTER 5

THE IMMIGRANT LOOKS AT COAL TOWN

THE immigrants who came to Coal Town [1] were largely from impoverished European villages. Some came from well-to-do homes and regions but these were exceptional. A few came directly from the eastern ports of entry of the United States, while others followed the trail of the expanding coal-mining operations. The immigrant in this community came to America for a variety of reasons. Some, for example, rebelled against the patriarchal patterns which characterized their homes in Europe. Typical of this group is the Lithuanian immigrant who reported as follows:

My family was not good. My dad used to beat my mother all the time. You see, over there in the Old Country they have a law that you have to stay together once you get married. There the woman is just like a dog. The man is the boss. He controls the woman and she is nothing but a slave. The man spends all the money and he does not have to give anything to the woman and children if he doesn't want to. I can remember that my father tried to whip me when I was about twenty years old and you can do nothing to your parents because of the law in the Old Country. I worked for my father on a farm for $100 a year. One time I went to dig a grave for a friend whose father had died on the next farm. I asked my sister if I could go and she said, "Yes." Well, I never told my old man I was going and that is where I made my mistake. You had to tell him everything. I forgot about it and so I went and buried my friend's father and came home about sundown. My mother came out to meet me and she said, "Don't go into the house because Papa has blown up." I had a couple of drinks so I could get mad at him and so I went into the house and asked him, "Papa, what is the matter with you?" Well, he was sitting on the bed and he started to get up to hit me, but I pushed him back. He tried to hit me, and I hit him back.

[1] See autobiography in Appendix D.

The next morning he was going to have me arrested. Now, I know what the law could do to a boy in that case. They could put him in jail and so my mother said that I should apologize to him, and so I did. The family life was not happy in the Old Country. The family is much better here than in the Old Country. There is more loving here and I am glad I came.

The vast majority of immigrants in Coal Town arrived with attitudes which made their assimilation, absorption, and identification with community life slow and difficult. To begin with, most of the immigrants came in order to escape military service and for reasons which were narrowly economic. They were interested primarily in earning as much money as possible and hoped to achieve a kind of economic security not possible elsewhere. We found few immigrants, as so often suggested, thirsting for personal, political, and religious freedom. The majority came from cultural backgrounds in which such values were relatively unimportant. The son of an immigrant claimed:

I would say that the immigrant was looking for a good future and the security was the number one thing that attracted him to Coal Town. You see, at that time that he came, the mines were working full time, and Coal Town mine was a good mine to work in. It was easy to get a job. Not too many questions were asked in order for a person to get a job.

Many of the immigrants who came for economic motives had no intention of remaining in the community or in America. Instead they planned to work a number of years and move on, or to accumulate wealth in order to return to their European villages and purchase land. Few actually returned, but hopes persisted for many years. An immigrant miner who arrived in Coal Town at the age of seventeen said:

Most of the people came here in order to get jobs. They came here with a mission—to make money and then to go back and live in the Old Country. But this is not what happened. The people had to stay here. They could not go back because of changes in the Old Country and because they never made enough. When I came to this country, I had a notion that I would go back. What I would do would be to make $300 or $500 and then I would go back to the Old Country to farm again, but after I had been here and after I had started in the coal mining, I just forgot about going home.

The son of a miner reported this problem:

I can remember my father made four trips to America. He would work a while and then he would come back to the Old Country and stay six months and show the people that he had a lot of money and he would have a good time. He did this and my mother did not like it. She always wanted to come to America so finally my mother sold everything and came over here. She brought the children with her and when she got here, she did not like the way in which my father was living and wanted to go back.

A second attitude which retarded the immigrants' assimilation and interest in Coal Town was their attitude toward change. The majority of immigrants had come from isolated rural settlements. Like the natives they were largely provincial and superstitious, with strong tendencies to resist change and keep their culture intact. Like the natives they were interested in the economic benefits of coal mining but rejected changes in their social system. The immigrants who expected to return to their native land saw no reason to change, while other immigrants thought they could remain aloof from the external influences. This both the English and non-English-speaking immigrants attempted to accomplish by living in self-imposed segregation. A native merchant reported this pattern:

I would say there was some mixing between the immigrant groups, but not much. For instance, the Greeks lived in one area, the Slovaks in another area, then there were the Polish, the Croatians, the Italians, the Montenegrins, the Irish, the Welsh, the English, and then the Lithuanians.

When new members of ethnic groups arrived there were established ways of orienting them. This was a common pattern in Coal Town:

The term that I used to describe the way all immigrants grouped together to live was colonization. There was a Frenchman who lived near a Polish friend. When the Frenchman came down here and got a job, he wrote his friend and told him to come down. This fellow invited more Poles and when they got here they lived together. This was usually true. One fellow went into a tavern and was looking for someone. He was Polish. They told him to go up to the next street and go to the Polish tavern. The bartender there took care of him and sent for his wife. They all lived together. They tended to colonize. All the Croatians would be here, all the Italians over here, etc. They would take inferior houses in order to live close to others of their own nationality.

In addition to residential segregation, each ethnic group had its own fraternal and social order. Aside from the usual sickness and death benefits which these societies offered, there were opportunities for interaction with persons from one's cultural background. Such interaction enabled the immigrant to perpetuate his values and customs, to learn American patterns through their being interpreted by his own group, and to receive new ideas filtered through at a tolerable rate which would not be personally disorganizing. An immigrant miner:

The foreigners stayed by themselves. In the early days we had a Croatian society. About four hundred belonged to this society. These Croatians would get their gypsy band and have a good time.

A Croatian remembered:

Oh, yes, there were many organizations here. There was a big Croatian organization here. Each group had organization. From time to time we have dinner, picnics every so often like that, you know. We was getting big crowds every time and we was making good money at that time. Now we got a branch of that all around here. But we used to have here in Coal Town 200 members. Now we got about 65. But half of that is in big cities scattered. Is only about 40 members here.

The son of an immigrant miner pointed this out:

These immigrants wanted to rise above their poor economic status but they have little chance to do so. This frustration got the best of them. This burden would lead to the formation of clubs, lodges. These were organizations where the immigrant could go to play a few games of cards and drink. They each had their own societies and would not have much to do with the other immigrants or natives.

The need to maintain cultural identity and homogeneity was associated with the development of a leader and spokesman for each immigrant group. These leaders served as interpreters of American culture patterns and generally occupied positions of prestige and respect. Many of these leaders manifested a deep interest in the members of their group. A highly educated son of an immigrant reported this conversation:

Y—— recalled that each immigrant group in Coal Town had its own intermediary, except the Slavs who all looked to one man. This man was a Slovenian, who was conversant in all Slavic languages as well as English, an experienced Austrian miner, whom they could trust to give them a fair deal despite the fact that he was also mine super at the time.

An immigrant noted:

Mr. D—— is in the position now what I would call an intermediary. Sometimes the immigrants couldn't talk good English and they would go to him. They get to like him. He is intermediary for these people and was counselor and give them legal advice and they listened to him.

One immigrant felt keenly the need for a spokesman:

Sure we still got some good men, too. Mr. K——, he's good to us. He's honest. He don't talk much. Some here say we don't need him but without a man like him the Americans might think hunkies don't need anything. That's why most of us vote for him in every election. There are some Americans that are good too, that you can trust, but not many. Some are real nice people—treat me nice. I got one good American friend. Another one a lady schoolteacher—she lets me plant her three lots over there.

Other leaders were unscrupulous and used the immigrant for personal benefit. A Croatian miner:

Immigrant people is hard-working people and honest but easy to mislead them by some crooks. You had plenty of people that would take advantage of them to get certain kinds of positions and this and that; using tricks to mislead poor people.

Many of these leaders fulfilled valuable functions for the immigrant. Others misused their power by perpetuating their authority and by playing on the underlying fear that "the big, bad native will get you if you don't watch out." This was not difficult to achieve since there were so many areas of conflict.

During election periods there was a tendency for the immigrants to vote as a block according to the dictates of their leaders. A native political leader made this observation:

Every nationality here had a leader. They would go to their leader for advice. They have used that in elections here. Each leader had a certain number of people who followed him.

Relinquishing democratic privileges meant little since there was no history of democracy for the immigrant. It was the individual leader who promised safety and security that had more reality than abstract political ideologies. The pattern of turning over privileges and responsibilities was a well-established one and became manifest in many areas of personal and social life. With respect to union membership we learn from the son of an immigrant miner:

Now, when the immigrant got into the union, they were followers. They were not leaders. They were afraid to do anything that might bring them trouble, more trouble than they had already experienced.

The pattern of giving up political freedoms underwent some change with the children of the immigrants. Nevertheless, the basic orientation of relinquishing freedom and responsibility to a leader existed for many years among these people. Even today an appeal for such a leader might fall on interested ears. Having said this we must immediately realize that we know very little about the social climate necessary for the integration of new ideas. Is it possible that the basic ingredients which might have enabled the immigrant to make the political transition from authoritarianism to democracy were lacking in Coal Town? Can we expect a people who for many reasons feel isolated and threatened to accept an alien ideology fraught with unknown consequences? To allow oneself to accept a climate of freedom and democracy requires the security and courage to relinquish ties to the past as well as a willingness to face the new and the unstructured. If these are some of the basic requirements for democratic participation they were not present for our Coal Town people.

During the 1920s organizations representing various shades of Socialism emerged in Coal Town. For the immigrant these organizations represented certain ideological interests with which he was already familiar, having encountered them in Europe. Nevertheless, our data suggest that for the majority of persons in these groups a nonideological motivation was present. These clubs represented social gatherings of lonely people in strange surroundings. Our general feeling was that the immigrants' attraction to the socialistic organizations grew primarily out of their need to mix with their own kind, and that whatever deep ideological convictions may have been present were felt by the leaders rather than the rank and file. For some fifteen years there were active affiliations of these organizations in Coal Town. A native merchant noted:

In the 1920s the doctrine of Karl Marx was quite successful in this community. He had a tremendous appeal to the immigrants. Many of the people who fell for the Marxism movement were the Slavs. It was a great appeal to them and they could be duped very easily. There were people here who went to regular meetings of this movement and one man was even sent to Moscow.

Another native:

We had many Socialists and Bolsheviks. Mr. J——, for instance, was a Socialist who mixed with some Americans, and in 1917–18 and the twenties they almost took over in Birdtown. The Anti-Socialists had to stick together and defeat them. The idea that was here was the Socialists were for the workers.

The leader for many years of the Socialist Labor Party in Coal Town was a man who had devoted most of his adult years to this organization. Originally he was a man of prestige and considerable following. Today, under different political circumstances, he is an outcast, considered queer and undesirable. This he senses. Although broken in spirit, he still maintains his ideological interests and believes in the inevitable overthrow of capitalism. In his speaking of his dedication certain insights are revealed which separate him clearly from the rank-and-file members:

I never married because I have devoted my life to the Socialist Labor Party. In this one cannot raise a family and lead an active life in the Party. I have a few friends that I can talk with, though I do not discuss this thing any more. Some of my friends I see less often now than before. I am somewhat isolated. I make my friends and I break off my friends. I haven't got very many. I feel alone. I cannot discuss these things I believe with other people, they do not understand. I do not visit any more, I just live alone.

The narrowly economic incentive for immigration, the feeling that they might shortly leave the community, the necessity to maintain their cultural identities, and their rigid attitudes toward change fostered an *exploitative attitude* on the part of the immigrants toward their surroundings. Furthermore, there was little concomitant responsibility or interest in the community or its problems. An immigrant merchant:

No, they didn't do that much [take an interest in city government]. I don't think the foreign people in those days cared much about city government and the community because they didn't know, they didn't know it was of benefit to them. Foreign people like a cleaner city now, but not then.

Feelings of impermanency, of mobility, of not belonging, of not being a part of the community emerged for the immigrants. Thus they were perpetual strangers, always on the outside looking in. Such feelings still persist and tend to perpetuate themselves. Any effort to change the immigrants was defined as an attack on their customs and precipitated considerable sensitivity and overreaction. The more isolated the immigrants felt the more negatively they reacted to outside interference, and this produced still more withdrawal. This facet of a minority group's way of viewing society may not be restricted to our Coal Town people but may well occur in other communities and is an important component in the social psychology of minority group people.

For these immigrants there was the belief that they might partake of the available wealth without contaminating their family patterns and their ways of behaving and thinking. This they were unable to achieve. The longer they remained, the greater the difficulty in keeping out new values and ideas. Subsequent chapters will reveal the consequences of these invasions of new patterns for personal and social behavior.

Although this isolation was the predominant pattern among the immigrants, there were those who actively tried to assimilate and change. A number of these were non-English-speaking immigrants in business. Their attempt at assimilation reveals an interesting pattern of change. For example, there was the tendency to adapt certain utilitarian business ways without concomitant change in personal life. Thus for these people two needs, the need for change and the need to maintain the status quo, were fulfilled. A native merchant:

If the immigrant kept his own customs it was very hard for him to get ahead, to become Americanized. Now, many of them were in business, whose personal life had not changed but their business life and their life with other people in the community had changed, and we usually referred to them as very successful businessmen. In other words, what they would do would be to adapt their commercial ways to the community but not their personal lives. There was not too much change in the personal lives of these immigrants but they did learn how to change their commercial activities and their way of doing things. They were good copiers and they used to copy business procedures from Americans and many times they were much better than the native-born Americans.

Other non-English-speaking immigrants in business tried to achieve complete assimilation. Many of these persons were self-effacing people. They had internalized the native prejudices toward the immigrant and held themselves in contempt. Their cultural identity was always in a state of flux. An immigrant describes his early motives for becoming an American and the aggressiveness with which he pursued his goals:

I came to America at the age of sixteen. I had read U.S. history, and I decided once I had read this history book to come to the United States. I was to go into the military service in the Greek Army because at the time the Greeks had captured our country. I served three months. During this time I learned the Greek language and I can still speak it very well. After I was discharged from the army I had arranged to go to Yugoslavia to work but I fixed things to come to America and when I escaped from my country, I went to Yugoslavia and then I came straight to America. I said even before I came that I would be an American and that I would forget my foreign ways. I always spoke English here. I never spoke my native language. It is not nice to speak Bulgarian in front of native people. You see, I don't pay any attention to the term "hunkie." I always got along with all of the people and you have to do this and you have to push yourself. That's what I did. I really pushed myself. I tried to stay by myself and be away from the foreign element. I wanted to do this because when I came to America I wanted to be an American. They say here that I am an American and even in Rock City when I used to go there after I settled in Coal Town, they would say, "George, what is the matter with you. You are too American for us. You are forgetting your old ways." They thought that it was not good for me to marry an American. I have been married twenty-seven years. I have never worried if I did the right thing. You see, I set my mind to do this and this is what I did.

The native American wife of our immigrant informant reveals her motives in marrying him.

My husband does not belong to the immigrant group. You see, he is different. If he had not been different it would have not gone over with me. I would not have married him if he were really an immigrant and if he had immigrant ideas. You see, he had American ideas. You see, among the foreign element, women had no say-so at all. They began to see that American families did not live like they do and there was a gradual change.

As we left these informants one evening after obtaining an excellent interview, our host followed us to the car. Now, alone with the interviewing team, our friend who had spent the better part of an evening describing how he did not want to be identified with immigrants made the following parting remark:

Fellows, I hear you have a Mr. Boolokov over there. Could you please bring him with you next time you come?

The marginal status which characterized our previous informant brought with it certain benefits but was always associated with feelings of guilt and uncertainty about where he belonged. Immigrants who tried to assimilate encountered the hostility of their own group. The educated son of an immigrant miner:

There was a tendency to reject the person who would Americanize. I do know that these immigrants who Americanized were usually talked about among the immigrant groups. For example, if an immigrant wanted to get ahead, he might marry a native woman. This might create antagonism in the immigrant's personal life, like my family, for instance. Now my wife and I have had some pretty terrible arguments on this basis and I know that there has been a great deal of trouble which could have been avoided if I had married a Croatian woman, but instead I married a native woman and this has caused some difficulty.

The very deep and painful social-psychological conflict which confronts persons in transition between cultural worlds is not in itself a new problem. It does, however, have some added significance for our immigrants in Coal Town. They emerge as a people with a sense of cynicism about the world which is nurtured by their life in the community. This cynicism appears as a component of our marginal people who attempted to bridge two worlds only to discover that such an attempt intensified inner conflict and turmoil. Many immigrants felt that for those who tried to assimilate, conflict and failure were inevitable. The educated son of an immigrant:

I think it is really impossible to make the transition a complete transition from the immigrant to the native side. For instance, you take the case of an immigrant man who tried to become American. Why, the immigrant groups just tolerates him and I used that word expressively. For example, the immigrant lodge just tolerates him. It's too much for a man to bear to be tolerated by his own group and not be accepted by the new group. At best, I think most of them are unhappy when they try this.

IMMIGRANT ATTITUDES TOWARD PREJUDICE AND DISCRIMINATION

We have discussed some of the significant factors in the immigrants' view of Coal Town and have suggested that there were active forces from within the immigrants' way of life which retarded their interest and identification with Coal Town. Further, we pointed out that movements in the direction of assimilation were retarded by the immigrants' emotional incapacities to make the transition and were actively rejected by some immigrants who defined assimilation as disloyalty to their culture. On the other hand, whatever tendencies the immigrants had toward assimilation and integration were easily discouraged by the active and pervasive prejudice and discrimination which they experienced. This prejudice intensified their feelings of isolation and helped produce even greater separateness. The immigrants sensed keenly the attack on their differences in national origin, religion, and customs. An immigrant points out the general native reaction to outsiders:

When the immigrant moved in, the native felt we were pests invading him. They had no comprehension and understanding of us. They thought we should all be Americanized and that meant changing all our ways. When we didn't we caught it. They attacked all our customs. They called us dago, wop, hunkie, and catlicker [Catholic]. They laughed and made fun of our being different. For a person to go to the Catholic Church was to invite trouble. The native was particularly interested in enforcing the law as it concerned the immigrant. But they were not particularly interested in enforcing the law as far as their own behavior was concerned. If the natives had helped the immigrants, I think there would

have been a totally different situation here. Some of the barriers might
have been broken down. Much could have been done to educate the
immigrant, to permit him to join native fraternal orders. Instead there
was contempt for the immigrant and the native had the tendency to
hold himself apart from the immigrant. I think that the world has
suffered too much from Germanic arrogance, Anglo-Saxon conceit, and
Latin connivance. Here it was Anglo-Saxon conceit.

Although the immigrant felt that virtually all natives were
prejudiced toward him, physical violence as a manifestation of
prejudice was experienced most frequently in relation to the miner
from the South, with whom he was in economic competition. An
immigrant miner's son:

Those blamed poor white trash from the South used to make it tough on
us. I've heard my dad tell many a time how they used to push him off
the sidewalks in Birdtown, call him a dago or a garlic snapper, even spit
on him. There wasn't anything he could do, he just had to take it and go
ahead, or get mobbed.

Prejudice from the native, previously unorganized, became
highly organized in the early twenties. This was a general period
of reaction in many communities throughout America, characterized
by a spirit of self-righteous bigotry, sweeping people of different
inclinations away; while the Ku Klux Klan saved the nation from
Rum, Romanism, and Rebellion. The native informants who were
interviewed on this question saw the Ku Klux Klan movement
largely in terms of their local situation. They defined the movement
as consisting of men banding together to keep people from drinking
too much, mistreating their families, or engaging in illicit sexual
practices. Although the natives recognized that Klan members
took the law into their own hands, they believed that this was not
a serious issue, since more good than harm was achieved and the
harm done was probably exaggerated. Force was necessary to stamp
out evil and evil was a matter of the Klan's definition, according
to the native. The native informant evidenced little understanding
of the movement. One had the uncomfortable feeling that nothing
had really been learned as a result of Klan violence and that under
a similar social climate an organization dedicated to the principles

of producing conformity through violence could still be nurtured in these surroundings. An immigrant's son:

I would say 1924 was the beginning of prejudice when the natives here declared war against what they called the four R's—Rum, Romanism, Rebellion, and Ruin. In this area they added a letter "R" and that was Ruin. And this meant the ruining that immigrants caused to the area. So that you had Rum, Romanism, Rebellion, and Ruin by the immigrants. There was a great deal of prejudice against the immigrant. He was blamed for the unemployment. This antiforeign prejudice was organized. It was used as a tool. The Klan used it in their meetings. I would call this a Klan psychosis, which has been particularly prevalent in this area. I can remember that it was in the Al Smith campaign that this prejudice against the immigrants and against the Catholics reared its head because most of the Protestant groups thought that Al Smith was going to deliver the country to the Catholics. Now, here the religious feeling was very intense because most of the Protestant religions here were Southern-inclined. The Catholic immigrant and the old natives were very much at odds on the subject of religion.

Many immigrants felt that Klan sympathizers were those with whom economic competition was keenest. An immigrant reported:

Now many of these people were illiterate and biased in religion and had a poor outlook on life. Their attitude toward work was not good. If you paid them $10 you would never get $10 worth of work. There was a great amount of absenteeism and these people would take off whenever they felt like it. They just wanted to get by.

A number of our immigrant informants reported a pattern in which prejudice and discrimination during periods of economic tension became intense. Differences between groups became distorted and hostility broke through. The pattern was something like this:

Now in the case of individuals there was very good friends between the immigrants and natives, not between groups but between individuals. I think that a sign of the emergence of prejudice is when the native became somewhat in dire circumstances and they are worse off economically than the immigrant, and he would become envious and jealous of his immigrant friend and would talk with other natives about the immigrants and how peculiar they were, how strange they were, how stingy they were, and how foreign they were. The individual personal quarrels appear.

There is for instance the insult of the immigrant by the native and the native gets mad and then he withdraws to his own group. This is usually seen in the fact that the native goes from one tavern where he used to hang out with the immigrant to a tavern which is exclusively the hangout of the native groups. When the natives refused to hang out any longer with the immigrants and would shy away from the immigrant and go to his own group, this was another sign that prejudice was aborning. One could see a widening rift, a gradual emergence over a long period of time.

Although prejudice was manifest in all areas of life, the immigrant, with a different set of cultural practices, reported that he was disliked and discriminated against because of his tendency to save and work hard. This theme appears over and over in our data and has been clearly suggested in the natives' attitudes toward the immigrants described in Chapter 4. The immigrant felt rather thoroughly misunderstood and indicted for embracing values and habits which were inherently natural and just to him. He felt frustrated and thwarted about being unable to communicate his feelings or his beliefs to natives. A native merchant:

The two factions, the immigrants and the natives, could not understand each other. It was heaven here for the native to work because he could earn a great deal of money, and he would earn this money but he would not save it. He would spend it and while he spent it he would not work and this would give him a great deal of leisure time. This was what he wanted. The natives called the immigrants tightwads because they saved their money.

Many of the immigrants viewed the values of thrift and industry as the only bases for a respectable life, but they were made to feel guilty by the natives' assault on these values. Hard work could bring more money, but seldom advancement in the coal industry. This appeared as an inconsistency which disturbed the immigrant. A native miner:

I can remember the boss saying about the immigrant that "As long as I am superintendent there will be no hunkie working on top of this mine, the only place for them is underneath."

One of our immigrant informants had this to say about working patterns:

The immigrant would work much more consistently while the natives would not. They did not expect much. They were not used to much. Why they used to say many times to us, "Why did you come here, 'hunkie,' because you take our jobs away from us. You should go back to where you come from." The immigrant would be more apt to save his money than the American. Well, the American people would have a good time. I won't say it was foolishness. They have nice looking cars to go places. In the early days the American boys would rather go hunting than work. They didn't care for the money. I don't blame him. But to have a good time you have to spend money. They used to get mad at us because we saved.

Another immigrant miner had this to say:

I would say that the foreign people were better miners than the natives. They told me that I was a very good worker. He said that I could do the work of two persons. He said that I was such a good worker that he hated to lose me when I moved from one job to the next. Sometimes the Americans would get mad at you because then they would have to work a little bit harder themselves and they did not like to do this. The boss liked me much better than he did the natives because he told me. The boss never called me "hunkie" in the mine and if they did I would have gotten real mad, though sometimes they say it out on the street. I can hear them.

The immigrant's habits of thrift created additional problems during periods of industrial strife. The son of an immigrant:

During industrial lags and strikes, the immigrant, because of his habits, was better able to weather the difficult period. The immigrant built his own house. He did not hire people to work for him like the natives. He saved money and for this reason he could weather the strikes much better than the native. It was the native who always kept yelling that strikes were too long and they were the first ones to give in, not the immigrant. For example, during a strike the immigrant was much better off than the native. You see, what the immigrant did was to save his money and live on only a small portion of his money. If his wages went up, that meant he saved more but he didn't spend more. But for the native, if the wages went up that meant he spent more and he always got into debt. This always made the native angry at us.

Working conditions were relatively unimportant to the immigrant, in part because he had no concept of anything better and in part because he felt impotent to change the conditions. The native had a different reaction. An immigrant's son:

The native was interested in two things. First, high wages, and second, better working conditions. Now the native was a stickler for working conditions because he had it easy underground and he wanted it to stay that way. I can give you one example. If a native was working as a digger with a pick and shovel and the union had signed an agreement with the Company that the car should be spotted at such and such a distance from the face of the mine very close so the digger would not have to move the coal more than once, this native would come down and find that the car was not close enough, so he would just sit down and wait for someone to come and lay the tracks closer. Now if this were an immigrant, he would not sit down and wait but he would go ahead and load the car. Now this was a sore point between the natives and the immigrants because the immigrant would tend to go ahead and work and thus violate the contract, whereas the native would not.

Still another dimension of the prejudice which the immigrant experienced appeared in the exploitation by the native of the immigrants. The tendency for the native to exploit the immigrant was a sore point with the immigrant, a pattern deeply resented which has not been forgotten. Many immigrants had this reaction:

The natives preferred to exploit the immigrant. There were some natives who were in a position to promote good will but they did not do it. They discouraged this between the two groups and preferred to exploit them.

The immigrants believed in caring for their own needs and resented deeply the practice of one person's taking unfair advantage of another. A retired immigrant miner:

A man's got to do this part, maintain his self-respect but not impose on other people, or take unfair advantage. Lots of us here were like that. We don't think much of a man who won't work hard. In this country they didn't give us much chance to use our brains. All they wanted was our muscle, like the niggers. That's what made us look like stupid boobs, like we don't know nothin'.

The immigrant's language difficulties made him vulnerable to exploitative situations. One immigrant reported this:

When we first came here, our first problem was with the language difficulty. It makes a person feel lost here. I would go into the stores and I could not make myself understood so then I began to go only to the stores that were run by the Lithuanian people and would not buy from the natives.

Another immigrant:

Before I learned to talk English, I would have to point to everything that I wanted to buy. One day I went to a store and wanted to buy some milk and eggs. They had a big wooden refrigerator and I couldn't see in it. I looked around and I looked around but I couldn't find what I wanted. The man asked me what I wanted but I couldn't understand him. He knew I was looking for something so he just let me alone. Finally I went over to him and I showed him what I was wanting. [Mr. P—— acts out a cow, then a hen laying eggs.] He understood me and got the milk and eggs for me but I never knew what it really cost.

One immigrant miner had this experience:

I had about three or four hundred dollars in American money hid in my clothes and in my shoes. I went up to a fruit peddler and tried to tell him what I wanted. He would point at the bananas and I would nod my head. He said, "Two dozen," and I nodded my head again. I didn't know what that meant. He would point at the oranges and I would nod my head. He filled a basket up with fruit and I pulled out a ten-dollar bill and gave it to him. He gave me back two one-dollar bills. I told my friend about the bargain. I told him that I had given the peddler one bill and he give me back two and a whole basket of fruit. He said, "What was the number of the bill you gave him?" I said, "Ten, I think." He looked at the two I got back and started laughing. He told me, "He charged you eight dollars for a little basket of fruit." I was a stranger here and I didn't know better.

Exploitation appeared most frequently in the business transactions which occurred between native and immigrant. An immigrant's son:

You've seen these native businessmen put up a sales talk to some foreigner they knew had money—trying to sell him something he didn't need or want. They had the notion that if only natives worked business would be good. The hunkies were too stingy. But they never figured the hunkie worked steadier and made more. Besides he always pays his bills.

Often a lack of knowledge of custom and law made the immigrant vulnerable. One native miner related this:

The natives, knowing the ignorance of the immigrants, would take advantage of them. One immigrant would salvage things and he built him a garage out of scrap lumber. He moved to a better home. While he was moving, a Southerner moved in and claimed the garage. The immigrant was afraid to take the garage then because he figured this fellow knew the law and what he was talking about.

The friendly, interested native was rare but not unknown. Some natives could respond with warmth to the immigrant's children. An immigrant's son:

One of the things that I remember about all this is that although the native was antagonistic toward the immigrant, they were fond of his children. I remember there was an old native who used to drive a dump wagon in the mine. As soon as he saw my brother and I out, he would let us ride in his dump wagon. I remember the landlord out there. He would make it a point to wait twenty or thirty minutes to take us kids to school. He would take maybe ten or twelve of us. We used to play in his sister's yard.

A retired immigrant miner told us about this:

I'll tell you another outfit too that was all right. The whole S—— clan. Why, I remember when the old man was running the feed store he'd deal with foreigners straight an' honest. He never made fun of the way they talked. He'd call 'em in an' talk with 'em an' try his best to please 'em. There were quite a few of those old gentlemen that you had to respect, but these damn, ignorant Yahoos, the damn, lazy, shiftless no-accounts. They were wild as a bunch of drunk Indians. That old man G——, I happened to hear him say one time, "Well, we sure got that old hunk's dough."

The scars of prejudice, discrimination, and bitterness appeared rather uniformly in our interviews. These feelings have not been eradicated. They are held more intensely by the immigrants than by their children, but to some extent by both. Many immigrants feel that prejudice and discrimination are still present. The son of an immigrant:

Joe, I can name you every one of 'em. I have to deal with 'em in business, in clubs, on the school board, and on the City Council. You think prejudice would pass and be forgotten but, by God, we've got it today. It crops up every now and then—that's the main reason I try to stay on the school board. Only a while back D—— came to me, said his boy wasn't bein' treated right in school. I took him an' the boy to the school board meetin'. The principal was there. I said, "Look man, let's be civilized, let's get to the bottom of this thing. We've got to educate these kids, no matter whose they are." An' we did get to the bottom of it, an' D—— was satisfied. When the principal apologized an' told him it wouldn't happen again. But Joe, those people are afraid. They don't trust anyone any more.

A social climate characterized by prejudice and discrimination brought with it deeply entrenched reactions to the native, reactions which promise to persist for a long time. The son of an immigrant miner:

I can remember, for instance, that an Italian gave me this statement not long ago, that a friend of his was innocently clubbed over the head in 1933 as he was standing on the street corner by a native simply because he happened to be standing on the street corner and he was an Italian. And then later on this Italian went on to say that when things got better in the community and promoters came around they were very interested in winning him over to their side and he said this statement—he told me this which I think is very interesting—it went something like this, "I don't care how much candy you bring me now, I am going to remember that you once hit me over the head." People won't cooperate. You can't crack a man over the head and tell him he ain't a full-fledged citizen one day and expect him to act l.ke one on the next day.

One immigrant felt this way:

But I got another neighbor over there on that side, one these call himself hundred percenter. Told me one time I'm not an American. I told that s.o.b. I'm better American than him. I said, "I come here on my own money, with my own belongings, to be an American an' I paid my way ever since an' do my part. (I served in the First World War.) But you, you're a bum. You come here with a bare behind an' never done no better since, only show it. You're too damn lazy to work, just chisel all you can on other men's work. You're a damn parasite." He call me a damn hunkie one time, too. I don't like that. He better watch hisself. I guess I'm a little crazy but when I get mad I want to knock hell out of somebody. I'll kick the hell right out of him if he doesn't mind his own business. I don't like that. I've been a loyal citizen an' I expect to be respected. I stay behind my own fence and mind my own business. I don't say any more than hello, how are you, to American neighbors.

Many of the immigrants feel that political democracy is an ideology which may apply to the native but which has no reality for them. Many feel quite hopeless about participation. Furthermore, fears regarding discrimination, of being easily dispossessed, are

present. Many immigrant informants were difficult to interview
because of this. One member of the research team had the following
experience:

I hastened to explain that there would be no personal identification involved and that they could feel free to say as much or as little as they
wished. But they were still hesitant. They exchanged a few words in
Hungarian and she began to explain to me and apologize in Croatian. Said
they had been in Coal Town many years, had seen many strange turns of
events there, had many troubled times, and had been the victims of much
abuse. "We don't know but what we may see similar events yet again,"
she explained, "and anything we say or do may be used against us." She
was profusely apologetic and begged forgiveness. "You are Croatian and
therefore you understand how it is with us, I'm sure," she said, "after all,
you know we both come from the Old Country and we are not what you
would call 100 percent citizens."

The majority of immigrants in Coal Town are now resigned
people. They consider themselves at the mercy of forces beyond
their control and hope that in some fortuitous way disaster can be
minimized. A retired miner:

Oh, all politics, we just are checkers on the board—if you're in the
right place you stay with the board, if not you get taken off. It's like being
a soldier in Franz Joseph's Army. If he gets mad at the Italian King you
go kill Italians or they kill you. If you're smart you try to accommodate
yourself to better situations and advantages within certain limits because
there is always someone in control higher up and you have to keep trying
to guess what the next move will be.

One immigrant informant, who came to America as a child,
summed up the reactions of his friends by suggesting that prejudice is not dead and may in the future become manifest in new
and different ways depending on the circumstances of the moment.

I think as the area sinks back into its provincial state prejudices will arise
once more. Prejudice is not dead here. It is being employed even gradually
now as the economic pressure becomes more severe. Whenever there is
tough competition for jobs such as there is at the present time here,
prejudice begins to appear. I would say that even today certain religious
groups employ pressure in order to get jobs for their members and keep
others out. They may be directed against other types of persons such as

new creeds, etc., and I think maybe that the liberal persons will be the target of much of the new type of prejudice that is characteristic of areas that sink back into their state of provincialism. This may result in the same person's, who is actually a liberal or different, being called a radical or communist. I think some of the signs of these are present in this area.

IMMIGRANT ATTITUDES TOWARD THE NATIVES

Thus far we have approached the problem of prejudice from the viewpoint of the natives reaction to the immigrant and the immigrant's personal experience of this. At this point it is necessary to suggest that the immigrant's basic disinterest in his surroundings, his lack of identification or feeling of belonging, and the overt discrimination by the native created a wall between the immigrant and the native. Barriers of prejudice, discrimination, and contempt for the cultural practices of the native emerged. Like all such cultural barriers they became general in scope, indiscriminate in application, and included all natives, regardless of person. Fear and anxiety were always present in relation to the native. Patterns of prejudice emerged in relation to observable differences in the culture patterns of the native. Even the friendly native found it difficult to penetrate this barrier. Personal relationships between the friendly native and the immigrant were often tenuous. A native schoolteacher:

I can remember specific instances in which the foreigners were suspicious that we might hurt them. For instance, I had a very close friend who was a member of the foreign-born group and he and I became very close, almost like brothers. But I never felt that he was too close to me. For instance, I would do some things for him and he would be suspicious that whenever I did it I didn't do it out of friendship but that maybe I had some angle, and I always had the feeling that he was suspicious toward me.

All natives were characterized as lazy, dirty, shiftless, and untrustworthy. Stereotypes of the native emerged which were readily applied to all. The native Protestant stereotyped the Catholic im-

migrant as professing Christian beliefs on Sunday and heathen beliefs on Monday. The Catholic immigrant saw the native in precisely the same terms. One son of an immigrant made this remark:

U—— characterizes the native as Christian—Evangelical, Methodist—
who believes it's a sin to drink beer in a tavern or go to a movie, but'
believes it's all right to make a sort of sport of "sneaking around to play
the deacon's or elder's wife." That seemed to be in the proper order of
things. Even if he got caught everybody would forget it in a little while,
it seemed.

A typical immigrant's concept of a native:

The mailman, he's really a good fellow. But you know how these Americans are. They won't make a garden but would like to have everything
they see someone else raise. He comes by, looks around—"Boy, what nice
tomatoes; boy, my wife sure likes those beans," and stuff like that. I take
his mail sack an' load him down with everything. Ah, since my wife
died, I can't can anything—nobody here to eat it. I give away pretty
near everything I raise. He does favors for me, and he's nice to me an' I
respect the obligation.

There was considerable contempt for the native's personal habits
of living, especially those of the Southerners, who were described
in the following terms:

We called the people from Tennessee and Alabama by this term in
Croatian, "cigani," which means gypsies. That was the closest Croatian
term in Croatian to describe how we felt about these natives. You see, this
group was also referred to in Croatian language as the "shoeless ones."
They were dirty and they were filthy. We also had some nicknames for
them. For instance, we called them "Monkey John," and they usually
were a very colorful lot. I can describe for you the typical Tennessee
family. They lived usually in a house on a hill and they liked to fool
around with their houses and make minor repairs, and usually tear off
things from their houses such as screens and doors and so forth. Usually
there were dirty and filthy kids running around the house. They were
never clean. They didn't have any screens on their houses. Now, most of
the people were mean, just downright mean. They all carried pistols or
guns. They seemed to be born with them. They resented any slurs on the
individual and on the family name. They were very quick to fly off the
handle. This is one of the important characteristics of these people from
the South, I think, and that is that they could call themselves anything

but an outsider would not dare to call the family names because everyone would get up in arms.

The immigrant looked down on the food habits of the native.

Whenever you had one of these from Balkan states he would have soup, meat, onions, and bread. An Alabaman or Kentuckian would have mince-meat and a lot of cookies. We called them cake-eaters. They would say, "You damn garlic snapper," and we would say, "You damn cake-eater." They would have more sweets. They would go to the store and get lunch meat. The foreign people ate better. Once or twice a week we would take chicken with us. We would fry chicken at home and take it with us to the mine. It took good eats to keep us sturdy and keep us ready for work. We knew that. The woman would buy all food for two weeks. After a while she liked the sweets and took up the food ways of the native, this was bad.

Bulgarians eat, well, I will tell you, it is different altogether from what the Americans eat. I would say that the dietary habits of the immigrant were much better than those of the natives. I think that they were under-nourished. The natives were very interesting in their dietary habits and that is they never had a well-balanced meal. They lived on bacon and beans. I would say "low down on the hog."

There was little understanding of the cultural traditions of the native. Many of the immigrants' observations had a strong element of truth, but there was an undertone of contempt and exaggeration in their remarks.

IMMIGRANT ATTITUDES TOWARD OTHER IMMIGRANTS

Prejudice toward the English-speaking immigrant was equally intense. The immigrant lumped all English together and viewed them as follows:

Johnny Bulls are hardest of all to get along with—too conceited. They don't like our people, Joe. They always try to fool them that they're friendly but they cheat and mistreat them.

The English were accused of shirking their financial obligations. In discussing a particular business enterprise that failed, this was said by an immigrant miner:

I'd put the Johnny Bull—I mean all of 'em, Scotch, Irish, Welsh—or whatever they called themselves—in the same sack with some of the no-account natives. They'd beat you just as quick. Why, those boys felt like if they weren't working good, or had spent their money for something else and didn't have it to pay you, you were just supposed to forget about it. An' the older the bill, the more you should forget. An' they were brazen about it. Take Old Jim (my wife's late uncle) and his wife, Ol' Beatrice, why they still owe me hundreds of dollars, all over town they owe, too, from forty years back. They owed L—— a couple of hundred for groceries an' never would pay him. Later they had the gall to come in his tavern to drink beer an' even ask for credit on that. Raised hell with him. L—— said he had half a notion to shoot 'em both, one time.

The son of a Croatian miner:

Not a single native or Englishman that Joe carried on credit has come across. I have the same experience here in the auto business. Once that those guys get in a place that's tight and get behind they simply won't pay you. They must think you're supposed to make allowances for them and just forget that they owe you anything. Boy, they're sure quick to forget.

The English-speaking immigrants, as previously remarked, remained aloof from the other groups in Coal Town. A native merchant noted:

The Englishmen were hardheaded and stubborn people. There was one big charge against them and that was that they held themselves to be better than other people and that they knew a lot more than other people. The Englishmen considered themselves apart from the immigrants and they felt that they were as good if not better than the natives. They mixed only among themselves and I think that the type of relationship that they had to most people was an overlordship, a sort of master-servant relationship, you might say.

The reasons for the aloofness of the English are complex but in part center around their marginal occupational status. Many of them occupied semiexecutive mining positions which meant that identification with either management or labor was not readily feasible. Many felt insecure about their status and refused to enter into associations which might in any way injure them. In addition to aloofness this brought with it loneliness as well. On the other hand, there was also a tendency for them to feel culturally superior to both native and immigrant. Their economic position was in almost all instances far superior to anything they had possessed in Europe. Although in the lower socioeconomic class in Europe, they became a powerful force in the Coal Town class structure, often obtaining top positions in the mining industry, and wielded influence in public affairs. The English-speaking immigrants' view of native and immigrant miners is perhaps best summed up in the following quote; an Englishman speaks:

Most of the mining board men that created safety for mines mostly came from England or Scotland and Wales. They had been miners for many years. Their fathers and grandfathers were miners. Our first mining books mostly came from England, as well as laws of mining. They have been mining coal since 1200 in England. A very small percentage of Croatians became efficient in mines. This was because of lack of knowledge of mining. The Italian people were just general workers in the mines. The Croatians and Hungarians about the same way. A very small percentage of natives and foreigners became efficient in the mines.

Whatever cultural patterns of prejudice emerged in Coal Town, they were never confined to a single group. Instead they became indiscriminately manifest in relation to all groups. Thus the immigrants who focused on the differences of the native developed a similar antipathy for people of their own group. The non-English-speaking immigrants had their own set of prejudices in relation to each other. One illustration:

The Serbs and Croatians had trouble. Serbs never like Croatians. At the time of the First World War the Serbs done some mean things to the Croatians. I see now that the Serbs know they did wrong then. I could tell you all but I don't like to say bad things about anyone ever. But I won't lie about anything either. I know they report wrong things about Croatians because they were Austrian enemy country, you know.

Many immigrant informants were envious of other immigrants who were successful. They often acquired native prejudices and learned to believe that the immigrant's business success was achieved through his own dishonest practices. An immigrant's view of a successful immigrant:

Quite a few cleaned up here in Coal Town. Pete got his start when he hit it lucky gambling. Now he is snobbish. Thought he was running a high-class place. If you are not well to do and well dressed he didn't want to have anything to do with you. He has little to do with his own people any more. Most don't like him.

Another comment:

He closed up the grocery store in 1928 and still has a fat bankroll. [Amused.] He is afraid for his money. He won't go to the bank if there are any Croats around where they can see him. He made it off them and is ashamed. Him and the one who butchered for him—they were good ones at weighing their thumbs. They must have made money aplenty in their time.

SUMMARY

Chapter 4 portrayed certain basic themes which characterized the natives' view of Coal Town. Significant among these was the marked impersonality which became manifest in alienation and contempt for immigrants and other natives. What was once the natives' land and country was now overrun by strange people with strange practices employed in what was at best a strange economic venture. With this they could not and did not identify.

The immigrant likewise, for perhaps another set of reasons, failed to identify with or to become an integrated part of Coal Town. His relations with respect to the native and in many instances other immigrants were characterized by impersonality and alienation. Which was the minority group—was it native or immigrant? Neither group felt it belonged, neither identified with the community, both had a feeling of impermanence and mobility. Both groups felt alienated and left out. Our data suggest that at least in the social-psychological sense both groups, irrespective of number, were in fact minority groups. They felt underprivileged and abused; indeed, they were. A native:

The natives felt that they were outsiders and the foreigners felt that they were outsiders too. This plus the migrant attitude, which both of the groups have, made them feel left out, both of them. The native white people were looked down upon as farmers by us and the foreigners. The term "farmer" was a derogatory term. If that was used against you, it meant that you didn't know much, that you had no clothes, and that you didn't know how to act. This occurred despite the fact that most of the people came from rural areas. You see, when I came here, everybody thought that I lived in a big city because of the way I talked. They would use such terms as "don't act like a farmer" or "don't dress like a farmer." The term "hunkie" was used against all foreigners. It was first used against the Hungarians and then it became a general term. Also the term "lugies" was used against the Lithuanians and we had such terms as "round heads" and "square heads."

Such attitudes crystallized into patterns of indifference toward and separation from other persons and the community. This orientation becomes increasingly manifest as we pursue our data, and it was intimately related to the character and stability of the political institutions which emerged. It is with this crucial problem that we concern ourselves in the chapter to follow.

CHAPTER 6

A WIDE-OPEN TOWN

FROM the very first Coal Town was cursed with a set of factors which retarded the development of a stable community. To begin with the community had the characteristics of a typical frontier settlement. The population consisted predominantly of single males who were without the traditional constraining influences of organized religion and family life. A certain proportion were "boomers," gamblers, and con men looking for the "fast buck" without work. These persons were devoid of any interest in the community or its people. A native miner:

The first people who came in were footloose. They were young men, unmarried, about eighteen to twenty years old. It was easy to get in bad company. These were outlaw type roughnecks when they came. Some had committed crimes and had come to this community. These boom towns are all the same.

A newspaper reporter made this observation:

Boom towns are more or less the same all over the country—they're rough. It's the class of people, I think, it's those that follow that line of work in coal mining that makes these towns so bad during the early days. There was just a lot of them that didn't care for anything one way or the other.

The coal industry attracted many persons who were highly mobile, without plans to remain in the community. Their behavior was explosive and predicated on their feelings of the moment. Real community feeling and interest was lacking and there was no concern for the social consequences of their actions. A native woman:

Now, on Saturday nights as high as four men were apt to be killed. You see, what would happen would be the men would float in here and work a week and draw pay and then pull out. Some of them, though, never made it out of town. You really had to watch yourself. There were many nationalities in here and these people that were the rough element were not too interested in the town since they were not going to live here and the good people couldn't do much about it. Now, most of these miners had not any future. About 92 percent of them lived from day to day and they didn't even think about the future.

In addition to the above-mentioned factors, common to all frontier communities, there were additional significant elements somewhat peculiar to Coal Town. The basic attitudes of native and immigrant discussed in previous chapters were conducive to the development of crime and lawlessness which characterized the community for so many years. Both groups were indifferent and impersonal in relation to each other and in a broader sense to the community. Our data suggest that these attitudes retarded significantly the development of a stable social milieu. Further, they suggest an important question to the research team. Can lasting conditions of law and order be maintained where relationships are impersonal and where a failure to identify with the society is marked? We do not believe so and suggest that the plight of many American communities with respect to compliance with the law and with respect to corruption and graft is related to the fact that there is no real interest in or affiliation with broader social goals. This we believe may be true regardless of size of community and can happen as readily in the rural as in the urban setting.

CULTURAL BACKGROUNDS

A third factor which retarded the development of a lawful community was the cultural background of native and immigrant. The native, as pointed out in Chapter 2, came from a cultural background in which violence and settlement of personal disputes by violence was patterned. Further, the immigrants who arrived in Coal Town brought with them conceptions of law based on conditions in their own countries where anything or anyone could be bought for a price and corruption in government was the rule rather than the exception. Our immigrant informants stated:

There was corruption in the whole community and the immigrant took this in his stride. He was very much inclined to take this philosophically. He knew he had already experienced patronage and corruption and so there was very little that he could do.

The fraud and corruption you had in the early government here in Coal Town fitted in very well with the picture of government which the immigrants had in the Old Country. You see, local politics was nothing but a lucrative gang. The immigrants were as reluctant to cooperate with the law as were the natives. The immigrant would seldom have recourse to the law.

Now, when the foreigners came, they had the tendency to settle the trouble by violence also and not to trust the courts because they couldn't trust the law in the Old Country.

Many immigrants had vested interests in perpetuating lawlessness.

The immigrant was somewhat indifferent to the law. You see, many of the immigrants were engaged in bootlegging. They did not take any interest in politics for the most part.

A marked fear of reprisal from the native intimidated some of the immigrants. An immigrant:

Some foreigners were afraid for the law and the law wanted them to stay that way because then they would be easy to control. They would not try to change things and they were not interested in having things changed.

In other instances pressures were brought to bear on those immigrants who "might have made it tough for other immigrants."

Among the foreign element I would say there was a good group that was interested in law and order, but you couldn't do anything about the situation. Immigrants were afraid to do anything because they would be picked out by their own group, and sometimes it was dangerous to be picked out by your own group.

The development of an orderly political life might have been furthered by the efforts of mining management. Instead, the combination of absentee ownership and marked preoccupation with production fostered an attitude of indifference toward the miner and the community. A native miner:

Then came a terrible person to the community and that was T——, the mining superintendent. He was a driver for production. He fought and knocked down a lot of people getting to where he did. T—— tried to buy over persons and he went to the union officials and bribed them on different occasions in order to keep the mine producing and to keep the coal coming out. He was that sort of person. Well, he had no use at all for the community.

Mining management's lack of interest in the community constituted a fourth factor which retarded the development of a stable community. Mining management, much like the native and immigrant, failed to develop a sense of identification with the community and actively discouraged its employees from becoming a part of Coal Town. Thus mining management was essentially unrelated to and unconcerned with the town's problems and development. This kind of attitude, evident over a number of years, had its effect on the subsequent attitudes of Coal Town people who became cynical and distrustful of mining management.

The coal companies did not want their officials to mix in with the townspeople and their affairs and I think that they wanted to bleed it dry.

The mining companies should have taken an interest in the town but they didn't. You see, no company store manager could stay here over a year at the company store.

Mining, you see, is all absentee ownership. The Company did not care about law and order. The Company didn't care whether or not things quieted down. You see, the Company backed up A—— (the mayor at that time) and they liked to have things wild and rough. I don't think that anyone wanted a quiet town, you see.

Our informants indicated that the mining company had an exploitative attitude toward the community and up until recent years was unwilling to support its institutions. A merchant:

There was no spirit of cooperation between management and the employees. It was a sort of "dog-eat-dog" proposition in coal mining. The Company thought that they did not owe the community anything. You see, the coal industry does not give a damn thing for the miner or the community.

Many reported that the Company did as little as possible to assist Coal Town with its problems of growth. A businessman had this reaction:

The Company people, that is, those who made money from Coal Town, never got together with the people in the community to talk over their problems. This was true in the past and it is true now. They did not get together with us. They paid us as low taxes as was possible and many of the townspeople today don't know this about the Company. It is only us business people that know this. We are the only ones that can lead in this community. The Coal Company has not done right about the community. All it did was to take the coal out and leave. It forgot all about it. We made millionaires of those people, some of these people who live in Lake City and other places, but they do not give a hang about this community then or at the present time.

It is not altogether clear why mining management possessed this attitude of indifference toward the community. One could argue that a stable political life could have contributed toward greater regularity in individual working habits, hence higher coal production. Others, however, insist that it was to the Company's advantage to have a social system in flux "where things were wide-open." Under these conditions spending is promiscuous and control of the worker through wages is facilitated. Furthermore, a general atmosphere of political instability is conducive to the bribing of various union and public officials connected with the industry. In this regard it is interesting to note that the merchants favored a wide-open town, since the general atmosphere of such a town was considered conducive to free spending. Prices were high, miners were encouraged to purchase silk shirts, fancy clothes, perfume, and gifts for the whores who inhabited the community.

The quality of life which became manifest in crime and disorder seemed to involve almost all of the members of the community. Either persons profited directly or they were victimized by the various crimes and vices. No one seemed to be untouched by the plague of lawlessness and destruction which permeated the community. The following descriptions characterize the conditions in Coal Town which existed until the late 1920s.

H——, who was working at the old mine, recalls that after the Coal Town strike was settled and the union took over, Coal Town was still a wild, lawless boom town. Many from New America used to go there for revelry. But it wasn't safe to go by any means. Holdups by highwaymen in the woods east of Frenchtown and along the road to the old mine were a common occurrence. Taxi drivers or even other motorists and foot travelers seldom went the route alone or unarmed.

No one was actively dissatisfied with the conditions so long as there was good money to be had for the taking.

We didn't care much about what was going on and we kept mostly to ourselves. With me and my husband it was all right because there was plenty of money; where there was plenty of money, we were always happy.

Coal Town was a good town, rough an' tough, but all the mine camps was like dat dem days. But he was the kinda town I like—everthin' open— the money was here—tings goin' all a time. Dis was bes' town for makin' money in Marshall County! I like to see big money—free spendin' like was in dem days.

The predominant ethos of the community during this period was one of pro-violence; marked indifference to law and order was persistently apparent. Women were often involved in street brawls.

Right across the house from us at one time there was a long shack in which two families lived in each end. Well, one woman accused the other woman of taking her husband away from her and both of them got pistols and went out into the street and began taking potshots at each other. Of course, they didn't hit anything and after a while some people got concerned enough to stop them. We didn't care much about what was going on and we kept mostly to ourselves.

When I first came to Coal Town everybody was drunk. There was full credit at all of the grocery stores. As far as I know, the government left us alone and I was not interested in what went on at the City Hall.

During the early days religion entered the scene occasionally.

Now, the people wouldn't get too upset with drinking unless some preachers would come by and get them all stirred up. They used to do this and it was somewhat easy to do, and then they would be on a rampage to get somebody to clean up the town but it usually didn't last long.

Out of these circumstances arose patterns of fear, fear of violence and fear of retaliation for complaining against lawlessness. All of this fostered in the population a pronounced tendency to withdraw within themselves, to avoid social responsibility, to create even more impersonality and cynicism with respect to the establishment of a stable community. Fear was pronounced.

There was a lot of people who were scared to death around here to come out and fight. If you did, you were apt to get knocked in the head for as

little as fifty cents. They tried out the Ku Klux Klan around here but it
didn't do any good either.

When I came here to work this was a wide-open town. It was pretty rough.
It was worse than any coal town that I have ever worked in. My wife could
hardly stand it here. She was really scared.

It was actually dangerous for a man to get out of the house at night at all.
You were liable to get knocked off. I never went to those picnics—too
much danger—I was afraid—always too much fighting in Coal Town. In
fact, there was one street, if you walked down it at night you could get
pissed on.

It was useless to take cases to court.

You didn't like to go out after dark. You see if you went into a tavern there
would always be somebody watching you and how much money you had
till you got ready to leave, or they might leave before you and knock you
in the head. They hardly ever tried a man for killing another man and it
was best for you to stay at home. You could never take anything to court
because the other fella could buy witnesses for anything.

If you took sides, usually it was a terrible thing. When I came here, you
had to keep your mouth shut. You never took sides and if you did, it wasn't
too healthy for you.

Heck, I had friends of mine who were holdup guys and different things.
We always had plenty of guns and pistols around our house and this was
true of most of the other people in the community.

Violence was usually met with violence. So pronounced was this
tendency that over the years it spread to all ethnic groups and became a well-ingrained pattern imbued with much pride and satisfaction. It emerges as a dominant ethos in the value orientation
of Coal Town people. The interviewing team at one point suggested to some of the informants that the official records revealed
less crime and violence than our interview material indicated.
These informants became annoyed at the inference and reacted as
though we were denying them a valuable chapter in their community history. We learned later that our interpretation was correct, for in fact there was and is considerable pride in the violence
which characterized Coal Town for so many years.

The people here get mad when you play down the violence of the community and it seems very strange that they do. The biggest battles here
have been told and retold.

Persons resorted to use of guns, fists, knives, or any other weapons handy at the moment. Fights, for all sorts of reasons, were constantly in process. A native miner:

It was rough and tumble then and I've seen them fight for the sake of fighting. Fights were a common occurrence at the mine. I've seen 'em lined up of a morning waiting for a cage and pretty soon a couple of guys would slip out of line, set their buckets down, and start knocking hell out of each other. After it was settled they'd get back in line and go on to work an' nothing was said. They might even be buddies, one of 'em ridin' trips for the other. But then sometimes a motorman and his triprider might get into it an' if the motorman was the kind of guy to nurse a grudge, he might try to rip his buddy's fingers or squeeze him between the cars, or even try to run over him in the day's run. More than one got put in the hospital that way.

It was easy to get people stirred up:

I can give you one instance of a very amusing incident this community had, and that was that some kids one day reported that they had seen a man murdered down here south of town. Well, immediately the community was up in arms and the posse was formed and the kids as well as the men went out. Well, everyone was excited and they were carrying guns and they got out to the place and they noticed a lot of brush cut and a lot of blood all over the ground and so they decided to form a line and go after the murderer. They were apt to shoot at anything that moved, too. Well, they finally discovered that it was a horse that had cut himself and that the kid had told a story. Well, that was really an amusing incident but somebody could have gotten hurt.

Whatever valuations for human life may have been present, they were diminished by the ever-present patterns of homicide and the flagrant indifference of the law officers.

No, she was a tough little town when I come here. It was dangerous to get out here at night. A fellow would get killed here or shot and nobody would even get arrested for it. Just like it was some dog or something. I don't know, the law just didn't care nothing about it. Toughs would come in here and if they got out, alright, and if they got killed, alright.

Oh, my Lord, yes, they was fightin' an' shootin' goin' on in Coal Town all the time roun' that drinkin' and gamblin'. Ever' time we hear a pistol shot we say, "They's someone else gone." Someone was killed ever' payday.

It was the dirtiest hole when I came here. I took a walk downtown and I heard a big old six-gun bang six times. Then I heard it again and I just turned around and come home. This was a hotbed for bootlegging. They was crazy for that booze all the time. The very first time I came in here one boy pulled a gun on another one, he drilled him right through the chest.

In the early days one or two niggers were getting killed every Saturday. There wasn't much concern about this.

Differences of opinion were settled with violence. A businessman stated:

There was always the hint of violence just around the corner if you didn't fall in with whatever was going on in the community. Why, I can remember that there were several fellows here that were responsible for actually shooting and killing a great many persons, merely because they didn't agree with them.

Even the schools were not immune, as a college graduate reports:

Growing up in this community, some kids would get all warped. They lost all sense of good manners. They would see people do violence and in the schools we used to have the roughest school system in any part of the state. Discipline was bad. I can remember that one time we had a woman principal and the kids grabbed her and threw her against the wall. Well, there was a principal, a man, who came in here and he settled them down. He used to bodily throw the boys down the stairs and it wasn't long before he jerked some sense into the kids' heads. There were plenty of big boys and they had to be punished. You see, you really had to beat them in order to get them to learn anything. The kids needed it. Why, one time, one had smeared tar all over the schoolroom. The books, the chairs, tables, everything had tar on them.

A native merchant:

At one time we had a bad bunch of boys in the high school. They ran the school. The teachers and the principal just couldn't control them. The boys got the upper hand and they told the teachers what to do. The School Board was aware of this and sent out and got a man who could straighten them out. He threw the boys down the stairs more than once. They really had some knockdown drag-outs, real fights. They never has been much learning in this school.

The reputation of Coal Town spread far and wide and organized gangs began to move in from metropolitan centers. When "the heat was on" many gangsters fled to Coal Town to hide.

There was a gang from Riverview that used to run things here. They used to rob the people on the streets and people would go home and keep their mouth shut about being robbed though they knew who robbed them.

There was much lawlessness going on here. There was an indifference to law. I would say that anarchy prevailed.

Back when the gangsters were battling in Lake City, it overflowed and came down here. A lot of the criminals would come down here and live until the heat was off. We had a fellow that lived right behind us. He gambled. He got in debt and his roommate shot and killed him and claimed that it was a burglar, at least he thought it was a burglar. They called it justifiable homicide. They couldn't prove anything otherwise. The jury recommended justifiable homicide and there was no disputing it. We had quite a few, about five or ten who hid out here. Sometimes they would work in the mine or in a saloon. I don't know what gangs they were. Nobody asked too many questions about them. They didn't do anything really out of the way.

Murders and killings were quite common in the early days. Remarks of the inhabitants tell us just how widespread such occurrences were.

They killed somebody every pay night. My first husband was killed and robbed. My brother was killed in Hartdale. Men from Coal Town killed him.

Well, as an example, here on Sunday night, I wasn't married and I was going to see a girl. I saw a man lying by the boardwalk and I thought he was just some Sunday drunk. I come back that night and found out that that bird had been killed out there.

I was living on S—— Street when the mayor got shot that time. I was less than a block from where it was. I heard the shot and the next morning I went out and —— had shot him down at Number 6 Saloon. One morning they went out and picked up two deads out in front of Number 3 in that ditch and took them up to the undertaker's and that was all you heard about it.

A murdered man in the drinking water!

It was a tough town here. They would hold you up, kill you, and throw you in a well. Why, there was a well over here in the north side of town and there was a man that was killed and dumped in the well, and the family didn't know it and they drank water off of him until he started to float in the well. Everybody thought that this one fellow had gone back to the Old Country. They found him in a well about nine days later.

Now, on Saturday nights as high as four men were apt to be killed. You see, what would happen would be the men would float in here and work a week and draw pay and then pull out.

When J—— and T—— first opened this place up, Coal Town was a wild place. They had a bunch that was in a room all by theirselves. They was all drunk. A fellow by the name of K——, that was sent down here to Coal Town to keep it quiet, he went up there and they quieted him down. They killed him right up there.

It was very rough times here. When at least one or two persons were not killed, it was not called a very busy night here in Coal Town. Two or three fellows were always lying around in the alley either drunk or dead.

Robberies and holdups were also common during the early days. It was quite the usual thing for miners to receive their pay checks one moment and be relieved of them the next. A case of mistaken identity:

Well, one time everybody knew that I was working, but one night I took off and went to the show, and after the show, I always took a certain route home, but this night I took a different way home. But some other fellow happened to walk by a certain place at the time that I used to, and the next morning he was found shot. He had twelve bullet holes in him.

Protection against robbery:

On payday you went home from the bank, another fellow with you—if you lived out by the mine—with one hand in one pocket on your pay, the other in the other pocket on a gun. That way if somebody came out of the bushes and said, "Stick 'em up," he didn't know what you would bring out of your pocket on either side.

Theft was so common when we first came here that you dare not leave anything out in the yard. This played out after the 1930s. I can remember that when we first moved here that you couldn't leave your garden hose out without somebody walking by and stealing it. You couldn't even leave chairs out. I remember I had some neighbors that would steal anything.

These criminal elements that came into Coal Town often had gotten into trouble at home. Now I remember one fellow who was a petty thief. He stole a cash register once from a store and then took it back and tried to pawn it. He stole a typewriter from me one time, I remember. When he was in town there was a post office robbery and he was suspected since he was playing around with a girl who would let him into the Post Office. We could never pin anything on him though and so he went free. One time he went to B—— and stole a set of tires. He put the tires on his car and then he decided that he would go to Riverview. He drove through B—— and got caught.

Gun-carrying and gunplay were an accepted part of everyday life. There were few homes in the community in which rifles, pistols, or shotguns of some type were not kept ready and waiting for use. Many times men got so weary of merely carrying arms that they had shooting bouts using any target available at the moment.

Everybody carried guns and the people used to get tired of carrying them and would fire them at night in the sky or in the ground. Men carried guns in their pockets and would shoot electric lights out just for fun.

I can remember that the people in this community used to always carry guns. Everybody had guns and they would shoot at anything that moved. They killed all the birds and they killed anything that ran or walked. I think this was part of the recklessness around here. There was a lot of shooting at night but I think most of it was just the fact that the men carried guns so long that they just had to shoot at something and the men merely pointed it in the ground or at the sky and let go. I know that people were always blazing away here with guns.

I can remember the first night that I was here. It was about ten o'clock and the guns were shooting all around and the people were screaming and the landlady was running up and down. Well, I didn't know what to do so I lit out through the park and I went over to get my brother, who was here at the time, and he said, "Oh, don't worry about the shooting. This goes on all the time."

I brought my wife down here in '24 and we both carried pistols.

It was pretty wild here when I came. I remember that the drunks would come down to the street at nights just shooting for all they were worth. I can remember dodging and hiding behind furniture in order to keep myself safe.

During the late twenties and early thirties personal property was purposefully burned in order to collect insurance premiums, a practice reported as being widespread in the general area. So pronounced was this practice that all bona fide insurance companies for many years refused to sell insurance to persons residing in Coal Town. A native merchant:

I can remember one businessman in New America who made it a business to set fires in the different communities, in New America and he also worked in Coal Town. He was working all around the area. Well, he was finally caught and sent to prison, but what it was interesting to note was that he was also writing insurance.

The "clever" person took advantage of this practice.

There was heavy loss in homes being burned down. I know it because I was writing insurance at that particular time. Now what happened is that many of these fires were set. You take, for example, if you tried to sell your house it would sell for $300 but if you burned it down, the insurance company, let's say, would pay you $1,100 or what you had it insured for. Why, you were a fool not to burn your house down in order to get that money, so the important question was, "Why not burn it down?"

Selling fire insurance was a tricky venture.

If you got a new customer for fire insurance, you were suspicious of him right away. It might be a legitimate account but you began to doubt it. For instance, if someone would come in and say, "Well, I want to buy $5,000 worth of insurance." You were immediately suspicious, particularly if this person was out of work or if he was planning to leave the community. You would worry about him and you would want to investigate as to how much money he had tied up, what his business was, and what kind of person he was, you see. Well, this fitted right in with the suspiciousness of the community that I have described for you previously.

Heavy consumption of alcoholic beverages was basic to the culture pattern of both native and immigrant. The native enjoyed his "white mule," while the immigrant favored beer and wine. With the passage of the Eighteenth Amendment full-scale bootlegging went into effect and Coal Town became the illicit bootlegging center of the area. Bootlegging was rampant throughout the community. A native merchant:

Through the prohibition times things were really rough. There was no respect at all for the law. It was from the top to the bottom a bad situation. These people, that is the gangsters and the hoodlums, owned the town and sometimes they would ask me in a kidding way, "Well, how is my town getting along?" The good people here cared but they were in a minority and couldn't do anything about it. The majority wanted these conditions or else they wouldn't have existed.

The local law enforcement agencies were indifferent.

Home brew was sold in the homes here in Coal Town, and to illustrate the attitude of the city officials toward that was this: The city got mad at the people not for selling home brew but for selling home brew in their houses so that they wouldn't be able to stick them for a license. They didn't object to their selling but only to the fact that they didn't have a license.

During the era of Prohibition, bootlegging could be found in every form of physical structure from the home to the so-called blind-pig. Consumption of alcohol was the expected pattern.

Why, you could get a drink in almost every house in this town, except the Post Office, and well, I don't know about the Post Office, you might have could in that, too.

When I came here in 1924 the town was wide-open. There was plenty of red-light districts and bootlegging. In fact, all the homes had a trap door in a corner in the floor for bootlegging purposes.

The bootlegging pattern was part of community life. The non-participant was the deviant.

Everybody was bootleggers. Everything was on a pay-off. They thought that if you weren't bootlegging you were silly. When they did finally get somebody, they would send innocent people to jail. Some people would go to jail for somebody else and when he came out they would take care of him. They done that. Bootlegging was really a big factor in this part of the country. They all was in on it. State, county, city, everything was in on it. Home brew was just flowing here. I guess these other towns was the same way, but we couldn't go to these other towns unless we walked.

We used to pay 55 cents a pint for white mule. Some of it was really terrible. I can remember when some of the people used to stand in line for the booze. We had a very good class of prohibition whiskey here.

One informant suggested that suicides were low because frustration was expressed in the drinking pattern. It is difficult to check this statement but the observation is an interesting one.

I guess the reason for suicide was the need to escape their problems, but usually in this community escape didn't take the form of suicide but instead drinking. Drinking was very much present here in this community. If you didn't drink, you were made fun of.

Gambling was a minor sport in relation to bootlegging but it was prevalent. Gambling took place on both levels, professional or organized and nonprofessional or unorganized. For the most part, gambling was controlled by gamblers who moved into the community to prey upon the pay checks of the miner on pay day.

We had a bunch of gamblers and crooks come in here to make a living gambling. They didn't come to work. They was all over down here. It really got rough.

Gamblers was just watching out to catch those poor miners. They were dozens of professional gamblers. They would take their money away.

Well, they was supposed to have law and order but they didn't use it. It was like it was an Old West town. Gamblers from Riverview and all over the country used to come in. They used to gamble big stakes too, Buddy.

A gambler reminiscing stated:

Yes, I remember lot of 'em—used to gamble, play casino, blackjack with 'em. They didn't know how to play—I'd just take their money easy as pie —good fellas tho, ever' one of 'em. They'd pay, buy the drinks, too. I try to tell 'em, show 'em till they learn, but they say, 'Come on play, play." There was one fella, I used to beat him all the time.

Prostitutes were imported to meet the demands of the male population. Houses of prostitution were established early in the history of the community and continued to flourish during the "rough" period.

In the early years the town was pretty wild on account of gamblers and prostitutes. Prostitutes would come in to town from outside and so many young, single people would just line up certain places.

There were houses of prostitution here too, five big ones. One particularly was a big house, why the whores would come in here for payday in taxis and on trains. This played out in the 1930s.

The majority of prostitutes were reported as coming from American families.

The whores that we had here were American born. There were no women directly born in Europe, though there may have been second-generation immigrants—that is, children of those immigrants who came to this country. Now I know none of the women who were in the houses of prostitution were born in the Old Country. Many of them were recruited from Arkansas and Kentucky. I can remember that we had two from Hartdale who worked here but who lived in Hartdale. The population of prostitutes would sometimes hit a peak of 200 and this was particularly during payday when extra help was needed to take care of the demand. The last whorehouse burnt down in 1938. Both Mrs. J—— and Mrs. S—— had very flourishing and prosperous houses of prostitution. T—— had eight or nine girls and his wife managed that end of the business while he took care of the tavern and the bar.

An old-timer reminiscing:

Like I said, this fellow never was married and I don't know how many
different women he had. He would keep one for a while. He always had
four or five or six girls there with him. He lived on the corner of C——
and H—— right on this side in that big house. Used to be just a rooming
house I reckon. I went in there one time and a little girl in there, she was
a pretty little girl about sixteen years old and blackheaded, just as black
as coal. The other girls was upstairs. I told this girl to get me something
to count out them eggs in. I just stepped into the kitchen in there and she
set me a pan there and I counted out the eggs there and I asked her how
long she had been in there. She said, "I have just been in here two nights."
I said, "I guess you are getting a lot of business." She said, "Yes, I am
just getting all I can do." I said, "As pretty as you are, you are liable to get
more than you can do." I got paid for my eggs and went on out. There
was some in there maybe twenty-five years old. They would get out and
get these younger ones to come in there and stay. I guess they made good
money. I expect they did.

Occasionally even a minister went astray.

I remember one Evangelical preacher who lost his job and joined the
police force, and he used to get the girls from the houses of prostitution
to sit on his lap. There were many houses of prostitution here and there
were saloons with girls in the back room. In fact, there was one across the
street. There are still a few prostitutes around here now, although not as
many as there used to be.

The lack of history of stable political institutions in the background of the native and the immigrant, the feeling of mobility
and impermanence, the major preoccupation with personal, monetary gains, and the inability to identify with the community resulted in a local government which bordered on chaos. It is particularly important to note that the government which came into being
was not superimposed on an unwilling populace. Instead it reflected
their will. People of Coal Town had a clear conception of the
political practices at work, and for many years voted in favor of
the "wide-open town."

The people here had the type of government that they wanted. They had
the type of community that they wanted too. You see, you didn't stick your

nose into other people's business. You kept to yourself and unless something bothered you personally you stayed out of it.

We wanted a man usually who would open the town to bootlegging and a
man that would go along with the majority. You know, that sort of thing.
There was plenty of corruption here then.

There were always some who could become interested in social
issues, but their numbers were so small and opposition was so great
that even these few became increasingly cynical.

You could get the people emotionally worked up for a period and then
they would become very excited about a community problem but after
that they could see that nothing had changed and they would get somewhat cynical.

There was very little respect for the law. The prevailing attitude
was one of distrust and disrespect. A native merchant:

I knew the U.S. Deputy Marshal. He called on me many times to find out
what was going on in the community. He said that if anyone knew what
was going on that I would know. I never gave him any information about
particular bootleggers because I never let it bother me. I never paid any
attention to it. You see, there was a lot of disregard and indifference to
the law here.

Not only was the average citizen involved, but the police were
corrupt and promoted corruption. Police cooperated with vice
operators in what amounted to a system of protection. A warning
system was set up so that police officials would not apprehend the
vice operators unless, of course, a particular operator happened to
be "in bad" with the law.

There would be sort of paternalistic raids on the establishments of friends
and the policemen would call and say, "Well, Joe, it's about time we
raided your place and we'll be down about four o'clock so have a bottle of
white mule and we'll catch you with it and take you down to the City Hall
and fine you about $5.00 and you can go back. We need a little money,
you see." They fined them whatever the city needed at the time.

Federal agents were handled in this way:

The bootleggers here were not bothered too much by the Federal officers
because the rumor system was used to warn the local taverns. The pro-
bation or the Federal officer would come in and immediately a runner

would be sent out and the word spread that he was here and the taverns would close up.

Not only did the law close its collective eye to bootlegging and vice operation, but many other crimes went unprosecuted or unsolved.

Men were shot, and you never heard anything more about it because this was the law in and of itself.

Kickbacks and pay-offs were common and extended throughout the entire law enforcement system.

You see, we never had any cooperation from the law in Hartdale. J——— and his group bought off the law and told them to please stay out of Coal Town and they would handle all the trouble over here. Well, that's the way it went and we never had any cooperation from Hartdale, the county seat.

The county law could keep the Federal law off of you if it wanted to. Now I can remember an election in Coal Town in which there were two bootleggers. Each held different factions and each was running on the ticket. One of them lost and as soon as he lost the police moved in on him and arrested him and all of the persons in his group merely because the other bootlegger had won the county election and was able to call in the Sheriff against the other fella, while he continued in operation. You see, that is an example of what I mean by patronage.

Law enforcement officials were no better than the way of life from which they sprung. An interesting report goes this way:

They had constables. They would not do right. They would go to the whorehouses and drink with the whores and then arrest them after drinking with them.

Policemen could not be trusted not to violate the spirit as well as the letter of the law. Often police took advantage of their authority. Since the police were products of Coal Town, arming them was tantamount to giving them a license to commit mayhem.

People in those days, especially you take law enforcing, it was just as wild as other parts. Whenever a fellow got a gun as a policeman he thought it was to use. They used it. It was nothing to see three or four people killed in one month. If none was killed in a month they wanted to know what was wrong. I saw Pete kill a man. I went to a lodge dance and I was coming home. He lived right across here. I said, "Hi, Pete," and he was a good friend if he liked you. Then a fellow came out of Number Three and said, "Pete, a couple of fellows inside took my money." He said, "You go in and tell them Pete said to give you back the money." He came back out and said, "They won' give me my money back." This fellow came out and he said, "Pete, that is one of the fellows that got my money and that is the other fellow behind him." He went over and said, "Did you take this man's money?" He said, "Yes, what are you going to do about it?" Pete pulled out his gun and shot him. "That's what I'm going to do about it," he said. The other run off so fast that Pete couldn't catch him. There was no such thing as justice, no trials. If you drawed quicker the other guy was dead.

A native miner:

One day I was down here at town. There was a fellow from Nobility over here. A policeman had this fellow over there and this fellow didn't know what he was doing, he was so drunk. The policeman shot him right through the foot there. He taken him up to the jail and I followed him and I said listen, "you ain't going to leave that man in jail. You take him to the hospital." He said, "No," and I said, "You will too. You are the law but I mean for you to take him. He wasn't trying to get away from you, he just fell." That made me so cockeyed mad I couldn't see straight.

Another example was that one fellow who was deputized shot up a wedding party and killed two people and wounded three others. There wasn't much law down here. In fact, there was no law at all.

Our informants reported that a person was as likely to be robbed by the police as by the common thug.

There was a time when you were afraid of the police in Coal Town. They would knock you over the head and they would shoot you. They were always ready to pull a shakedown on the poor immigrants. The persons who were elected into public offices were usually the big liars and they didn't care at all about the people. We had two policemen who used to rob all the drunks and roll them. They would do this, especially to the foreign element, and when they didn't find an immigrant drunk enough to roll, they would usually hit him over the head and then roll him.

I know that you have heard some of the stories that the people used to worry about the policemen around here. I guess they used to roll drunks but the attitude was that if a drunk was rolled, then he didn't have any business getting drunk in the first place. There was no sympathy for him. This is the same old thing I was telling you before. Besides, they didn't have too many intelligent people here who would be policemen and the policemen wouldn't be above going in a house and searching for white mule and then taking some money. He thought that that was all right. The police were like all of the rest of the people here. They just didn't give a good goddamn, nor did the city itself. The cops were drunkards and pretty near anything you want to call them.

Coal Town citizens felt that the police were thieves and just as much to be feared as any criminal. On the other hand, there was no real concern about this because of the prevalent attitude that the police had just as much right as anyone else to get in on the graft and the illicit money-making.

When we first came here in 1923 a person could get his throat cut in the alley and his money taken away. I know this because this actually happened. Police protection was really meager and the police, you see, were in the bootlegging racket themselves. You had to worry as much about the police as you did the crooks. The law did not take too much interest in the welfare of the people.

An accepted part of government in Coal Town was the fixing of elections. Honest elections seldom occurred and all manner of dishonest techniques were employed.

One time, during an election, I asked J—— how he was running. He said, "Well, I was behind today, but I took the ballot box down to my house and this morning I am ahead!"

When T—— ran against W—— for mayor, a mob of us went down to the City Hall to see that the election ballots were counted correctly. We almost had a riot there, because W—— wanted to appoint the election judges, and well, if that happened you know what the result would be.

It was common practice to bring in voters from other communities in order to win elections. A case of too many votes:

In the early days you had to vote right. You knew who was going to win an election even before the election was held. I can remember one time there were only a thousand registered voters here in one of the wards and one man got twelve hundred votes, and then in addition to that his opponent got some votes too. Something was wrong somewhere, I guess.

Vote buying was also common.

People got votes in many ways. They called it here red-light votes. One year there was a bought election. This was, I believe, when C—— ran for mayor. He spent a couple of thousand just to get elected as mayor of this little town.

In carrying on election campaigns, the politicians were willing to promise anything to get elected. A former mayor stated:

Now when I ran for mayor, I would promise the people anything just to get elected. It didn't make any difference what you promised. I never believed a word of what I said to the people. I ran against that notorious hoodlum, K——, and I beat him. Now what I would do would be to go around and kiss the babies and maybe pat the ladies on the back and promise the men anything.

A citizen reported:

You know the bad government often rubs off on the people and this was what happened with me. These officials would promise you everything in order to get you to vote and then forget about you after the election. There are crooked people everywhere. They would come to me and ask me to vote for them and I would tell them yes, but I would know in my own mind that I would not vote for them and I would not when the time came.

Purchase of votes through outright grants of money was rare. Often it was a matter of dispensing liquor, jobs, and favoritism.

I can remember one miner complaining bitterly to me that L—— had promised him a pint of whiskey to vote for him and that he had voted for him but that L—— had never given him the pint of whiskey and he was very mad about that. This is what they would do. You see, they would promise you anything, and then they would never pay off once they got in office.

Election victories had nothing to do with the issues involved. A defeated candidate said:

You see, in order to win an election you had to get up some sort of scandal about the administration and then they would often get up a scandal about you. Why, they had a big scandal out on me and that was that I was a sex pervert. They even got the whores in this town to swear to this—that discouraged me. Why, you could get witnesses for anything, no matter what it was. Now you could buy those witnesses and get anybody to swear to anything.

Persons were motivated to run for public office by the lucrative profits which were readily available.

Now you could make money when you ran for office and this was one of the reasons why people used to run.

Civic projects were very often a front for graft. In fact, the argument that there was money to be gained was used as a point of persuasion to get community improvements.

Now what usually happened was that civic improvements were merely used as a front in order for certain persons to make graft and a tremendous amount of money for themselves. This was one of the reasons why immigrants did not trust any type of civic improvement except schools and this they could see for themselves.

Administrative officials cooperated with the vice and bootleg operators and received their share of the reward for doing so. Like the police, they extracted sums of money and material pay-offs for their protection. Often they engaged in vice operations themselves.

I can't remember an honest mayor in this town. At one time there were sixty licenses for drinking parlors. They were called soft-drink parlors but what they did was to sell white mule. You see, Capone borrowed his ideas from Coal Town. It wasn't the other way around.

We had bootleggers here. It was really rough. Everybody was coming into town. When R—— was mayor, he catered to the bootleggers and you had to pay him so much money to keep in operation. The same thing was true with prostitution. It was organized and they used to import new girls and deport the old girls from here about once or twice a week.

Our best mayor was R——. He said, "I'm a bootlegger, and I don't rob anyone dishonestly." He operated his own bootlegging establishment, but he came right out and said that he did, and he didn't hide behind anyone else. He was honest about it.

It was difficult to "buck" the law even though the law was illegal.

Conditions were so bad here that the mayor and his thugs used to go out and slug anybody that they wanted to. The mayor was a killer. He was as mean a man as I have ever seen. He tried to have me assassinated once but it didn't work. Everything was bad about him. You see, I sold people houses on installment plans where they would pay a little down and then a little each week or month. Well, the mayor got one of the immigrants to come to me and say that he wanted his money back. Well, I happened to know this immigrant fairly well and I said, "John, why do you want your money back from the deposit that you made?" He said he just did and finally I got the true story out of him and it was something like this. The mayor told him to go to me and ask for the money back. Now, the mayor knew that the money was not here in Coal Town that it was in Lake City. If I couldn't give the man the money back, then the mayor would have it spread around that I was taking the money and not giving the people a good deal. This immigrant said that the mayor told him that if he told me that story he would cut his tongue out—and he really would. He was the will power here and he was the power behind the throne even after he went out of office. The union people liked him and he was in good with the public officials in Hartdale. The law would not try to help us decent citizens out here. This way nothing was ever accomplished about cleaning up the town.

For instance, this man S——, who was mayor, was a first-class louse. You couldn't believe a thing he said. He hung on around here for four or five years. He stayed in power largely through the use of fear. He made persons fear him and if you didn't go along with him, why you damn well knew what would happen to you.

A mayor dedicated to the elimination of vice in the community said:

I really put the whores and their pimps out of business. That is, those who weren't on my side, but I took care of those that were on my side.

A friend of the mayor engaged in the following practice:

I can remember, for instance, in which at one time a friend of the mayor used to lie in wait along the main railroad track that led from town to the homes and on any dark night he used to waylay the people and rob them by hitting them over the head. Though he was a friend of the mayor, mind you! That is a good example of some of the life that was present in Coal Town during the early days.

THE PRESENT

Over the years the basic patterns of violence and corruption diminished. Nevertheless, it is interesting to note that the period of violence and corruption coincided with the period of greatest economic prosperity. Likewise, as money left the community, violence and corruption diminished. With little opportunity for profits from corruption, crime, and vice, persons so disposed moved on. Thus by the late twenties and early thirties things were relatively quiet.

We do not mean to imply a simple cause-and-effect relationship between community prosperity and political instability. Over the years there were many factors which precipitated change. People grew older, married, and settled down. The general cultural milieu changed and in some ways so did the thinking of the people. Nevertheless, residues of the past remain. A citizen reported the following practice:

There is a system here in which persons are fined by the policeman making the arrest and the Justice of Peace, and in many instances they just get the fine and there are no records made of that. I can give you one example of this occurring. A man was going downtown the wrong way. It was about eight o'clock at night. The policeman flagged him down and arrested him and took him over to the Justice of Peace and fined him $20.00. The man didn't think anything about it until the next day when he realized that in making the arrest the policeman should have given him a ticket to appear before the J.P. at a certain time. So the next time he was through Coal Town, he asked to see the city records. He then got a lawyer and by that time the city officials were only too glad to give him his money back.

Distrust of police remains.

Now there is another example where if you play along with the police you can get by with anything. In back of me there is an old woman who lives with two older men who are on pensions. These two old men keep the old woman and neither of them are married to her. I have seen the policeman go over there and he knows what is going on but they don't do anything about it. In fact, the night policeman sometimes goes there and has sex relations with her.

Seizure of political power for financial gain and in order to control the behavior of others was common in Coal Town during the early days. The financial incentive is gone but power to control others still has appeal.

You see, these big shots are in politics for personal power. They have the money. It's not because they need money. They have enough of it and there isn't too much money to be made, but they're in it for personal gain. You see, the clique belongs to these clubs you read about in the community.

It is reported that if one is not a member of a pressure group, winning an election can be difficult. The following was related by a father whose son was running for public office.

I don't think my boy had a chance to win the spring election. You see, the man that ran against him, Y——, belonged to the —— and he is a member of the —— religion. Both of these groups support him. My boy was not supported by the —— Church because he has not attended church regularly. I wanted him to get to church because this would help him in his election and he told me that if he had to go to church for that reason, he wouldn't go at all.

Deeply entrenched political convictions are practically nonexistent and people commonly believe that votes go to the highest bidder.

Now you can take a sum of money and you can put over anything you want to in this town. This was true in the past as well as the present. It has always been that way. All you have to do is to buy them a little beer and maybe pay about ten or fifteen dollars and you can put over any deal that you want to. The plant was a good example of this. Why, you could have built that thing for a third of what it cost and the end result was that it raised the taxes here. Why, you can still buy votes for about fifteen dollars. A little beer and a little money will change the minds of the people. The people are gullible here and will fall for anything. They fall in with all sorts of crackpot schemes. I explained it on the basis of ignorance.

I can give you one example of recent corruption and buying of votes in this community and this was when we were voting on the bond issue for building of the reservoir to supply a better source of water power for this community. I was talking with a woman who was opposed to the bond issue and she was telling me why she was opposed to it because it would mean a raise in taxes. Well, I was opposed to it for the simple reason that the cost was too much. They could have done the same amount of work for much cheaper. Well, on election day she came by the house and asked me if I had voted and I said, "No, I haven't." She said, "Well, I have a car here and I will be glad to take you to vote and I would like for you to vote for the bond issue." Well, this sort of surprised me because I had just seen her a few days before and she was so violent. Well, she began to tell me why she had changed her mind and it was $15. They had made her an official on the Board and so she had given them the vote. You see, that is typical of the way this community is run at the present time.

Cynicism with respect to reform and change is well entrenched. Our informants feel hopeless about community life being different —"Things are just that way."

A lot of patronage still goes on here. There is a great deal of talk about it on the street, "so and so gets a job and somebody else doesn't," but there is not concerted action against anything. You have a feeling, you see, that life is like that. You could not depend on anyone following through on anything. Most people don't want to ask for any trouble. They keep their nose out of other people's business.

SUMMARY

In this chapter we have suggested that the cultural backgrounds and personal attitudes of natives and immigrants, including cynicism, impersonality, alienation from one another, and lack of identification with the community, were significant factors in the kind of political organization which arose in Coal Town. Equally significant were the life experiences of Coal Town people which reinforced certain basic premises. Motivation for the development of an orderly political life was without foundation. Thus the personal needs of each person became predominant, and what sense of social feeling there was emerged after years of corruption and exploitation. These people are today devoid of any real interest in government. They are cynical and suspicious, they expect the worst and feel that any official, regardless of position, has his price. Corruption in places of high office comes as no surprise to them. Such occurrences are more consistent with their view of the world than the picture of self-sacrificing patriotism portrayed in history books. Coal Town's development is hardly conducive to the assumption by its citizens of the democratic responsibilities which confront them. Democracy for them is, in the final analysis, an abstract ideal which is celebrated on appropriate holidays with the display of fireworks and the consumption of liquid refreshments. The emotional integration is still to come.

Although the cruder forms of violence and aggression have disappeared, these patterns are merely the outer signs of the inner malignancies of community life. What have been the effects of growing up in such communities—the nondramatic effects, so subtle that they pass us by?

A woman who spent the first twenty-five years of her life in Coal Town developed an outlook on crime expressed below which is fairly typical of our Coal Town people. Particularly pertinent is the notion that the criminal is not really a criminal but that, like most people, he is a fellow who "got sticky fingers."

It was a wild west town here but we took care of our own family. Why, it was terrible the way they used to do here. They had women coming in ever' two weeks to whore around with the men. I can remember old man B——. He was a good man even if he was a crook. Why, everybody knows where he is. I know my sister has seen him. The people here, they just kid themselves when they say they don't know where he is. Sure they know where he is but it's too much trouble to bring him back. He was a good man but he got sticky fingers. Most people start out as pretty good in offices like that, or head of big companies or things like that, but they get sticky fingers. That's one reason that I voted for Y—— rather than E——, because old Y—— had already made his fortune seven times over. E—— with a big family, he has to make his fortune yet in terms of graft and corruption. So I think it's best to vote for the older man who has already his money. He is not apt to take any more as the new man. That was why I voted for him in the Lake City election.

The data gathered from our informants are certainly consistent with the "cultural theory of crime" proposed by several criminologists.[1] In effect, such a point of view suggests that within our culture values may be found which create "criminal proneness."

At another level we may ask what are the personal and familial consequences of growing up in such surroundings, replete with cynicism, hostility, and unrelatedness to others? What are the effects on human personality? At the deeper levels of personal organization cynicism, hostility, and unrelatedness become sources of inner turmoil and conflict; disturbances in human motivation, in families, in marriages, and in the life goals of people. The toll on human life was far greater than the official or unofficial indices of crime and corruption. Successive generations were injected with a value orientation antithetical to community integration. These are the psychic weights and pulleys—the residues for Coal Town people.

[1] See Mabel A. Elliott, *Crime in Modern Society* (New York, Harper and Brothers, 1952), Chapter 1; Donald R. Taft, *Criminology* (New York, Macmillan Co., 1956), Chapter 2.

CHAPTER 7

THE MEANING OF MINING

IN previous chapters we have been concerned with certain personal, social, and cultural values which were responsible for the pattern of life which emerged in Coal Town. We now turn our attention to the nature of coal mining and examine its effects for the people and the community. As we work through the data we shall point out how the essential ingredients of industrial life contributed to subsequent patterns which evolved in Coal Town. Here one finds five major themes which contributed to the way of life which emerged. These include violence, impersonality, authoritarianism, corruption, and insecurity—physical, psychological, and economic. All of these themes, already existent in the community, were accentuated and fostered by coal mining as it functioned in Coal Town.

VIOLENCE

From the first, violence was associated with mining in Coal Town. Either mining management was in conflict with labor when it wished to organize; or miners of different unions were in conflict with one another. The fact that the community was beset by violent strikes helped matters little. During the period 1908 to 1925 at least five major strikes occurred, each associated with marked violence.

During the early days of labor-management strife, management, well organized and backed financially, resorted to violence and coercion. The use of guards, well armed, with "touchy fingers," contributed to the ever-present tension. The son of a native miner:

That's the way it was at Coal Town. The Old Man ran everything. He was
the czar down there. He used to go down to the mine with two 45's
strapped on him. All the officials an' bosses stayed in that building where
the offices were. The guard up in that little blockhouse on top with a
machine gun an' searchlight would watch the Old Man all the way to
the mine. They had guards with rifles posted along the way too. I wish
the old boy was still livin'. He could tell you a book full about Coal Town
in about five minutes.

Patterns of violence and coercion characteristic of management
applied equally as much to union activities. Settlements of difference possessed undertones of violence and physical force. A native
miner:

Most of the boys didn't like G—— [a union leader], even the ones that
finished upon his side of the fight. They were wrangling about G——
at the start. I was at a meetin' one night about half lit up an' I told 'em
the strike would cost people in this area millions of dollars. I said, "Hell,
we could get one of those gangsters from Lake City to kill the old s.o.b.
for five thousand." I guess I shouldn't have done it, shootin' off my mouth
like that, but hell, you know me.

At another meeting this occurred:

Now, I've seen some rough union meetings here and I can remember one
in which we almost rioted in the Miners Hall and they wanted to get
J—— on the end of a rope and drag him out of town. Well, I opposed this
move and I was the only one that was brave enough to get up and suggest to the boys, if you do this, you're taking the law into your own hands
and that would be a bad situation. Well, I opposed this move all on my
own and then after the meeting many of the men came around and shook
my hand and said, "Well, that was what I wanted to do but I just didn't
have the guts to do it."

Shooting and killing often followed disputes.

There was a shooting down the street from our house during this time.
The union thugs told this fellow to get off the streets or else they would
kill him. Well, apparently he didn't move fast enough so they shot him.
He didn't die but several were killed during this time. You see, the union
had the law on their side and you had to stay close at home unless you
wanted to get hurt or get into some kind of trouble.

A jurisdictional dispute between two rival unions in the 1920s
ripped Coal Town wide open and initiated a period of violence

and lasting hatred equal to anything previously experienced in this community.

We had a period in the late twenties when they had this union trouble. That was the worst thing that ever happened to this town. A lot of the men never did get back to work at all.

The issues are not altogether clear but some of our informants reported that mine mechanization necessitated a reduction in mining personnel and that the leaders of Union A, the dominant union, in an undercover move sponsored a rival union, herein called Union B, in order to create trouble over the mechinization issue, thereby justifying the elimination of a large section of mining personnel.

The Union B trouble, I think, was caused by mechanization in the mines. You see, we had to have some friction to do away with the miners and this was what happened. These foreigners could be led and many of them joined the Union B movement. They lost their jobs and this was what was wanted by the higher union officials.

I think that the Union B trouble was stirred up and trumped up because the union had the companies tied down and the companies had to keep the men hired. The problem was how to get the new machines in the mine and when the new machines came in, that meant that many men had to be cut off from the mine so this was where the Union B trouble started.

You ask me about the Union B difficulty and G——. I would say that the story is absolutely true. I know this to be a fact. I know that G—— paid the Union B men to stir up trouble. The issue involved was this. There was not enough jobs to go around and the men had to share their work. When there was six days of work many men shared this. Then when it got down to only two or three days, the men could not earn enough money. This was the basic cause. I know this story sounds weird and unusual but I would say that it is true.

Other informants believed that the dispute centered around the dictatorial policies of Union A. Still others believed the problem was one of personal struggle for power between union leaders and that ideological issues were not involved.

The Union B trouble went something like this: There was a group of miners that did not like Union A and G—— and they wanted to form a dual organization in order to get rid of G——, so they formed the Union B movement.

It is difficult to tell which of the points of view expressed is true. All of these positions are held by a substantial group of our informants. The jurisdictional struggle was in its very essence a most basic "bread and butter" fight for the miner. Regardless of the outer issues, the miner realized that his economic security was at stake. Moreover, the fight was in many ways a last-ditch stand for economic security in an industry which at best was never economically secure. Out of this struggle a period of lawlessness reigned for some two years. Scenes like this were common:

Union B tried to stop us but we went ahead and worked anyway. Why, they would come and tell a person what would happen to them and what they would do to them if they ever caught him working. Well, this frightened the people and I know one Union A man who used to tell his wife every morning when he left to go to work to run through the Union B lines that she knew where to bury him in case anything happened. I can remember one example of when I used to get off work at night and walk from the mine to this house here which wasn't too far; there was a car that would always follow me home. Well, it would drive along slow behind me and as soon as I would get in the house, it would turn in the driveway next door and go back to the mine. I could tell that there were four or five fellows in the car and so I happened to mention this to the superintendent one day. He said that was a deputy that the Company had and his helpers, to protect me from the Union B people. Well, I told them, "Thanks a lot but they had caused me a lot of worry since I thought it was some of the Union B men."

A miner's wife made this observation concerning the strike:

I can remember one time that when we lived down the street here, the union had a house right across the street from us that had six machine guns pointing over toward our house. Well, it was really terrible living across the street from that and I was always frightened that my children would get hurt. I can remember that my daughter used to have the front bedroom and we moved her out to the back bedroom. We were very glad when that house burned down. Of course, we don't know why it was burned down but it was very fortunate that it did.

The miner was frequently confused about the issues involved and intimidation by both sides was common.

Many persons were scared into joining the Union B movement. They were afraid of bombings, shootings, houses being burned down, and many of them did not know what was going on. One side would say, do not go down [to work], and many of them did not know was going on. And the poor miner did not know what to do.

A number of our informants who were members of Union A believed there was communist influence in the Union B movement. Thus they found it easy to dispense with civil liberties.

In fact, there was a communist who did come here on the train and set up a printing press. Union A destroyed the printing press and gave the old boy a beating and put him in the Hartdale jail. They held a kangaroo court there for this communist. By the time that communist left the area he was no longer a communist.

The majority of adherents of the newly formed Union B were reported to be immigrants. Many of them stated that any union in which the native had control would not be one where they could expect to be treated fairly. Thus, in light of their own experience, more could be gained by joining the opposition. Many of the natives saw the conflict in terms of the immigrants' attempt to take over the mines. Thus the basic native-immigrant hostility was brought into focus once more. Old wounds were reopened. The son of an immigrant miner made this observation:

The native was already predisposed in a highly prejudiced way against the immigrant and this offered a good chance to attack the immigrants.

It was easy to incite the native against the immigrant during this period; anarchy reigned. An immigrant reports:

There's always been about 60 percent of the natives, ignorant as horses, who were prejudiced. After they got whooped up with propaganda their members increased about a hundredfold and their prejudice and hatred did too. After they found out they could get away with anything, they even went into homes—made arrests without a warrant. I was there when they took my brother-in-law out of the house. I asked 'em where their warrant was an' they told me to shut up or they would take me in too.

There was little room for neutrality; people were forced to declare themselves as favoring one side or the other.

When the pressure of prejudice was on, it was interesting to note that many of the Union A workers were deputized and acted as deputies in the trouble against Union B. I can remember these workers would go in to hardware stores and requisition ammunition from the stores to be used against the Union B men. In one particular case, this happened to be a relative of mine who owned a hardware store, he was very fearful that the Union B men would take it out on him. You could not be neutral in this situation. You had to be declaring yourself as to your side and this was very difficult for the person to do. I would say that prejudice was used as a deliberate device in order to get persons to declare themselves. As I mentioned previously, most of the immigrant group took the part of Union B rather than Union A.

The merchant was caught between rival factions.

You see, you could not say anything because if you did that would mean that they would not trade with you. I would have gotten into a lot of trouble if I had said anything one way or the other. You see, if you opened your mouth here, you would lose business. Why, they could boycott you and your store. That's what saved me; I never said anything. One time a group of Union B men came in and they wanted me to let them have a meeting above my store. I would not do this because it would mean that the Union A men would burn my store or bomb it.

Many merchants suffered financial loss during this period.

Many businessmen here went broke because of what the people owed them and the fact that they lost their jobs. I lost over $6,000 during that period. Most of the foreigners here were Union B men and they lost their jobs. Many of them had to leave the community.

Crowds and mobs were a frequent occurrence; anything might happen. A native miner:

I got home from D—— one night. I thumbed a ride back. I got home about twelve o'clock. There must have been three hundred or four hundred people in the center of town. I didn't know what in the world was the matter. That was during the union trouble. They said these Union B fellows are getting ready to go down to the mine and stop the examiners from going down. The law was there. The sheriff here had deputized several men from the county for Union A and they let them have it with buckshot and they scattered and the mine examiners went ahead and worked. There was one kid here around eighteen years old. He didn't have anything in it, he didn't work in the mine or anything, but he went with these Union B guys and they picked buckshot out of him up at the filling station. That is just the life that you lived around here.

In the end Union B, the rival union, was crushed. With it the jobs of the vast majority of immigrant workers were lost. The reverberations were pronounced in all phases of community life. Vindictiveness against the immigrant and his family was marked.

Retaliation against the immigrant for his union affiliation was severe and persisted after the settlement of the conflict. With jobs at a premium many informants, both native and immigrant, reported that foreigners were chased from the mine.

When the mines reopened under Union A, there were some immigrants who wanted to work in Coal Town. They were driven away from the mines at gunpoint. The natives would not let them work in the mines after they had reopened.

I went to work at the mine in 1922. I got my leg hurt there and was off work a long time. Then came the union strike. When I got well enough and went back to work they wouldn't let me. Those American officials sent me away with a gun. Told me, "You hunkie, get to hell out of here." Many of us got raw treatment. Someone had to go. There weren't enough jobs. They framed our people here.

Many innocent persons were penalized. Other members of the family suffered when a miner was on the losing side.

If you were on the wrong side in the union trouble, that is the losing side, you were out, and in that year at our school there were nine teachers let out of our service system. If you had any affiliation with the losing side, you were out.

When they had the union trouble between Union B and Union A all teachers whose parents or whose husbands belonged to Union B lost their jobs. I know this for a fact. The girls were let off of their jobs because their parents were Union B people.

I could not get a job here in this area because my father was a Union B miner.

Personal relationships became uncertain and tenuous. Close friends could no longer be trusted.

Individual natives felt some pressure put on them to remove the immigrants from their jobs despite the fact that these immigrants were their personal friends. I would say that this was a sort of jungle in which the strong one won out. When the contest for the jobs came the people's ethics shrank away into nothing. Now some of these persons were actually hungry. Some of the immigrants were bought off by the nativistic groups and these immigrants were forced to spy on their own people—their own immigrant groups.

Immigrants turned on one another during this period.

Then the foreigners all got a raw deal, were badly misled, terrorized, and abused and even were turned against one another. No one could trust anyone else then. I got chased off the job and was out of work for eight years. They called me a Union B man and wouldn't let me go back to work. They chased us with guns—nothing we could do. Some of us were mad enough to fight and kill but we had others to think about.

Families paid a price too.

There was a very strong feeling about this trouble between Union A and Union B. Why, even families broke up because of this and members of the family did not speak to each other for many years. In fact, some of this still holds true today.

In the end the basic native-immigrant cleavage, characterized by hostility and resentment, remained more firmly entrenched than before. Interpersonal relationships became even more unpredictable, without order and stability. Finally the marked suspicion and distrust of friends, in some instances family members, helped foster cynicism and impersonality among these people.

IMPERSONALITY

The development of impersonality was furthered by problems stemming from absentee ownership. As noted in the previous chapter, the coal company was production-centered rather than community- or miner-oriented. The coal company lacked real interest in the community. One informant put it this way:

The Company wants to make money and there is no two ways about it. I can give you one example of the difficulty that we are in at the present time and the reaction of the Coal Company. As a member of the Board of Education we were interested in trying to put a kitchen in our school. The Company owned a house not far from here with a kitchen in it and we wanted to see how much they wanted for the house. They told us that they would sell it to us for ten thousand dollars. I got mad. I told them that they should donate it to the city for all the city has done and the fact that now the city is in need, the Company should help them.

The many years of characteristic absentee ownership tended to foster in Coal Town people a feeling of futility regarding their future life. Their destiny was always at the whim of the mining industry, and changes in production method or policy could easily wipe out a community on short notice. At a deeper level there was the haunting fear that there was no concern for them as people, for their needs and their aspirations.

AUTHORITARIANISM

Authoritarianism and violence frequently appear together. Coal Town was plagued by both. By authoritarianism we simply mean "domination of the many by the few." From the very first, mining activities in Coal Town seemed to lend themselves to authoritarian ways. During the early days the coal camp, previously described, was rigidly controlled. Any phase of economic or personal life which might threaten the status quo was curbed and eliminated. Often individual liberties were easily expendable. An early description goes as follows:

You know how it was, a guy with the money wanted to start a mine, he'd hire somebody to run the whole show, build the camp, rent it out, police it, get help to run the company store an' keep books an' manage the mine. Hire—fire as he damn pleased. That's what the Old Man was used to. You didn't have no freedom. Whenever you come to Coal Town they wanted to know why and what your business was. You had to mention name when you come here. They find out quick what is your intention.

In time the coal camp expanded and became a coal town. Overt violence diminished over the years, but the fact that Coal Town remained a one-industry community meant that economic power, which was centralized, became a potent weapon to control and regulate behavior. In Coal Town such power resided in the hands of the mining superintendent and his associates, who controlled the economic life of the community. Although always important, the significance of these people grew as unemployment increased and the community deteriorated. Our informants repeatedly referred to the power of the mine superintendent's clique and the need to handle them diplomatically. Some superintendents reputedly treated the miners with fairness and justice. Others exploited them and took advantage of their position. Many superintendents believed in arrogant, authoritarian ways, demanding homage and subservience from the miner. During a period of economic decline, belonging to the "right church" became a factor in employment.

I do not attend church any more. I used to but I didn't feel at home in that church recently and I'll tell you why. It was something like this. When T—— came in he sort of took over the church and many of us just had to drop out and not attend because of his personal power. It is well known in the community that if you want to get a job working at the mine of which T—— is superintendent, that you must be a member of the —— Church. I, being a Methodist, was told that I belong to the wrong church. It went something like this. I was out of work and I got a call from Mr. T—— to come over to his house at five o'clock. My wife took the phone call and she told him that she would give me the message. Well, I went over there at five o'clock and he asked me if I wouldn't like to work at the mine rather than going all the way over to Hartdale to work. I told him sure, I would much rather work at the mine and then he told me something that really made me mad. He said, "Well, you know, Jim, you belong to the wrong church, that's all." I didn't say anything for a minute and then I sort of controlled my temper and I told him that, well, if I had to change my religion to get a job, I just thought I'd go on working where I was. He didn't say anything but sort of grinned, then turned around and walked back into the house. That's the last time that I've had anything to do with him. I know of two families in the —— Church now who joined that church in order to get a job. When the mine was hiring, the qualifications to get a job was —— Church membership.

Authoritarianism stemmed not only from the policies of management but from union policies as well. Regardless of the benefits accruing from union activity, and our informants reported many, authoritarian practices emerged. Struggles for power between union personnel and management occurred. Struggles within rival union groups likewise took place. For many years the union in Coal Town had considerable power in the community, power over individuals and merchants which was not always judiciously used.

The Company did not have any power because of the powerful strangle hold of the union. The union was the controlling factor here for many years. The city officials were all approved of by the union.

The union officials had sufficient power to bankrupt a merchant, if they so desired.

The union was so strong here that the merchants would be scared of being boycotted. They used to threaten merchants with putting a banner in front of your store—that is, a picket line—and if they ever put up this banner, why you were ruined. You were out of business because no one would ever cross the picket line. There were no real cases in which this was actually done but there was always the fear that it might be done. You see, everyone was scared. It really haunted the businessmen and there was always the hint of violence just around the corner if you didn't fall in with whatever was going on in the community.

CORRUPTION

A fourth community theme fostered by coal mining is associated with corruption in management-labor relations and intra-union activities. The overwhelming number of mining informants who reported such activities were stalwart union men who spoke in laudatory terms about the benefits of the union. Many had witnessed and survived the early struggles.

Unions were a good thing for the miners. They are good for everybody in all these factories and things. You take now the operators and workers in the factories, they don't fight one another like they used to. They see it is best to get along. In the coal mine they ain't had a strike in five or six years. They settle things between themselves. You got to give it to G——. Union A will never get another leader like that. I am a charter member of Union A. I joined Union A when I was sixteen years old. It cost me fifty cents to get in and that was all. I have never dropped my card since.

The miner had considerable pride in union membership, as is shown by the following remark:

There was one unspeakable name in this community and that was "scab." You could not call a man that in jest. If you did, that was the worst insult that you could give. No one joked about this term.

Nevertheless, miners readily admitted that corruption entered certain union activities.

The majority of older miners reported that union leadership had changed drastically. Many of them believed that the early leaders were essentially idealists interested in the broader social meaning of unions. Whether this is a romantic conception which appears in retrospect we cannot say. The son of an early union leader points out this change in union leaders:

I would say that the early union leaders were very enlightened persons. This leadership was true during the period of my father's interest in the union and later the leadership was the very reverse of this. Now the union has no educational program that I know of. Though I do remember hearing during regular union meetings about the contract and how things should be done and the interpretation of the contract. This was to help the workers. I would say that the union leadership has become demoralized. They became cynical, particularly during the 1940s, and all that they were interested in was in holding a job and they did not care what happened to the worker.

As union leadership deteriorated many of the early enthusiasts lost interest. An English miner:

I would say that in this new group the bottom of the barrel sought positions of leadership and this was a somewhat radical group. Now the Kentuckians and the Tennesseans were part of this group that took over and the group that took over was entirely composed of the native group without any foreign born. The good citizen, for instance, lost interest. He lost interest in the job. He lost interest in the union because he could not respect the leadership and because he could not believe what the union leaders said. Now I would say that part of the leadership in the Kentucky and Tennessee group were very aggressive but at the same time it was bad.

A mine boss suggests that the ethics of union leaders underwent change:

The union leadership has changed a great deal. When I first came here, it was based on honesty and a fair deal. The Company, you see, was very much opposed to the union, but now the unions have gotten rotten and they are even worse than the Company. They do the same things that the Company used to do, only do it a little bit worse. Why, in the later years that I worked, you could not even fire a man. You see, what happened was that the union got strong and you would have to bow your neck to the union.

The union, designed to eliminate labor-management evils, created its own. A native miner:

It's dirty now. It's really dirty. It's just terrible. What happens is that the Company and the union officials get together and work against the good of the miners.

Many believe that union officials could be bought.

Why, the coal operators could buy off these union officials at any time they wanted to and they usually did. The union officials had control of the union machinery and they wanted to hold offices so that they could have power. These union officials double-crossed the men many times. They sold the miner down the river.

INSECURITY—PHYSICAL, PSYCHOLOGICAL, AND ECONOMIC

A fifth community theme is manifest in the essential insecurity which underlies the personal organization of our Coal Town people. Psychological feelings and cultural patterns of insecurity emerge as a result of different factors. At this point we wish to assess the significance of the hazardous nature of the mining occupation itself. When we turn to the nature of mining some interesting attitudes appear. There were those who openly professed to enjoy the work.

I am not sorry about having mining as an occupation. I would choose mining again if I had it to do over. We saw better jobs in the mines. I had ambition. One of my boys also worked in a mine for a while.

During the early days of hand loading a miner was paid for the amount he loaded. Thus each miner, working for himself, was in a sense his own boss. Many reported that during this period individual skill was exceedingly important and that the miner had personal pride in what he was able to produce. With the shift to a daily wage, much of the personal pride and satisfaction began to disappear.

This old sociability is now gone. It was true in the old days because an individual was on a piecework basis. That is, each digger had a certain portion of the mine to work. The diggers were on a competitive basis with each other, but a digger would work with two or three other men, and between these there was cooperation. The digger felt a personal satisfaction in his work. He sort of felt like he was in business for himself. He had a room down in the mine for himself. He was the boss of that room. All he had to do was to get out that coal and he could do this quickly and get out or he could loiter and loaf and take all day, so that he actually felt as if he were in business for himself.

Many of the miners reported that they enjoyed mining for still another reason: avoidance of unfavorable weather.

Well, when I was able to work I used to enjoy it. I first put in four years on top. The boss wanted me to stay on top. I decided I wanted to go below and to get out of the weather. We loaded coal there for a good while and I got another buddy and we loaded till they got the machines and then I went to running a motor. I worked on the night shift and that wasn't agreeing with me. I got on a motor and I stayed on that till the mine closed down. I like it better on the bottom. You are out of the hot weather and bad weather and you get more money.

Another miner had this to say:

Well, that's what I liked about the coal mines was that on hot days like this you were down there and you didn't have to suffer this heat. Well, I would say that is the main thing. You can go down there and work pretty hard. You get up a sweat while you are working but when you stop you get chilly. A fellow could work and it wasn't hurting him too bad. Eventually they made the mines safe. They put up lots of safety lights and everything. Mining wasn't too bad then. It was pretty bad before that. A lot of them would enjoy that loading. It was 92 cents a ton. They would load about five cars. Each car held about five tons. That would be about $23 or $24. It was good money and the work wasn't too bad. If you had to do that work out here in this heat it would kill you. It is just like getting in one of them air conditioned stores, I like that. I would like to work there all day.

Many of the miners were fearful of the hazards but were ambivalent toward mining and reluctant to leave it.

The dust is bad. It is dirty. You have never seen anything like it until you go down inside one of those holes. This type of work kills a man. I know, I started in when I was nine years old at 45 cents a day. This coal mining, though, becomes a part of you. Despite the bad part it is attractive to you. It just becomes a habit and you can't live without it. It's sort of like smoking.

The overwhelming majority of our mining informants reported differently. The data to be presented suggest a set of deep and penetrating fears in the average miner—fears which are cumulative,

fears which over the years leave certain residues on the personalities of miners. In order to appreciate the significance of these fears
we centered our questions on such topics as: "Does a miner worry
about his work and about getting hurt?" "Would you want to be a
miner again?" "What does it do to one to be a miner?" In answer
to direct questions—"Does a miner worry about getting hurt?"
"Would you want to be a miner if you had your choice?"—65 percent of the miners interviewed reported that they were fearful and
would not chose to be a miner again. The remaining 35 percent
reported they did not worry about their work and would choose
mining as an occupation once more. A qualitative analysis centering
on the "feeling tones" expressed reveals a greater discrepancy, however. For these remarks were in response to direct questions which
the researchers put to the informants. In this regard it is important
to note that on the whole we found the miner to be a person with
marked sensitivities which became manifest whenever discussions
centered around personal questions regarding self-feelings and
personal worth. Any implication that mining as an occupation was
inferior to other occupations or that miners were cowardly, or not
as fine as persons from other occupations, brought much defensive-
ness. Our informants spontaneously felt it necessary to speak as
follows:

You see, the miner is not such a bad person. They work hard at their
jobs but some people don't think that we are human beings. Why, many
persons think that coal miners live like dogs. Why, I am as clean as you
are. There is no difference between a miner and other people. They're just
as strict as anyone and just as good as anyone. We have a bunch of louses
who are miners, and we have a bunch of good people who are miners,
just like everything else.

One informant went so far as to recommend coal mining for
tuberculosis.

There has been much said about tuberculosis as a result of coal dust but
I can give you one example. For instance, a local doctor said at the time
that there was no connection between tuberculosis and coal mining. In
fact, he had tuberculosis and he went to work in the mine himself so
that he could recuperate from tuberculosis since he felt that there was
nothing connected about mining and tuberculosis.

It was necessary at this point to move cautiously in dealing with our informants. We tried to understand the defensive comments which appeared at this time and probed for the deeper meanings which were not always apparent. As we listened to our informants, we felt that the general quality and content of their remarks were far more indicative of their real feelings than the direct responses to direct questions.

Here is a miner who reported he felt safe in spite of his misfortune:

I felt just as safe in the coal mines as when I worked on top. I have had my hand broken, some ribs broken, and I've had my teeth knocked out, but I never worried about my life as a miner.

One informant suggested that miners never worried—but:

The miners did not worry about their occupation. The miner, though, was pretty damn scared. He was always scared. He always worried about his occupation. I can remember some of these miners who would start from home to go to work, and then they would get scared and then they would come back and they wouldn't even go to work and the family members did not know if the man was coming home from work after his shift or not. Something might always happen to him.

One miner who spent considerable time informing us that miners never worried ended his remarks with this statement:

You know, I don't think a coal miner worries. I think that is the farthest thing from a coal miner's thoughts. If you worried about it, you couldn't go. I think that is one of the farthest things from a coal miner's thought is leaving for work and worrying about his job. I think he just goes to the mine as a matter of course. When he is in the mine, he worries about himself and the conditions above him. I will say that.

Another made these comments:

A man with plenty of experience down in the coal mine, he doesn't worry about getting hurt. At least it seems to me that he didn't worry. I knew I never did. You see, when you're a coal miner you have to take lots of chances, and you just don't think about getting hurt but your family does. Your family worries about you when you are working in the mines. Now I've been in some mighty dangerous places in the mines. I've been in several squeezes, as they call 'em, and I've been so damn scared down there that I've shook all over and the hair would stand up on my neck. I was in really some dangerous places and I wouldn't do that now.

Although there were those who professed little fear of mining, the majority of our mining informants were quite open about their fear and dislike of the occupation. Our data are replete with descriptions and accounts of personal fear and experiences such as these:

I would not be a miner if I had it to do all over again, it's too late now and too dangerous. You see, you never step on that cage without wondering if you're going to come back or not. Being a miner is just like going into battle. There is always this fear of the mine.

I don't guess there is ever a minute but what a miner worries. I don't see how he can keep from it. You can set there and hear falls, maybe like thunder. They sent me up to X—— to pump a mine out that had been shut down for nine years. We made a scaffold and after we got this water pumped down it was a good place to lay around down there. We was trying to get it so we could get back to another section. We was going to make some boats out of inner tubes and float across this and then we could walk on the other side. The next morning we went down there and there was a hundred and fifty ton of rock right where we were sitting. I think every miner has got that same fear. Well, whenever you see a bunch of men covered up it takes a long time to forget it. That does something to you. My wife's brother worked there a long time at the tipple and he reached in to get a grease cup and it ground off his arm. It took them an hour to get him out. He was just hanging there. You see, when I was driving every time somebody would get hurt you would drive down to get them and they would die on the road and all that. I don't want to live over again, that is too much to live. I would be something else. I am sixty-seven. If I got to go through my life again, I wouldn't want it. I would be something else.

I would not work in the mine today. I got hurt. My arm was broken and the air that we breathed in the mine was not good. The working conditions were poor. We used to have to load from thirty to forty tons of coal by hand. That is a short life. A person dies pretty quick. If a man works on the outside like I do now, it is a good life. I feel better. The miner's worry is about getting hurt.

Fears of injury and death do not diminish but increase with time.

The miner never knew if he was going to come out of the mine alive or not. Now when the miner is a young kid, he still has his courage. This is not true with the old miner. For instance, from what I know now I would say that the young miner did not have sense enough to be frightened. I worked in the old coal mine when I was a youngster with mules and I recall that I was not as afraid as the old-timers who worked there who had more experience. The old-timer would know more. I was not afraid because I didn't have sense enough to be afraid.

The danger is constant.

The miner is concerned with the problem of getting hurt. You see, when anybody gets hurt, this bears on the men's minds. Now, you really have to watch yourself in work around a mine either on the bottom or on the top. I always look for the dangerous spots in the mine and you particularly have to watch for them when a shift goes off because many of the men are careless and are apt to leave things in any sort of way, and if you walk in there without looking, you are apt to get hurt. It is a dread all right.

Many miners feared the consequences of accidents for their families.

The miner sure did worry about getting hurt. I know that they used to think about their children and what would happen to their family if they got killed or injured. One example was a fellow that had one arm cut off and one leg and then a second time he had his other leg cut off and all he could say was, "Oh, my poor family and my poor children." I've hauled many men home on the wagon from the mine that was injured or killed. The Company wouldn't take care of them in the early days and it was really terrible.

Every venture into the mine was a gamble. One never knew if he would return.

Oh, yes, I guess most of them worried. You see, they have seen these accidents and heard of them. You kisses your wife good-by and you don't know if you will see her again. I kept putting off quitting and my wife wanted me to when I was old enough to get a miner's pension. My kids raised cain with me. One day I told my wife, "This is the last bucket you will have to fix for me." I told my wife and she didn't believe it till I brought my clothes home that night.

Many miners feared injury more than death.

Personally, I took it somewhat fatalistic. Some of the miners had a tendency to be more concerned about injury rather than death. Many of them had aversions to certain types of injuries, for instance, chest injuries, and they would often prefer to be killed rather than to be permanently injured.

Feelings of anxiety were quite common and effects on personality ensued. For example:

Now, miners do worry. Why, I can remember that everytime I would step on the cage to go down in the mine, I was afraid that maybe something would happen to that cage, that maybe the cable would break or else the man who operated it would have a heart attack.

Some had this reaction:

I think a miner worries a great deal about getting hurt and particularly at night. At night you're down there in the mine by yourself and it's very scary. You can hear the coal fall and you hear it crack worse. You can hear a lot more things at night than you can during the day when there's a lot of noise down there. Well, you study about this and you worry about it and it sort of gets you down. The family worries too. You see, if I let myself think about it, I guess I would go crazy but you can't do that. You can't let yourself think about what might happen to you down there because if you did you never would get anything done. I've been injured three times in the mine myself.

A good many of our informants told us that miners became fatalistic.

If you worry about your job in the mine, what are you going to do? You have to get used to this. I forget about it, this getting hurt and getting killed. It is fatalistic. It could happen on the street even, any time. At explosion times the wives and the families would get very worried. I know many men who have gotten scared after an explosion and they do not go back to work in the mine.

I used to worry every time I heard a loud noise. It made me uneasy. I was uneasy because I used to work in the mines in C—— and they are much safer mines than the mines were here. My father told me that the mines here was full of gas and some of this I found to be true. That is why I did not stay in the job as a miner. Now some of the family members would worry about their menfolks who were in the mine, but you know that if it is going to happen, it will happen anyway. I don't think that the worrying does any good.

One sixty-year-old miner summed up his feelings by pointing out these things:

You asked me what happens when a man becomes a miner. I would say that he is in poor health. To do this work results in the degrading of a man. Many people get sick because of lots of dust. The lungs fill up with asthma. People die. They become discouraged, hopeless. There is no future.

A retired native miner:

This work in the coal mine makes you grow more irritable as you get older. It affects one's physical strength. He just gets run down. He does this because we have what we call in the mine "make-believe air." It's really not good air at all and there is a tendency to get blue and down in the dumps. I know. I have gotten blue many times and so down in the dumps that I just didn't care whether I lived or not.

The families of miners lived in constant dread of what might happen. A wife of a miner stated:

I used to worry a lot. I would think what I would do if they brought my husband home a corpse. Why, you never knew that when he went to work if he would come back that evening. It was this sort of worrying that really was hard for the woman. The families, I would say, worry more than the miners.

Apprehension mounts when the miner fails to return on time.

Now, during the explosion over at W——, my husband wasn't working at that time and he went over and helped carry out some of the men that were in the explosion. He left on Sunday morning real early and he didn't come home till real late Sunday night. I worried more that day than I did all the rest of the time that he was in the coal mine. Of course, if there are times when he is a little late getting home, I worry. He usually is so prompt and if he is just a little late, I worry about him.

Some miners felt that the work itself plus the danger contributed to family difficulties.

This affects the family of the miner in a bad sort of way. You see, when the man comes home, he's tired, he's done a back-breaking work in the mine and he really works in the mine. Don't kid yourself. This is apt to start arguments. You have been down in the mine all day and you would like to get out on top and breathe some of that good clean air, but your wife has been home all day and she wants to go somewhere. You don't feel like going. There are arguments and these build up and there is a lot of difficulty. You always come out of there with a headache. There is a lot of noise and vibration. In the winter it's warm down there and you're sweaty. When you come up, you freeze to death before you can get a shower. In the summer, it's cold down there and when you come up it's like opening the door of an oven. It really blasts you right in the face. It's really somethin' when that hits you.

An ever-present dread is the possibility of explosion or accident which may inflict destruction to life and limb. These were more than idle fears, for the history of mining accidents in Coal Town was such that death was always a possibility. The majority of miners interviewed who had worked in a mine possessed some physical disability; sometimes it was as minor as a smashed finger, other times it consisted of back injuries which were almost totally disabling. Official records indicate a total of 211 fatal accidents and 2,977 nonfatal accidents in the period 1904-53 for the two major Coal Town mines. These statistics, in and of themselves, mean little, however. We had hoped that it might be possible to compute an accident rate for five-year intervals, but this was not possible because the state mining statistics dealing with employees failed to differentiate mining personnel from office and management personnel, and for one ten-year interval there are no records. Nevertheless, it is our impression, based on information from our informants, that the above figures underrepresent grossly the actual incidence of fatal and nonfatal accidents. Reporting of such activities was for many years conducted in a haphazard manner and oriented toward presenting mining conditions in a most favorable light.

Typical statements regarding fear of injury and death went like this:

A miner worries about his work. It is a dread that is always with you. You see, there are so many ways of getting hurt. You can get hurt from the walls, from the sides, from the machines, or anything. I know of many miners who have been killed or injured in the mines. I would say that 75 or 80 percent have been hurt in some way in the mines.

I have never been in a mine disaster and if I am ever in one, it will be my last. I expect to quit. Why, these blasts are really terrific in the mine. These cutting machines that we use weigh from eighteen to nineteen tons and that blast that they had over in the mine turned one of these machines upside down. That gives you some idea of how dangerous those explosions are.

The danger of coal dust is ever present. A description:

We try to avoid getting hurt, you know, but it comes, you know. They furnish the respirators for you and everything like that. This rock dust is a kind of ground limestone. The idea of rock dust is to render this coal dust into a nonexplosive state. Once the coal dust starts it goes along and ignites all the time. It travels with a speed of five thousand miles per hour. I went down after the explosion and some of the men were badly battered up.

Concentration of smoke is usually a sign of danger.

Well, right after I got my new job there was this explosion and I guess I considered myself lucky that I'm still alive. I can remember that it began to get good and smoky one day down there and the men kept on coming down and they couldn't get the fan fixed at the air shaft to blow the smoke out. Well, we didn't work the next day but some of the men went down and the mine blowed up and when it blowed up all the men were killed in the mine and there were 57 in there.

Our informants reported they worried about explosions in the winter and falling roofs in the summer.

Your most dangerous period of getting hurt is when the roof falls in, that is in the summertime. In the summertime, the mine takes in moisture and all workings are wet. When the weather changes in the fall everything gets dry and dusty. All your explosions were in the fall or winter. The moisture has all been taken out of the mine. There are several gallons of water enters the mine every day in the summer. Now, right now at our Number Three we have a terrible time on account of rock fall.

When the roof starts "to work" the miner is in real trouble.

Whenever you hear the top begin to work and move, then you had better get out from under there plenty fast. Another sign of trouble in the mine would be when the props began to break and you always had to step out and back. I like a good sound top to work under and I would not work, for instance, in Number Three Mine down here. They don't have a good sound top, instead it's wet mud and when that thing gives, it doesn't give you any warning.

The roof is likely "to work" in the summer.

I would say that the most dangerous thing about coal mining is the roof falling in. Now the roof always warns you before it falls in. There is always a cracking and some noise and you can usually have time to get away if you listen for it. Now, in the summertime the mine is much more dangerous than in the winter. Most of these roof falls are the result of air hitting the coal and the rock and causing them to contract. In the winter it seems not to affect the roof as much as in the summer.

Fear and excitement take over when disaster occurs. In the early days it was a "short blast" on the whistle that informed the inhabitants of Coal Town that a disaster had occurred.

When there was a mine disaster here in the early days before they had telephones, the mine blew a short blast on the whistle. This meant that a fatal accident had occurred, either that someone was injured or that someone was killed. The women would start to worry right away whether or not it was their husbands and they wouldn't know until their husbands came back. When telephones came in, they used to call the mines and try to find out who was hurt or who was killed. I was in three mine disasters myself. Word spreads from person to person in the mine.

News of disaster travels fast abetted by very real concern for one's friends.

You see, in a mine the men are scattered all out over the bottom. They may cover several acres. If somebody is killed in the mine, the news goes all over the mine. This increases your fear because they don't tell you who was killed and this makes you worry because it might be a good buddy of yours or maybe a relative, or a friend, or a son, or something like that. That is a bad situation. Everybody tries to get out of the mine at once when that whistle blows to say that someone is dead. When you have a death in the mine you have all of the men getting upset. The other men lose confidence.

Fear and uncertainty mount, then a group moves in to recover the bodies—an experience that few ever forget.

The wives really worried about this all the time. There was always a dread. I don't know how to explain it. For instance, when the whistle used to blow to indicate an accident, that meant that somebody was hurt or killed and the whole town would hear this and they would begin to wonder. The men in the mine would hear this and dread would fill the mine. You could just feel it and then it was really terrible when you had to go in and get the dead men out. When you did go in, you didn't know if you yourself was coming out alive. Because if you go to move that man, some more coal or rock might fall down on you and kill you if you do. It was a terrible thing. You get sick at your stomach when you do this. I know. I have rescued many men from the mines and I have brought them out with every bone in their body broken. I've put them on the motor car and hauled them up and that warm air would blow over them in your direction and it would make you sick. It's a mighty horrible experience. I would say that there is always this fear that a man had. It was with him all the time.

Bringing out the bodies is bad. These bodies are in all sorts of shape. Why, I've seen the undertaker around here sew up the bodies like they would a sack of grain. It was like building up a snowman. You had to shape the body back into what the person sort of looked like. It was awful to crawl in there and get the bodies because usually you had to take some back entry or go through an air shaft in order to get to them. Then after you got to them, they were in all sort of shapes. They looked terrible and you would often get sick.

Another description:

Oh, that was bad work, go in there pickin' up pieces—a arm here, a leg there, here a fellah with his belly done blow open, a man with no head, his brains splashed agin' the rib, dead pit mules blowed all to pieces. They pay us $1.50 a hour, if I remember, it was worth it. Couldn't eat after that.

The daughter of a miner reminisced:

I can remember one time when Daddy was hurt in the mine. I was just in the second grade. He was kinda crushed in the chest. I didn't know him, he was so black and it was just terrible. I just cried.

After an accident the following procedure was used:

They would go down for a little bit and come right back up when they first started. They would put some birds on the cage and see how far they could go down. When the birds died they knew they had to come back.

A miner reported this experience after an explosion:

I went down after the men when the explosion was over and when we got down there, all the inspectors were down there and they kept asking us to go in and find the bodies. Well, I wasn't too keen about going down and going on in but I stood near the shaft and we used to hand up three of the dead men at a time. There were four people that could ride on a cage and we would have one of the men on there and we would throw up the bodies to him and he would take three of them up. Well, these mine inspectors wouldn't pay any attention to us and they went on down further into the mine and pretty soon we found them dead. They died of what we call "black damp."

A miner who has spent fifty years below wrote this poem:

The Old Miner's Story

Deep down in the earth
Far from the light of day
Nature stored the coal
For the use of man today.

In eons of ages past
Beneath the earth sod
We pause in awe to contemplate
The wondrous work of God.

For fifty years as boy and man
I've worked down in the mine
Toiling in the darkness
Where the sun does never shine.

The miner's life's a roughly one
And full of danger too
I have a little story
That I wish to tell to you.

'Twas in the month of June
Just thirty years ago
We stepped upon the cage
And swiftly went below.

We proceeded to our work
And soon were at the face
Each man strapped to his buff
And in his working place.

'Twas just about half work
We heard an ominous sound
The crash of rocks and timber
That shook the very ground.

In dire alarm we stood
And listened to the din
Then very soon we found
That we were barred in.

We got ourselves together
In number we were five
We wondered in our hearts
Would we get out alive?

When our lights died out
To God we then did pray
As we knealt in total darkness
I remember to the day.

Then we heard a knocking
Our rescuers were near
To us poor hapless souls
A pleasant sound to hear.

Five days we were entombed
Men worked with might and
    main
Broke a passage through the fall
Then we were safe again.

We all got on the cage
The cage was rapped away
We soon were up the shaft
Back to the light of day.

Then everyone was happy
Gave thanks to God on high
How beautiful it was again
To see the bright blue sky.

Our informants reported that danger is present in all phases of mining regardless of the particular task. The mine examiner had his dangers:

Now a little something about my job as a mine examiner. You see, we go down into the mines of a morning before the men go to work and look for gas. We also look for squeezes. A squeeze is a top that gets heavy and crushes the supports. Now, I was examining the squeezes in the abandoned section of the mine for accumulation of gas the last few years that I worked. This was a particularly dangerous job because there wouldn't be any persons in these abandoned sections of the mine for a long time and this would make a lot of gas accumulate and it was pretty dangerous work.

"Shooting shots" is particularly dangerous.

You see, when you do the kind of work that I did, such as shooting down the coal, you are apt to get killed, not only from the falling coal but also from the shells that bounce back from the coal. The smoke is thick and the gas from those shells really does smell. It's a terrible thing. You can't see anything and if you do hear the wall beginning to crack, you don't know which way to run because you might run into it as well as out of it, so it seems that it's most of all guesswork.

The most dangerous job in the mine was shooting the shots as it was called, in which you had to remember how many shots that you had set off and then be sure and count them because if you went into a room and a shot hadn't gone off, then you might get killed.

Those who were motormen and tripriders had their problems, too:

The motormen and the tripriders are the ones that have the most dangerous jobs. You see, they have to go down as soon as somebody gets through shooting the coal and load up. Now down in the mine every worker tends to blame somebody else. Everybody blames somebody else except the motorman and the tripman. They don't have anybody to blame and they have to take it.

Those who worked on top had other difficulties. Each occupational group felt that its particular task was the most dangerous.

At the mines, I have worked only at the top. I would say that there is just as much injury on the top as below. In fact, in proportion to the total number of men who work, there are more accidents per man topside than on the bottom. My brother was killed on top when he was trapped in a big bin of coal dust and smothered to death. You see, on top there is plenty of machinery and wherever there is machinery, there is plenty of danger. I have been a load rider, that is riding the coal cars as they come up to the washer, and this is a very strange and dangerous work.

Through the years safety measures were increased. Nevertheless, with the introduction of new machinery mine hazards increased also. Each machine brought with it its share of accidents.

You see, this new machinery makes so much noise that you couldn't hear the roof if it did begin to crack. That's why in many cases most of the injuries today are from the roof falling in. Used to when the machines weren't in, it was very quiet and you could hear the wall crack and that would give you time to get out.

All the machinery is down there now and it's pretty dangerous. It's more dangerous now because you can't hear anything. You can't hear the top working and you don't know anything about what might happen.

Many of the miners reported that safety precautions could have eliminated the probability of mining accidents. Nevertheless, safety measures were reported to have been ignored by both management and labor. There were those who claimed that management ignored safety rules in order to increase production. A miner reported this:

There's a lot of truth in that business about safety. The Company didn't care at all about safety when the men were below. The only way that you could be sure and be safe would be to stand for your own rights. Now, not all the people have the guts to do this but I did. I would not do any dangerous work at all. When I found out that a room was not ready to cut, well, I would not cut it. You see, the boss would try sometimes to impress you with his knowledge and say, "Sure this room is safe," but I wouldn't go in there because I knew that it was dangerous and that somebody was apt to get killed or hurt. Lots of things like that goes on all the time in the mines and I didn't want any boss to run over me when I was working in the mine.

The miners were never impressed with the Company's safety program.

Now, what happened was that during slack periods the Company will ask the miner to go to safety meetings. But after you go below in the mines, the Company don't want you to pay any attention to safety. It's all for the public eyes. Why, they teach one thing at the safety school and then boss comes running around and saying to you to hurry up. Me, I don't pay much attention to that safety program because it isn't the practice at all.

The Company once threatened me with a discharge because I wouldn't go in and cut a roof. Well, I told them that it was not safe in there. You see, the Company was guilty of this and they used to hire some of the workmen as bosses and these workmen would make it hard on you and many of the bosses then used to keep themselves from the men and this was exactly what the Company wanted so that the Company could use these men.

You see, you can't follow all those safety rules with the face boss right on your heels all the time, and he doesn't care whether you violate them or not as long as you get the coal out.

Quite apart from management's responsibility, it is important to note that miners themselves were reluctant to follow safety rules. The mine examiner often tried to create working conditions that were safe.

I was an examiner and I used to go to work at 2 A.M. I examined the mine, everyone's little room in which they worked. Looked for gas and bad tops, and then I came back. If I found a place where there was gas, I would put a yellow check on the man's tag and that meant that there was gas in his room and that he had better not go on down. He would be told by the mine when he reported that there was gas and that he had better not go to his room. I was always very careful about finding gas, and whenever I did, I would block off the room and mark three chalk marks, which in the mines means danger.

Often the miner himself was more interested in production than in his own welfare.

We all used to do things that we weren't supposed to do such as ignoring the safety rules. I've been on a safety committee more than once and you will take more chances, I think, to make a dollar than you do paying any attention to any safety rules.

Some miners were simply reckless. A native miner:

I would tell lots of men what to do. The trouble is that most of them wouldn't listen. Some of the miners didn't care. When you got marked there, "Stay Out, Gas," you have to wait until the gas man comes and checks. When they take the sign off you could go to work. I was careful.

One informant bragged about his recklessness.

You see, these mines were filled with gas and it was really scary down there when you would see that gas around and you would want to get out of there as fast as possible. Now, you were not supposed to smoke in the mines but I did. I just didn't give a damn about anything and many times I broke black powder with a pick and I had on an oil lamp too, and I don't know why I never did get killed or blowed up.

Miners were reluctant to accept changes in safety regulations. A mine examiner:

We had oil lamps first in the mines and then carbide lights and it was hard to get the men to use the battery lights. They didn't like the hard-shell hats either. They said it was too heavy or else it gave them a headache. The same thing was true when we introduced the hard-toe shoe. We had an awful time getting them to put them on.

Some miners felt that wearing safety equipment was almost a sign of fear and weakness.

I can remember the example of the new skull-hats. When they first came in there was a lot of opposition to it. Well, it was proposed at the union meeting that any union man wearing a hat would be fined $5.00. Well, I was the first to wear one of these hats and it was to my benefit to wear it too. I was an opposition to this movement and I spoke my piece.

Out of the hazardous nature of the occupation friendships emerged. These sprung in part out of the essential fear and danger which the miner encountered in his occupation. They were also fostered by the general impersonality in the community as well as by the hostility felt in relation to mining management. At times the friendships were tenuous and fragmentary, but nevertheless they indicated certain positive feelings which the miners had for each other.

It was the fear in the mine that usually resulted in a miner forming some fairly good friendships with other people. You always worked with a companion and this companion was called a buddy. The miners used to mix outside the mine and they usually had very good times together.

During periods of catastrophe, barriers between persons were dropped and archantagonists came to the aid of one another as well as to the families involved.

Men form close friendships. It is surprising that they can argue about things but when a man gets hurt, all come to do what they can. It is an unwritten law among them. You are good buddies and you never do forget them. Just like in the war. I have an old friend in the other part of town.

He is retired now and we are still buddies. When I go to German Town they will stop and talk to me.

People in the mining industry build strong friendships. You will see this in a catastrophe or even in sickness. When one got hurt in the mine when I first came here, it wouldn't be half a week until a collection was taken up for him. This was true in England, too.

For instance, in the event of a crisis or a mine explosion all barriers were down between the natives and the immigrants. Even the natives took this position. Even Victor had some pity for the poor immigrant miners who were killed in the mine. The work of coal mining creates a personal interest in the worker for the other worker. There is an ever-present danger. This makes fatalists of men. This coal mining occupation has much of the same effects as war on a man. It forms strong friendships between the men.

The friendships formed gave rise to the term "buddy," so frequently heard in mining camps, and these friendships were the basis for structured cliques. These sub-societies functioned not only as personal units within an impersonal milieu but became an effective unit in controlling management. Thus there were informal rules regarding the amount of work one ought to do, methods of control for those who deviated, and ways of getting back at management for grievances.

You see, you have to go along with the boys and do what they want if you want to last very long. There is a lot of jealousy down there in the work in the mines.

In spite of the positive elements involved in friendships, they were easily terminated.

The coal miner builds up a lot of friendships but they don't seem to stay with you as you grow older. These friendships do not seem to last but they seem to play out.

Well, yes, if you are working with one group and you are all buddies and you respect one another and help one another out, strong friendships build up which continue after they get out of the mines in some cases. Lots of them don't. One fellow working with me, I thought I was a very good friend of his. Somehow he don't like me so much any more. I haven't seen him for a long time. Maybe he feels he is higher up. I never was that way.

Patterns of interaction characterized by humor are typical in Coal Town. Such patterns, however, possess a destructive undertone, well recognized by the participants. Even among friends humor which bordered on being destructive was involved. For example:

You see, the miners are great hands to pull jokes on each other. For instance, it is not unusual for a fellow to hang his coat up on the timber in the mine and for somebody else to come along and drive three or four nails in it. The same things happen to shoes if you leave them in the washroom somebody is apt to nail them down on the board.

A practical joke that was almost disastrous was this one:

There was a little Italian got to bitchin' with his buddy one time and his buddy threatened to squeeze him. The little guy told him if he did he'd kill 'em. I guess the motorman only half meant it, but before the day was over he did accidentally catch his buddy between a couple of loads. When he heard him holler, he just left the motor and went to the bottom and took a cage out. Didn't even pull the loads off him. The guy wasn't hurt but he stayed pinned a long time. Boy, you'd laugh to hear him tell about it.

We will deal more fully with the implications of destructive humor in a subsequent chapter.

Insecurity in many forms characterized life for the Coal Town miner. There were not only the insecurities previously discussed but also the constant threat of economic deprivation. Our informants reported that even during the prosperous years, which were not numerous, the miner never worked more than nine months.

You take the cycle of the way these mines work. It is either a feast or a famine. It is a period of good work and then it slacks off. It runs in cycles and your children are better off in a steady industry.

A seven-month working year, or less, was common. The employment history of the Coal Town miner reveals the following patterns: [1]

1. There were 6 years during the period 1904-51 when miners did not average more than 129 working days per year.

[1] Data compiled from official state mining reports.

2. There were 12 years during the period 1904-51 when miners averaged between 130 and 169 working days per year.

3. There were 14 years during the period 1904-51 when miners averaged between 170 and 209 working days per year.

4. There were 8 years during the period 1904-51 when the miners averaged between 210 and 249 working days per year.

5. There were 8 years during the period 1904-51 when the miners averaged between 250 and 289 working days per year.

Thus economic security was always precarious and likely to be completely upset at any change in other branches of our economy. Then, too, there was the ever-present problem of being in debt:

Hell, I would not be a coal miner again if I had it to do all over again. It's a hard life. It's heavy work and you lose from three to six months of the year. In addition to that you are always in debt. Why, I know some friends who never got out of debt. All they used to do was draw their little coupon books and take it to the store and they never did see any money for a long time. If I had my life to live over again I would be a carpenter. I think I would go to school and learn all I could about carpentry, I like it and it is very interesting work. I never would be a miner by a damn sight.

As in other heavy industries, the man past fifty is no longer employable.

When I quit the mines I know then that if I ever tried to get on any more I couldn't because of the age. You see, when you get to be fifty-two or fifty-three and they let you go, you can't get a job at the mines. I know that I could do a good job.

As time progresses what visions or hopes for changing his occupation the miner possesses become narrowed. In spite of certain expressed undesirable features of his occupation he becomes increasingly insecure about venturing out into new endeavors. His outlook becomes constricted and he continues to settle for less and less. Even though a mine is to be closed, many miners remain in the hope that in some miraculous way the mine will reopen. A miner:

They have some very interesting attitudes toward their work. They will stay at a mine and work despite the fact that they have been given notice that the mine will close. They feel that if they can stay they will have a few dollars saved up. Something holds them to the mine. If they were smart, they would quit early and then go to other places such as big cities like E—— or Lake City to get jobs, but this does not happen. They know the mine will close but they stay on.

Other occupations and economic opportunities may be available, but these have no reality for the miner. They are too removed and distant, not in the geographic sense, but in the psychological sense. Some miners break through these self-imposed barriers which restrict and retard, but only after coming to grips with their own anxieties and fears.

In part these problems may be viewed in light of certain general emotional insecurities, but an equally important component of the personality of miners is the self-contempt which lies beneath the surface impressions. It is difficult to pinpoint the origin of such a complex attitude. Nevertheless, it is our impression that the many years of tenuous living associated with mining foster in the miner futility about his having any control over his life or his destiny. This attitude of futility added to the general social definition regarding the menial nature of mining creates feelings of unworthiness. Again we note the marked sensitivities of the miner which were revealed. A merchant who has dealt with coal miners all his life pointed this out:

I've heard of this expression "niggers and coal diggers" and it is a derogatory term. I can remember the time in which the niggers were brought in; and when the coal miner uses this term it is a form of self-depreciation. There are many such terms here in Coal Town and it seems to be characteristic of the miners to try to make light of themselves as persons.

SUMMARY

We have tried in the present chapter to analyze certain dominant themes associated with mining as it functioned in Coal Town. The themes of violence, authoritarianism, corruption, impersonality, economic insecurity, psychological fears of catastrophe, and tenuous interpersonal relationships all had their effects on the personal organization of the people involved. The themes so clearly fostered by mining were in part a reflection of factors unique to the occupation, but they were well reinforced by life in the community. Thus the industrial patterns and the patterns of other segments of community life created a social milieu in which families were reared in accordance with the kinds of values we have just been describing.

What are the consequences? In the chapter to follow we concern ourselves with a phase of this question—the emergence of family organization.

CHAPTER 8

FAMILY PATTERNS IN COAL TOWN

IN the preceding chapters we have pointed out basic trends implicit in the behavior of Coal Town people. Many of these were reflected in the family life which evolved. Thus the general impersonality found in Coal Town permeated relationships in the family. In a circular fashion the family configuration resulted in personality types which reinforced certain values in the community. Family life in Coal Town reflected two broad sets of influences: the ethnic backgrounds of the people and the cultural experiences encountered while living in the community. In this chapter we shall be concerned with two major family types, the native and the immigrant.

During the early history of the community the disproportionate sex ratio and high rate of mobility produced relatively few marriages. Bachelorhood for both native and immigrant was the rule during this period. One of the early recreational patterns consisted of the performance of a mock wedding in which two males, one dressed as a woman, went though a token marriage ceremony usually followed by drinking and festivities. A newspaper editor recalled this:

One thing they used to have quite a bit of that they don't have any more. They put on a womanless wedding. The men were characters in it. It was money making, you know. They would have some little man to be the groom and some great big man to be the bride. They used to get large crowds when they had those.

With time the pattern of singleness changed but women were scarce and many men during the early history of the community married women who had originally begun life in Coal Town as prostitutes. A merchant made this comment:

There were many whores here who married and settled down in the community. Most of them never went into many social groups in the community but they stayed where they were and gradually were blended into the background. Some joined the churches and were accepted. Others tried to do this and failed—that is, they lapsed back into their old behavior. They got loudmouthed, for instance, and drank and whenever they would do this it wouldn't go over very well. The people would say, "Well, remember she is nothing but a prostitute."

THE NATIVE FAMILY CONFIGURATION

MOTHER-CENTERED [1]

The native family which emerged represented a configuration of traits we anticipated along with characteristics which were new and different. For example, at the outset of this phase of our analysis we expected to encounter a traditional family—father-centered. Such was not the case; instead we uncovered a family type which was mother-centered.[2] Our analysis reveals that in our sample of 70 native families approximately 60 percent are mother-centered, 40 percent are father-centered, and 10 percent are democratic. Our informants believe that for the entire native community the mother-centered family has been in existence for some time.

The pattern of family rule is at best difficult to determine and our approach therefore was particularly dependent on the depth material obtained in the interview. Here we attempted to examine the problem from various points of view. We asked direct questions regarding family rule; we probed for the pattern of family rule not only for informants but for their parents and grandparents as well. Further, we inquired into the patterns of arriving at everyday decisions, family goals, discipline, and other areas of husband-wife

[1] The terms "mother-centered" or "father-centered" are used to designate a social arrangement in which family activities and goals are primarily organized around the wishes and power of the mother or father.

[2] We do not plan to deal with the father-centered or democratic family since our investigation revealed no data not already well known.

interests. We were particularly careful to observe familial interactions during our interviewing sessions and we derived inferences
regarding the relative positions of persons in the family. We found,
for example, that a pattern in which the wife kept interrupting her
husband and correcting him was a far better index of relative dominance than a direct question regarding family rule. In order to
illustrate this point more effectively we can take the case of Mrs.
A who interrupted her husband repeatedly during an interviewing
session. She questioned his judgment, criticized him for his behavior, ordered him around, repeatedly told him that he was in
error; but when asked who was the boss at home, immediately
withdrew and said, "My husband, of course." [3]

Our native informants evidenced little hesitancy in discussing
the mother-centered patterns in their families and openly agreed
that the woman in the native family was the boss. In speaking of
her ancestral family a woman stated:

You see, our family was divided in the Civil War. In the family both man
and woman were supposed to be the boss but I can tell you that it was
my grandmother that ran things. Among the natives I would say that the
women were the boss in the family. You see, women had more to say
than the men even in the early times.

A retired native farmer:

In the old family in Coal Town the children were expected to work. The
mother was the boss of the family.

A male generalizes about the group with which he is familiar:

Well, you asked me about the boss in my family. Well, my wife is boss
and she keeps us all in line. The woman is the head of the house rather

---

[3] Part of our inquiry was hampered by the age brackets of our informants.
We found, for example, that the majority of elderly informants (sixty-five and
over) reported almost consistently a mother-centered pattern. We were frankly
unsure as to whether the report was based on the over-all life patterns of the
couples or whether they were based on their lives since retirement. In many
cases the relatively younger age of the women made them appear to be more
dominant than the male at time of interview. In arriving at our family rule
percentages we assumed that in 50 percent of these cases (age sixty-five and
over) the mothered-centered pattern was one that appeared in the marriage
since the retirement of the male.

than the man. I think that it has always been that way, at least in our group, the people that we associated with have.

Consistent with the mother-centered pattern is the reversal of traditional roles for husband and wife in the family. A woman suggests that one is trained for the mother-centered role:

Most of the women belong to clubs and organizations but the men don't at the present time. They tend to stay at home with the children. I don't think that the men are joiners because I guess they get sick and tired of their wives being joiners and going so much. As far as my husband is concerned I don't boss him. I know just how far I can go with him. In my age group I think the women are the persons who take more initiative than the men. When you come from a family in which the woman is the boss, then you are trained for the job. It seems to be handed down and that's the way you start out. I think that is important.

The mother-centered families have interactions of this type:

I know that I am the boss in my present family. I always direct the children and control them. My decisions are always heeded.

In disagreements the woman wins out.

I know that if I wanted something done and my wife said no, it wouldn't be done. She generally does win out in most of the fights and arguments. Whatever the wife thinks is good for the family is all right.

The purse strings are usually controlled by the women in these families, a practice not uncommon in mining families, both in this country and abroad.

In the family the women would be the boss at home and around the house. I think that it was usually the woman that would win out. The woman holds the money and she takes care of that sort of business.

The native men were reported as being "henpecked." Our informants suggested that this is a typical pattern in the native family in Coal Town. A merchant:

The men in this community, I know, are henpecked. You see, we do a lot of work such as installing air conditioners and things like that. Why, it is always the wife that tells the husband what to do rather than vice versa. You take, for instance, today; we were installing an air conditioner for one of the worst henpecked husbands in town and that is Mr. T——. You probably know him. Well, his wife was ordering him around and it was somewhat painful to see the way that he jumped around when his wife asked him to do anything.

Of all the mother-centered families we encountered one stands out as epitomizing the qualities associated with authoritarian family life. In addition to the aggressiveness with which this orientation is pursued, one finds an emotional pride in ruling and a concomitant disregard for other persons in the family. The quote below, taken from the most outspoken female in our sample, exemplifies some of these qualities.

I first met my husband when he was a boarder in the Johnny Bull boardinghouse. I chose my husband and he had to fulfill these requirements: (1) he had to be a Republican, (2) he had to be a Methodist, and (3) he had to be an upstanding citizen. So that you can see I had some requirements before I would marry my husband. Why, I am the boss in this family. Why, next door it was terrible. There is a man over there who is lord of the manor. Why, he even buys the groceries. I sure wouldn't let that happen in my house.

The findings with respect to the mother-centered family raised a number of interesting theoretical questions, some of which will be taken up at this point.

In our opinion the common assertion that the traditional American family has been father-centered in form is an oversimplification and must be reexamined. The common acceptance of this belief is based on what may turn out to be insufficient evidence. The social scientist who asserts that the American family was father-centered without any qualifying statement assumes that rural America was homogeneous; a homogeneity that may never have been present. From the very first our society possessed the seeds for the development of cultural and regional diversity, and while we recognize the existence of cultural and regional variations, we tend to ignore the implications of this for an analysis of family life. Thus it is entirely possible that certain sub-cultures may have developed family patterns consistent with their own historical and cultural circumstances.[4] In addition to father-centered families, these may have been mother-centered or democratic. Even the

[4] For some excellent corroboration of this point of view with respect to England see: Michael Young and Peter Willmott, *Family and Kinship in East London* (London, Routledge and Kegan Paul, 1957); Raymond Firth and Judith Djamour, *Two Studies of Kinship in London, Kinship in Southborough* (London, Athlone Press, 1956.) It is to be noted that many anthropologists are of

scanty evidence currently available, including letters and diaries, probably has never been exploited to the fullest. The whole pattern of frontier man-woman relationships with the markedly disproportionate sex ratio and ever-present destructive forces confronting men of that period suggests the possibility of a nontraditional pattern of family life. Here we certainly have a thesis worthy of more consideration than it is currently given.

If historical materials must be reevaluated, so must our orientation for the examination of the *present scene* be revised. For a second error which we may have committed in postulating a father-centered family for rural America has to do with the personal and professional orientations which set limitations on what we are capable of observing. Can it be that sociologists, predominantly male, are emotionally repelled by mother-centered patterns and so fail to observe them? Furthermore when the sociologist examines the question of family rule it is usually approached from the point of view of *form*, avoiding *content*. By the term "form" we refer to external criteria of male or female dominance. Attention here has centered on legal codes regarding the relative rights of men and women or on the formal patterns of associations between family members. From such indices we have made inferences regarding the existence of family patterns. While we recognize that there is a relationship between legal codes and the ways in which people order their lives, we are equally aware of the discrepancies which are present. We can also suggest that the preoccupation with form has been grossly misleading and has kept us from examining the *content* of family life. By content we mean the entire pattern of interpersonal relations within the family, subtleties and strategies between persons, mechanisms for arriving at solutions, and method of control of persons (see long quotation near top of page 152). We believe that an examination of such internal family criteria viewed from the standpoint of social psychology may demonstrate that once the outer forms and appearances have been removed, certain pronounced mother-centered patterns may be uncovered,

the opinion that the prevalence of the father-centered family in American society has been overstated.

both historically as well as in the present.[5] Further we believe that for certain sub-cultures the trend may be one of a movement from a mother-centered to a democratic family, rather than, as now viewed, from a father-centered to a democratic family.

In turning to an explanation of our Coal Town data, we would like to suggest that *mother-centered patterns are fostered whenever the continuation of the father's role is threatened by the socio-cultural organization.* This may include situations in which occupational hazards resulting in injury or death are ever present. Or such conditions may involve institutionalized practices of feuding and fighting which allow the male greater freedom for personal movement and freedom from family responsibility. Finally, we may have instances in which a dominant culture utilizes authoritarian cultural practices to intervene and remove the male from a minority group culture. The Negro father, for example, in the plantation economy had little control over his destiny. His role as a father could be interrupted at any time the slaveholder saw fit to uproot him and ship him elsewhere. Under these circumstances family life becomes organized around the mother, who represents in her own way stability and predictability in the home. The development of mother-centered patterns is not an idiosyncratic development, but instead probably represents a culturally defined way of dealing with unstable familial conditions of the character we have described, when these conditions have repeated themselves over a period of time.

Although this is in effect an important component in the explanation of the Negro mother-centered family, we have ignored the lesson to be learned for families of whites. Nevertheless, it is precisely these conditions which we believe help explain mother-centered patterns in Coal Town families and perhaps mother-centered patterns for other groups of families. The native culture had historical patterns of violence and personal instability, with physical injury and death for the males an ever-present danger. The precar-

---

[5] For an illustration of this pattern in an American Indian culture see forthcoming publication: Charles Lange, *Pueblo of Cochiti, New Mexico: Past and Present* (Austin, University of Texas Press; to be published in 1958.)

ious nature of the males' existence changed little when they moved to Coal Town. Here the nature of mining itself and the general hazards of community life previously described could cut the breadwinner down at any time. Thus the effect of life in Coal Town was to accentuate an ongoing mother-centered pattern rather than to change or disrupt it.

If there is validity to our analysis, might not one find mother-centered or democratic family patterns in cultural circumstances which approximate those we have described? We hope that this analysis may be suggestive and provocative to the point of encouraging other investigators more fully to explore ramifications of the problems outlined.

INTERPERSONAL RELATIONS IN THE FAMILY

The impersonality and alienation which characterized life in the community was consistently reported in the majority of our native families. Parents were preoccupied with monetary pursuits in various forms and were immersed in a way of life not conducive to the growth of close familial relationships. Thus warm, meaningful associations between husband and wife and parents and children appeared in few instances.[6] What might have been a positive influence counteracting the harshness of the external milieu failed for the most part to devolop. Instead familial values reinforced certain basic patterns. A typical husband-wife relationship was described this way by an insightful informant:

I know that me and my husband were never too close. He never did know me as a person, what I really was like, and I never knew him. He always wanted his way and I guess I was afraid of him but I guess you think it's funny after we have been married for fifty years that I can say that I never really knew what kind of man my husband was and I guess he really never knew what kind of woman I was, either. But I guess I have been able to stand it.

A woman described family life as she experienced it:

[6] Our findings with respect to impersonality in familial relations are borne out by a report on a mining community in England. See Norman Dennis, Fernando Henriques, and Clifford Slaughter, *Coal Is Our Life, an Analysis of a Yorkshire Mining Community* (London, Eyre and Spotteswood, 1956), Chapter 5.

My husband was the boss. I had to listen to what he said. Whatever was done, he did it and whatever he said he was going to do, well it had to be done. He was determined that he was going to come to Coal Town and that was all there was to it. I stayed at home and took care of the children. This, I think, was what he wanted. I never had any close heart-to-heart talks with my husband. He never really knew me and I never really knew him. The children did not know him either. He was so strict with the children.

Family members fundamentally were strangers to one another. Interpersonal relationships were distant and some integration appeared only when outsiders intruded; this was a pattern common to native families in the area.

The feelings of persons within the family was one of distance. It seemed that each one was going his own way. The emphasis was on the kin. You were always loyal to your family whenever any trouble came but within the family itself we were not close.

Parental indifference was reported by many.

I think that children and parents grew apart from each other because parents didn't take any interest in the children. This was true of a lot of families here. This was not good for the children to grow up in this community because they ran around and nobody took any care of them. It's still true today.

Expressions of affection were discouraged by the family as well as by outsiders. To be kissed by one's mother in the presence of peers meant certain ridicule. A number of our informants reported that they had to learn to keep their feelings to themselves, a lesson which created problems for adult man-woman relationships.

Love and affection in the family was a sign of weakness. There was no outer signs or demonstrations of affection whatsoever. For a boy to be kissed by his mother after he got to be seven or eight years old was really a mark of shame and the kids would really let you know about it. As far as demonstration of affection was concerned, it was definitely out.

Wealth served as no immunity against the patterns of interpersonal relations which emerged in the native families of Coal Town. Families in all economic strata were somewhat similarly affected. For example, disinterest in the child was an ingredient of upper-class family life. A son of an economically secure family comments:

There was a great deal of family neglect of children in this community and particularly even within my own family. For example, my mother was so busy that she didn't have any time for us children. My father used to get up at six o'clock in the morning and be gone all day. He would come home and eat and then go back to the office in the evening. He worked at night. Mother was busy with the younger children and they really didn't have much time for my other brother and I. Finally we got Dad to go down to the river with us one time to go swimming but he was not too interested in us and he was quite surprised to learn that we could swim. We dived out of the boat that we were in and he thought sure that we were drowning and he said, "Why, you boys, I didn't know that you could swim." We told him, "Yes, we can swim, we have been swimming for some months." If he had spent a little more time with us, he would have known that we could swim.

The impersonality that was present was perhaps more pronounced in upper-class families. The parents of the handful of Coal Town upper-class families were in all instances very ambitious. Their lives were almost completely oriented toward the accumulation of personal power and wealth. Their families suffered. In a number of cases children of these upper-class families developed serious personal problems which were well recognized by other persons in the community.

The Q——s were a very prominent family in Coal Town but it seems interesting to study what happened to them. One of them turned to drink and died in the state institution. I can remember when he was running the tavern there in Coal Town, how he used to get drunk and run off all his help as well as the customers. I can remember that one time my husband and I went in for some coffee and we didn't know that he had run off his help the day before, but we did notice that he was in there alone and there were no other customers. Well, it was very apparent then that he was drunk and I wanted to leave but my husband said that this would only anger him so we sat there and drank our coffee and it was real cold. I finished mine rather quickly in order to get out but he came over and wanted to give us some more coffee so we had to drink two cups.

In still another upper-class family with several children, one became a successful businessman emotionally aloof from his parents. Another is single at the age of fifty, rigid and reactionary in his views, while another purportedly drinks to excess. In still another upper-class family we found a rigidly patriarchal father with marked contempt for his sons and his wife, a contempt felt equally by the family toward the father, according to reports.

SEXUAL ATTITUDES

Sexual attitudes of native Coal Town families typify a basic theme in the life which was established. The destructive tendencies prevalent in the community are considered natural. Sexual impulses, however, are defined as unnatural. Using the terms cautiously we might postulate that for these people natural things became unnatural and vice versa. Sexual relations were identified with promiscuity and prostitution. For married persons sexual activity became part of marriage but with the feeling that "none of this was quite right." Often such attitudes led to the following situation:

My wife is sort of cold. I think she could live without sex. This is not true of most miner's wives, though it is true for some of them, not all of them.

Although the overt attitudes toward sex are significant, we may at a deeper level ask whether families that manifest emotional distance are capable of transmitting healthy sexual attitudes and feelings? Or can unhealthy personalities have healthy sexual feelings? It is well recognized that healthy sexual attitudes, and ultimately healthy sexual adjustment, cannot emerge in personalities emotionally barren, where positive emotional feelings are repressed and destructive impulses are the rule. Sexual expressions are considered by many to be expressions of the total personality. If this is true, personalities who are aloof and contemptuous may manifest such feelings in the most intimate relationship of all. Can healthy sexual relatedness emerge from these circumstances?

The young male in Coal Town developed attitudes toward women which made sexual adjustment in marriage difficult. This was true in the past and it is still true. The prevalent notion that in some strange way "good women" do not indulge in sexual relations retarded greatly the male's own marital sexual adjustment. These attitudes often led to the male frequenting houses of prostitution. A fifty-year-old male who was born and reared in Coal Town:

A boy in this community would grow up with a pretty mixed-up attitude toward women. We were taught that there were two kinds of women, the good and the bad. I think that this hinders the adjustment of boys in marriage later on. I know that I should have had a sister to help me out and it would have made a lot of things for me easier later on, but I sure didn't. I think that this attitude that was prevalent about women in this community is responsible for a great deal of trouble that men have today after they get married. I know that it was true in my case.

Sexual information was rarely received from parents. When it was it might take the following form:

We never did discuss sex in the family with my children. I never mentioned the subject to any of the boys. Now, one time I did jump on the oldest boy because he had taken the car out and had a girl out in the car. Well, he came back to the house that night and put the car in the garage and the next morning his mother went out and found a rubber in the car and she almost had a fit. Well, this made me mad because what he had done is thought he had thrown it away but it had dropped down to the floor of the car. Well, I really jumped on him and told him that he should be ashamed to bring something like this home and disgrace his mother. All he did was just hang his head. He knew that he was in the wrong.

Coal Town people believe that premarital sexual relations occur frequently among present-day youth. The girl who is still a virgin at marriage is considered to be an exception. In spite of the early history of sexual promiscuity in the community many older citizens feel that the younger generation is "losing its morals." One such citizen became indignant toward police officials for failing to control the sexual behavior of youth:

The city here doesn't do anything about sex relations of the younger people or of married people with other husbands and wives. The police know that it goes on but they just don't care. Why, two or three carloads of the kids will go out to the outskirts of town here to the forest to engage in necking and petting and sex relations. The boys like to brag about this and if they know that a girl is putting out, they will tell the others about it. Now, when I was a kid it was different. If we knew this we didn't say anything about it. We might want to go back ourselves. Now, all the boys seem to take a hand in it.

CHILD-REARING PRACTICES

Although family rule among the native group possessed marked mother-centered patterns, discipline of the child was and is largely the responsibility of the male. Thus an interesting pattern of family relations developed in which the mother, who is dominant, is nevertheless seen as the child's confidant while the father in effect becomes the outsider. We do not know whether this pattern had a rational origin. It does, however, allow the mother to rule in an authoritarian way, while diverting the hostility of the child to the father. Often in these relationships emotional dependency on the mother developed, and this pattern made emancipation for both mother and child difficult. The son of a native:

My dad was the disciplinarian in the family. We could get by more with mother than we could with him. He was pretty strict. We took our problems to our mother.

A native father:

The woman sees them everyday in and out and, of course, she is a lot closer to them than a man. The father is always at work and the kids would go to the mother with their problems. She understands them more and she knows their ways much more than the father does. I think that the kids would run to the wife whenever they had anything that was bothering them.

Discipline was reported as harsh. In some instances this occurred:

The trouble with me was that whenever I started in on the kids, such as giving them a spanking or beating them, I didn't know when to stop and I got scared one time when I actually drew blood from one of my kids that I was giving a spanking to. I think the kids need a good spanking. I'm a strong believer in "Spare the rod and spoil the child." I think that children are born mean unless you begin to teach them right from wrong. Sometimes you can do that.

Some parents believed that harsh discipline was one way to develop respect.

I always whipped the children and even today my boy who is a grown man will mind me because he has a lot of respect for me. He visits with me all the time.

The rearing of children in Coal Town during the early days reflected to a large extent the general chaos of the community. Children were left alone and expected to care for themselves.

The people were busy and had little time for the kids and the kids just got along the best way they knew how. Some of the miners lived in tents and the mother had the washing, the ironing, and the cooking to do. All of this was done by hand. She had to carry water a long distance and if there was a hydrant in the yard, why this was something that was exceptional. The older kids took care of themselves and many of them didn't even eat meals at noon but some of them that had charge accounts would go into the stores and maybe get some crackers and cheese and bologna and put it down on the bill. Others of us just didn't even eat meals at noon but we ate such a big breakfast that it held over until dinner. Usually in the miner's family hot supper was on the table by four o'clock and the boys really ran home for that. No one would miss that meal because it was something to eat.

Breast feeding was common regardless of economic group. Some of our informants observed that such feeding was conducive to the child's good health.

The pattern here was breast feeding of children. We remarked about it at the time. When the children were breast fed, they were in good physical condition and good physical shape.

Weaning was reported as being sudden and traumatic for the child.

When the kids were weaned, I know they used to get mad. The time of weaning, I think, was about one and one-half years old or at the time that the children began to walk. After they were weaned they were in rather poor disposition.

Parents were concerned about bladder control and punishment of some sort followed infractions.

Why, I know that some kids are three years old today and still wetting in their pants. Why, if I had done that when I was a kid, I would have got a spanking. Now when I did wet my pants, my mother would shame me out of it.

EMPLOYMENT OF WOMEN

Many married women in Coal Town are today employed in submarginal industries. It is our general impression that the husbands are very much in favor of this. In cases where the male is unemployed it allows for a leisurely existence and minimizes the pressures to find employment. The picture so often presented of the

American male, whose ego is disturbed because his wife wishes to support the family, does not apply generally to native males in Coal Town and may in fact not apply to other sections of the American male population.

There are nevertheless some men and women who are disturbed about this development. A woman speaks:

I don't think that women should work if their husbands are working. She ought to be at home. I think that if she does work she will have much more difficulty between herself and her husband. In the past I know that there were very few women who were working but today there are a lot of women working, and a lot of the women here in Coal Town work. I think that most of the men would prefer to have their wives remain at home and be housekeepers.

Some men were concerned that outside employment would foster emancipation.

You see, when the woman works you always have trouble. Your meals are never ready for you when you come home. When I got out of those coal mines, I was tired and when I came home I wanted my supper right there on the table. It makes a woman independent to work outside.

There are those who believe that children are neglected under these conditions.

If a woman goes out and works, this usually leads up to trouble at home because she doesn't take care of the children and she doesn't care too much for the home. If she goes to work, she'll turn out bad.

There has been a good bit of family irresponsibility in this town toward children. Some of it is due to the fact that women work and in some cases it's all right. I think that they have a right to work. But in other cases in which they neglect their children, I think that it's not too good. Now my own wife works, she never neglected the children in order to work. But some of them do here in this community.

Much of the resentment which members of the community have about women's working is also based on the economic deprivations experienced by the men. If there are jobs to be had, men should get them.

The women ought to stay at home and leave the jobs to the men. There used to be an issue in this community against women working. This was long ago and it showed up during the Depression. They thought that if a man and wife were both working that the wife should not work because this was taking up the place of another man and the wife should quit.

FOOD HABITS

The dietary habits of the native families were very similar to the dietary habits of the early settlers discussed previously. Whenever possible, meat in some form was used, garnished by a few greens of some type.

I would say that our diet was made up of biscuits and gravy, fried beef and chicken. Sometimes we had bacon and ham. We used green beans and vegetables. Our breakfast would be fried eggs, bacon, and rice, and we had biscuits every morning. For lunch there would be some boiled foods. For the evening meal we would eat leftovers. The main meal was during the noon meal. You see, my husband usually came home for dinner and that was a big meal. Now, sometimes when he took his lunch, then the evening meal would be the big meal. We believed in eating a lot of fried and boiled foods. When we could get fish, we would eat fish. They were catfish and then there was also another kind of fish that the boys used to catch. You could reach down with a gig and pull them out with their gills. I don't know what kind of fish. I think it was called a hogfish. Anyway it was ugly as sin and looked like a hog. We always enjoyed fish.

The preferred meat was pork, while the preferred beef was round steak, which was considered superior to any section of loin steak. A favorite saying: "I think I'll go home and fry me a round steak." The pattern persists.

Dietary patterns have remained essentially the same. During times of economic prosperity the pattern is one of purchasing the same foods in greater quantity rather than attempting things that are new. Innovations in food habits tend to be resisted.

VIEWS OF PRESENT-DAY FAMILY LIFE

Our older informants reported that family life has undergone great change. The older generation believes that the younger generation is "going to the dogs." Thus they refer to such things as the emancipated behavior of parents and children as disturbing signs. For example, children no longer respect their parents.

The kids have changed a great deal now from what they were in the past. They don't have as much respect for their parents now as they should. Things are too easy for them. They have not been trained to work hard. They are less responsible now than in the past. The change in the kids, I think, is a fault of the parents. They are being spoiled. You see, they have everything now and they want everything done for them.

There is a difference in the families of today. They have no respect for their parents. I think that the parents are to blame for this and I think one reason is that their fathers don't play with the children very much. All they do is quarrel and growl at them and I think this is the real reason. Why, my son always hunted with me, and I always bought him guns and we would pal around together. I don't know what's the matter now except that these new parents give their children too much privileges. You see, my boy was eighteen years older than my girl, which was my second child. I always ruled my children with an iron hand. That's the way they learned to respect you.

Children are allowed too much freedom.

The children these days tell their parents what to do. Why, the kids never stay at home and they talk back to parents. That is what happens to those children across the street over there that you can hear even now. Whenever they go anywhere today, they go without asking parents. Why, I can hear some of the parents calling their children around dark. They don't even know where they are. They've gone off all day and then don't have any idea where they are. I was not rough on my children, though I would say that children today are allowed more freedom than we used to give our children. My children never asked to go out anywhere after dark. They always stayed home. They would go to bed.

Children fail to address their parents properly.

There is a big difference in rearing children today than it was when I was rearing my children. When it was dark, I can remember, my kids were in bed. This was what happened to me, too. I can remember that I said to my father, "Sir." I didn't ask him "what" when he told me to do something, I would do it. This is a good policy for anyone raising children, especially now. You see, too many parents have turned their children loose. I would say that the family is very weak now and this is certainly bad for the children. You have to be strong with them if you want them to be any good.

Some of our informants believe that children can no longer be trusted.

The kids say one thing to their parents but then they do something else. They have cars now to get in and they stay out more and they stay out later than they used to.

Many feel that familial relationships in the past were close and harmonious but that *today* life is impersonal.

My family is different from the family life of which I remember as a child. Today the family members are not as dependent on each other as they used to be. The family had greater unity than it does today. The change is in the people themselves, I think. Parents and children are not as close as they used to be and the same thing goes for husband and wife. In the past the people were concerned about their family much more than they are now. Why, parents think nothing of running off and leaving their children with a baby sitter and go out of town to dance and carry on and so forth.

Families used to do things together but today our native informants feel that each family member is out for himself.

I think that family life has changed quite a bit. In the old days, Mother got up and fixed breakfast and Father called us boys and we got down and we ate what was set before us. Now it seems as if the family is never together for a meal as a unit and it seems as if the kids fuss a lot about what is put before them, they don't like this and they don't like that, and it seems as if the parents go off and leave the kids now more than they used to. The family used to do things together. Now one will get up and go in one direction and one will get up and go in another direction. Everything is changed.

Many older informants are disturbed by changing values and motivations which they observe in their children. To be content with what you have is a virtue for many.

You asked me about family life. Well, I know that it has changed a great deal since I was rearing my children. The children now are not as easy to please as it used to be. It seems that they are always striving for better things. This goes for parents as well as for children. The parents and children today never seem satisfied. I was always taught to be content with what you have.

How can we evaluate the criticisms made about family life by our older residents? Certain superficial changes in family life reported by our informants are undoubtedly valid. Nevertheless, the writer feels that family life today is no worse or more impersonal than it was before for these natives. Harking back to the "good old days" represents for our informants a gross distortion of the past. And it is an interesting illustration of how an environment which was essentially antithetical to warm human relations may over a period of time become twisted and distorted. Family life for the native who resided in Coal Town in the early days was chaotic. With family members unequipped to block out the disintegrating forces, emotional ties within the family, barring an attack from the outside, were usually loose and without deep commitment. The characteristics which appear today are not replicas of the past, but they assuredly have grown out of the past and are guaranteed continuity by a similar set of values in the present.

IMMIGRANT FAMILY PATTERNS [7]

In turning our attention to the immigrant family we note at the outset that the immigrant was slow to marry. Native women preferred native men while immigrant males likewise preferred women from their own backgrounds; such women were not available. Many immigrants remained single and never married, while others, who had been married in Europe, failed to bring their families to America. Some established casual alliances.

There were many foreign people who were married in the Old Country; some came over here and then they began to live with someone else.

Many had plans to marry but were unable to do so.

We have a lot of old bachelors here. They was especially foreign people. When they come to this country they think they going back to Europe and marry over there. They spend money and can't go back home and not marry here in the early days and they stay here and die.

On at least one occasion an immigrant sent for a mate from Europe.

Why, we had a man I remember we nicknamed him Stockhandle Pete. He sent over for a woman from the foreign country and when she came here, she would not marry him so he told her that if she wanted to, she

[7] The immigrants from the English-speaking countries tended to be evasive with respect to family organization. Therefore this analysis is, by necessity, incomplete.

could marry another man; provided the other man would pay for her passage over here. She got someone to do this and it was agreeable with old Stockhandle.

Some brides from Europe were confused by the interpretation of American culture given by their husbands, as in the following occurrence. The son of an immigrant:

As I mentioned before, the foreigners had very high ethical principles. However, when a foreigner dropped his ethical principles he could sink mighty low. For instance, I remember in the case of one incident in which a man brought his wife over to this country. She was somewhat naive and he prostituted her in order to get a better job in the mines. This was a good job that he wanted and he told his wife that she would have to submit to the advances of company officials and his boss and the supervisors. And when the wife objected to this, he told her that this is the way that we do things here in this new country.

Many immigrants viewed with considerable favor the development of an integrated family life. Potentially it afforded an opportunity to maintain certain cultural values and to counteract the harshness of the external milieu. Furthermore, it shielded the members from an abrupt introduction to an alien value system.

The plight of the single, immigrant male, without familial affiliation in an alien setting, was often difficult. A native:

A lot of them came over without any family ties here. Their country had not fastened on them. That is, the Old Country ways hadn't. They came over here and intermingled and they clashed to beat the band. They had no permanent viewpoint and they were mixed up.

IMMIGRANT FAMILY CONFIGURATION

The traditional father-centered pattern was much more in evidence for the immigrant family than for the native. Nevertheless, we were surprised at the number of deviations that were uncovered. For example, using the same methodological techniques employed for the native family, we calculated that 70 percent of the immigrant families in our sample (40 families) were father-centered and 30 percent were mother-centered. None had a marked democratic orientation.

Of considerable interest, nevertheless, was the relatively high incidence of mother-centered families encountered among a European population, which historically has been father-centered. The explanation for this presents us with a set of formidable problems. At the outset we raise an old question. Historically speaking, have we in this instance ignored the possibility of diverse cultural and regional settings which may have given rise to diverse family forms? Have there always been pronounced mother-centered strains among certain European families which have been ignored? We believe also, however, that the hypothesis (see page 155) which purports to explain mother-centeredness in the native family is pertinent at this point. Many immigrant families were placed in precarious situations by the ever-present danger of injury or death to the father from the hazardous nature of the occupation as well as from the unstable character of community relations. We believe that mother-centered tendencies may have been accentuated by these conditions.

MOTHER-CENTERED FAMILY

A large number of the immigrant families found to be mother-centered had been so for many years. Some mother-centered tendencies were present in almost all immigrant groups, but appeared to be most pronounced in the Irish and Greek families. The native daughter of an Irish family stated:

In the Irish family the woman is the boss. I wear the pants in the family and I just let my husband think that he wears the pants. He does not know how to boss. Now my mother was the boss in her family, too. The discipline would be cared for by my mother.

The same informant continues her observations:

My mother is the boss of us. There was a great deal of devotion of us children to our mother, you see. My mother's philosophy was, "Don't do nothin' that you would be afraid to tell me," and none of my brothers ever had to get married and none of us girls ever had to get married because we were pregnant. Why, I would tell Momma everything. She put us on our honor. We would go out and be gone all night but we could come in and would wake Momma up about four or five o'clock in the morning and we would tell her what happened. I would tell Momma who pinched me and I didn't know the meaning of that at that time. I was about fifteen or sixteen years old, you see. Well, Momma really told the boys that had pinched us to stay away. None of us girls ever did anything bad, you see, because she put us on our honor and now we take care of our mother just like she took care of us.

Some of our Greek families also displayed a mother-centered pattern.

The man in the Greek family is responsible for the earning for the family while the woman serves as the head of the household. The woman always handles the money of the household and she was responsible for disciplining the children. I always gave my money to my wife and whenever I wanted to buy something I would just ask her for the money and she would give it to me.

You ask me who was family boss. I believe the women were the boss. Mostly women make the decisions in the Greek house. I think that the woman is head of the house in Coal Town. Women rule the house. The women told the men how to do things and I think that it is true the woman is the real boss in the family.

FATHER-CENTERED FAMILY PATTERNS

The immigrant families with marked father-centered patterns appeared to be more authoritarian than the native family with a similar orientation. One immigrant:

The men were the boss in the family. The women wouldn't talk back to the man or she would get the hell beat out of her. That is the Balkan tradition. I am not talking about their kids now that married. It was a man's world.

The patriarch possessed rigidities of character which were difficult to change. The daughter of an immigrant:

You see, in some of the immigrant families the man is king. He would never give his wife any money of her own. He didn't believe in any conveniences in the home. In some cases, I remember that the woman was very unhappy. Some used to come here and visit me and cry and tell me all of these things. You see, the reason that the man did not want any conveniences is that they did not have them in the Old Country. This was a pretty common situation and many of the women were unhappy.

The patriarchal orientation carried with it certain attitudes toward family members. One Bulgarian informant, in speaking of family rule, points out a basic attitude toward the mother which is common to persons from his background:

It is often said in Bulgaria that one is raised by an ignorant mother and an educated father. That about sums it up.

In the event of the father's death, the affairs of the family were taken over by other persons.

The oldest son usually took the responsibility with the help and guidance of the mother in case of the immigrants' father's death, or in some cases the godfather. Now, there was one relationship that was very strong and that is the godfather-godchild relationship. This was important among the Croatians and also important among the Greeks who settled here. You see, in the event of a disaster in which the father was killed the godfather assumed the responsibility for the raising of the children.

With time even father-centered patterns have undergone some change within the immigrant family. An embittered patriarch sadly comments on changing times:

The woman is the boss—in any nationality. It's not like it used to be. Men are becoming sissies. Of course, all the law is on the woman's side. Immigrant men sought a good cook and homemaker for a wife. Now everything is for looks, divorce is easy, women are careless, bumming round at night drinkin'. That's why you got juvenile delinquency, it's parent delinquency. The kids are not to blame. This free American divorce is bad business, can't raise a good wholesome society, it should be prohibited. Croatians were not allowed to divorce. I never see anything like that in the Old Country. Once in a great while you would hear about some scandal among them. Now most Croatians was never bad to monkey around with another woman if they're married. They stay home where they belong. They were taught over there that way. Sure, there are exceptions. But a man or woman who do that never had a good name any more with their own people. Now it's different. You know that Dalmatian woman over there across the tracks, that widow? She try to get me in there. I would marry her if she was right kind of woman. But I know her. What she gonna do when she gets tired of me an' see some other man she likes better? [In Croatian] "Not for the love of God, she's the devil personified."

INTERPERSONAL RELATIONS

Many immigrants were able to establish families with warm, meaningful interpersonal relationships. Thus the impersonality of the community was partially counteracted. Familial relationships in one such home were described by the son of a Croatian immigrant:

Home, for all of its shortcomings, was a sanctuary. Parental love and religious piety leavened the barrenness of it and the quarreling and bickering and meanness common to a family of ten crowded into four small rooms. Up to school age and a little beyond, I still knelt at my mother's knee for my evening prayer and reverently bid each parent good night. I was avidly interested in my older sisters' and brothers' work on their school assignments and their recapitulation of school adventures. I learned to recite and to love the homely poems of Whittier and Longfellow before I went to school and imaginatively fitted vivid phrases to my own environment. Less than scholastic excellence was shamed at home and I often wonder how much more the less studious of immigrants' children felt the sting of prejudice than we did. I wonder, too, how badly the harsh environment of the camps would have warped my personality, except for the counterinfluence of the home, family, church, and school. My older brother had a strong influence in my early life. He was a sort of policeman in the family as well as a shining example. He was of a very studious nature, a genius perhaps, who set examples of achievement and behavior that none of the rest of us ever quite equalled.

The majority of immigrant families were not so fortunate. The external milieu unleashed forces which attacked and assaulted any attempt at integration which might have been present. Youths and adults alike were exposed to alien and contradictory points of view. Separation and individuation arose. Further conflict was precipitated by the immigrants' attempt to be individualistic in some segments of life, while maintaining conservatism in others. We refer specifically at this point to the tendency of the immigrant to be quite outspoken in favor of radical economic changes, while at the same time diverting much of his energies toward maintenance of the status quo in his personal and familial life. The tendency to compartmentalize in the manner described above frequently appears in our data.

Some struggled with the conflicts precipitated by new values. A few of our informants changed markedly and developed broader horizons for their children.

It worried my wife more than it did me. I did not want my children to become miners. My wife and I feel that education is important to the children and that there is no future in the mines for the young people.

Some were aware of the potential talent which often went undeveloped.

No immigrant father wanted his son to be a coal miner and the most deplorable thing is that these immigrants were wasted. A great deal of their talent was wasted. In many instances these immigrants were geniuses and today their offspring do well in cities.

The majority of immigrant parents we encountered, however, were slow to accept innovations. Rigid and insecure in their personal organization, they were often indifferent to opportunities for personal development. In these families children were viewed as economic commodities from which a monetary return was expected; the effect of this was to foster in the child a kind of cynicism about the motives of others. A native merchant:

The immigrant youth did not get any encouragement from his own family. They thought only in terms of money. I know that a man would calculate what he had spent on a son in terms of dollars and cents. Not because he really loved the son or because he wanted to do this for him. The intellectual and the cultural interests were limited and they were definitely not encouraged in this community. The economic factor was all that was important. Affection was absent in the immigrant home as well as in the native home. The people here, it seems to me, though I may be somewhat cynical, were interested in only two things, that is, money and sex.

Many families were actively hostile toward any effort of a son or daughter to improve through the development of personal talent.

I can give you one example of this in terms of an immigrant family and this was a boy that I helped to give a scholarship to in N—— College. The boy had a Polish father and a Russian mother. He hated the coal mines but his father did not want him to go to college or to finish high school but to start to work in the mines and give all the money that he earned to his father. Well, he and his family grew apart after he got the scholarship to N—— and he went on his own way. He was never encouraged by his parents but later on he held a much better job financially than he could have if he had been a coal miner.

The above quote suggests an important source of emotional conflict for the children of these immigrants. Many of them had inter-

nalized two sets of values, mutually contradictory. In part they
felt that development of their personal abilities was a legitimate
pursuit, while on the other hand they had also acquired the feeling
that self-improvement was egocentric and fraught with personal
frustration. The values were in conflict and precipitated anxieties
in these people.

THE ECONOMIC INCENTIVE

The quest for economic security always appeared to be pronounced. Little opportunity for personal pleasures was available.
The son of an immigrant recalls the past:

I am close to my mother now. My brother does not come home very often.
We never did do anything as a group. We took no trips, no vacations, no
parties, and so forth. We always had to run the store. This store was open
from early in the morning till late at night seven days a week. I would
say that my attitude toward my parents was a sort of mixture. It had a
little bit of fear and a little bit of respect.

Many of our informants who had worked in the mines stated
that they did not wish their sons to become miners. Our general
impression is that while such an attitude applied to some, the
majority felt differently and would have been happy to have their
sons follow in their footsteps, had mining continued to offer opportunities.

I don't think that what you have heard about the immigrant keeping their
sons out of the mines is true because I know a lot of immigrants whose
sons went right in there and began working in the mines, just like their
fathers.

PARENT-CHILD RELATIONS

One of the major orientations of the immigrant family was the
achievement of uniformity and conformity among its members, a
tremendously difficult task at best. Thus inculcation of basic immigrant views was attempted by many parents. Discipline in various
forms was employed. The son of an immigrant reports this:

Father was responsible for the discipline. He could make you feel like
you were a heel. He would always start off on this sort of routine that
"I've done all of this for you and all of my life I have done things for

you," and that sort of thing. The children would usually not come to their parents with teenage problems. I know that we never did and that many of our friends in this community never did.

The eldest male often served as a father surrogate.

The punishment in the family depended upon the character of the father. The family always had to have an accounting of where I happened to be at any time. For example, if I was to miss dinner I was supposed to tell the family in advance. If not, and I was somewhere and did not come home to dinner, then I would have to give an accounting of myself. The older boys were used by the father to enforce some of the discipline in the family. This was particularly true of the oldest boy. He was almost like a father and the thing that I did not like was my brother's discipline of me. I resented this much more than I did the discipline of my father.

The efforts of parents to shut out alien values and maintain the status quo was doomed from the first. In time parent-child relationships in the immigrant family, regardless of ethnic group, were characterized by rebellion on the part of youth. Rebellion of children was based on the many areas of conflict between native American and European patterns. Equally significant, however, was the fact that many of these children felt tied to a value system, which for them was stifling in their present surroundings. What appears as rebellious behavior, often destructive, was one way in which many immigrant children tried to establish a meaningful life of their own out of a milieu replete with contradictions. That such efforts often resulted in misunderstandings and isolation of immigrant children from their own group was perhaps an unavoidable aftereffect.

As contact between the children of immigrants and natives increased parent-child conflicts became intense. Some believed the automobile to have been a significant factor in hastening this process.

There were young persons who rebelled from the authority of the parents. I would say that the automobile caused a great deal of this breakdown in the immigrant family. The main conflict came in the immigrant family when the son wanted to live different and to spend his money. I would say that over in Europe the father had more power over his son. Here he could not because the son could leave the house and leave the home and live elsewhere.

At a later period contact with city life became a factor in parent-child conflict. An immigrant's son:

It began to dissolve when work became scarce and when the boys left home for the city. When these boys came back, they dressed differently and acted differently. This, I think, was the beginning of the breakup of the close-knit immigrant family.

In some instances immigrant families were sufficiently flexible and were able to shift perspective and reorganize their values. Here rebellion was at a minimum. Other families were more rigid. In the majority of homes active rebellion occurred.

There were some real problems in the personalities of these immigrants. That is, some of them were easygoing and others were not. Some of the families were easygoing and others were strict. In those cases in which the family was easygoing the immigrant children usually rebelled and ran away.

You would not get rebellion of the children when the family and the parents were too strict in holding the children to the Old Country traditions and patterns. You got a breakdown of the family when this occurred. Sometimes the children would leave the family for good and would never return. I know of such a case here in D—— in which a boy left the family because the father was too strict and he didn't come back until his mother's death.

Situations like the following led to conflict.

You asked if the immigrants were ever confused about the different ways of life that they found in this country. Well, some of the immigrants were determined that their ways were right. The children sometimes chafed at the ways of their parents and this did cause some confusion. I remember particularly in my own family when my sister was going with a boy that my father did not like, he made her stop seeing him. The brothers would be asked what kind of boy is this that your sister is going with and if they did not like him, they would turn thumbs down on him and that would cause difficulty.

BOY-GIRL RELATIONSHIPS

Major conflict between parents and children centered on boy-girl relationships, which were a constant source of friction. Such relationships were always considered solely as preludes to marriage by the parents and they wished to control them rigidly. In spite of the ever-present disunity, parents still saw control of the marital arrangement as one means of perpetuating their values. Parents unfamiliar with native dating practices were disturbed by the casual manner in which boys and girls met one another. The daughter of an immigrant:

Sometimes the boy would meet the girl at a dance, if the parents did not like the person that the girl was going with. Many of these meetings were apart from parents.

From the parental point of view there was little room for personal selection in the boy-girl relationship. Further, suspicion and distrust of the young people's motives were ever present.

The parents here do not trust boys out with their daughters. I know that this has been the case of many of the immigrant boys who go with other immigrant girls and the girls' parents do not trust these boys at all. Now, what happened in the immigrant family was that the kids rebelled against the customs of their foreign parents and it was easier for the boys to sneak out and run around than it was for the girls because the foreign-born parents used to keep a strict hand on the girls.

Hasty marriages characteristic of natives in this setting were a constant source of concern for immigrant parents.

There was prejudice against hasty marriages and by hasty marriages I would say marriages in which the two people knew each other for only a month. There were some cases in which parental approval could be obtained for marriage after a period of six months. There was a tendency to have girls marry at an early age in order to remove them from the family, but this was never done at the cost of a hasty marriage.

The manner of personal conduct, particularly sexual conduct, troubled parents.

The boy and girl relations were serious for us. It was a very serious matter to have sex before you were married.

Immigrant parents worried about their daughters.

There was a great deal of concern over the conduct of daughters among the immigrant group and the daughter who did not comply with her parents' wishes was talked about by her friends, and this was very true if she engaged in sex before she was married. The unmarried, pregnant, im-

migrant woman was looked on with pity instead of anger and avoidance
and the family would feel responsible to rear the child.

THE WEDDING CEREMONY

The wedding was another culturally defined way of maintaining
the immigrants' traditions. The immigrant wedding ceremony during
the early days was an important event for the surrounding neighborhood. It was the cause of much celebration and for the immigrant
affirmed the existence and maintenance of certain cultural traditions.

Most of the foreign people would have weddings and they seemed like
young girls would marry older men. I don't know why. They used to
dance down here. Everybody that danced with the bride was supposed
to give her some money. They would have squeeze boxes and fiddles
going and sometimes them weddings would last for two weeks. That was
how the young brides used to get enough money to set up housekeeping.
They used to have a dance band up there and they would play all night
sometimes.

The barriers between immigrant and native were temporarily
dropped during such occasions.

If an immigrant had a wedding, he invited all his neighbors. This was
only for special occasions, though. The closest contact otherwise was
when the man would work with a native. They wouldn't trust their daughters with native boys.

The only meeting with the foreign element was at weddings. They used
to last for days and weeks. They used to be a big attraction. It was all
the booze you could drink and the food you could eat. You had to give
so much to dance with the bride, so at the end of the week she was pretty
well in the pocket. They would invite everybody. They had a kitty in
there and you fed the kitty. The bride got enough to set up her house
when everyone got through.

Although the patterns associated with the immigrant wedding
were designed to produce conformity, they contained the seeds for
diversity. Out of the interactions between immigrant and native
friendships emerged and beliefs were exchanged.

THE ROLE OF CHILDREN IN THE ASSIMILATION PROCESS

In time many children were able to effect changes in their parents.
Their efforts, marked by a quality of desperateness, often involved

some ruthless tactics. The children with language facility became the interpreters of American culture for their parents. This pattern served as support for the immigrant children's rebelliousness but it was also a means of controlling the behavior of parents. The daughter of an English miner:

Now the interesting thing is the relationship between the children of the foreign-born and their parents. You see, the children would get loose when they would grow up and they would take advantage of their parents being foreigners, they would put over things on them. They learned to use their parents and to look down on their parents. You see, their parents did not know where to draw the line on training their children and they were very much confused over what the children should do and what they should not do. The parents did not know what it was all about and the kids would see this and stand off. They would not let the parents know what was going on except what they themselves wanted the parents to know. The kids would actually tell the parents what to do. You see, the parents were really confused. You can't blame the parents for this situation because they could not speak English. I have seen these advantages being taken of parents by the children time and time again. The children misrepresented things to their parents and took advantage of them. Now when these children themselves have had families they either tended to become too strict or else they were too lax.

Often the children of immigrants, in the process of assimilating, internalized native attitudes toward immigrants and became anti-immigrant themselves. Finally many of them tried to shame and humiliate their parents into becoming Americanized. An immigrant's son:

The youngsters were too powerful for their immigrant families and the youngsters became the interpreters for the family as far as the larger society was concerned. The foreign parents were concerned with the moral teachings of their children and as the children frowned on the old customs and practices, the parents were pressured to change into the American patterns. The parents began to go out of their way in order to act American and the foreigners were sensitive about their nationality groups. You see, they could not stand shame and shame was one of the means used to get them to come over and change their habits.

The attempt on the part of the children to dissociate themselves from their parents and to assimilate precipitated the usual problems of marginality. Many of these immigrant children tended to accept the natives' views of their own people. A native merchant:

It is the desire of the children, I think, to get away from certain habits which their parents have had. Examples of this, for instance, has been that when the English came over here they had a blood pudding. Well, to the children this seemed very bad and the boys used to want to get themselves away from these habits. You take another example and that was the homes of the Bulgarians that used to be plastered by lime and cow dung. The Italians were garlic eaters and it was told to the boys that this was bad. The boys, you see, picked this up from the native boys that they wanted to change from their old bad customs.

The assault of the native community on the immigrant customs and the immigrants' inability to accept themselves for what they were led to self-contempt and self-rejection. Eventually there was for some a loss of identity. An immigrant:

The children wanted to be American and to keep from being shamed they would go American; and then their parents would go American with them in order to keep from being shamed also. There are many cases of people who didn't belong anywhere. There was a great deal of turmoil in the personalities of the children. You may delay the process in children but you cannot stop it, you see.

Often these feelings led to situations in which parents were openly rejected.

The customs were different. A lot of the immigrant children were very embarrassed about their families not being able to speak English. The children didn't even want their parents to talk to them because they were ashamed of them and they would use rough language sometimes.

One of the means of solving the psychic trauma associated with marginality was to return to the Old World values. A woman who tried to reject her background points this out:

Immigrant children, I think, try to take on American ways. They learn to speak the language very quickly. I think it would be nice, though, if my children knew more about the Old Country background which my parents had. You see, my parents did not change too much even though my father read a great deal. When I get older, I think that it would be good if my children could remember some of the things that my parents used to tell me.

Although the effort suggested above was attempted by some, the majority of children who underwent assimilation fundamentally remained marginal people.

THE DIET

In general contrast to local native diet, dietary patterns brought from Central and Southern Europe were built around a meal of bread, potatoes, beans, spaghetti, and meat. The preferred meats were beef, veal, or lamb, rather than pork; each was prepared differently depending on the ethnic background. These food habits have undergone little change for the immigrant themselves. Bread, especially, was important.

We used a hundred pound bag of flour every two weeks. Now, to the immigrant group bread was the staff of life. The entire meal was built around the bread. I can remember that we had loaves about ten inches long and from six to eight inches high. We would consume one of these loaves of bread at one meal. The foreigners used to buy a great deal of veal and lamb.

During the early days each ethnic group had its own store which handled its ethnic specialties.

Food was different. There were stores that handled food for their own people. The Polish, for example, imported their food.

The fact that few of these stores are left testifies that the majority of immigrants have moved out or have passed away. Although the children of immigrants are in the process of becoming assimilated, the immigrants themselves retain, very much, their Old World practices.

SUMMARY

In this chapter we have tried to point out the major threads which made up the pattern of native and immigrant family life. Both family types made some effort to achieve stability and order in a milieu characterized by chaos. The native family, in its efforts, manifested marked mother-centered tendencies as one means of achieving such order. In this connection we suggested *the hypothesis* that *whenever continuation of the father's role is made uncertain by dangers in the cultural milieu, mother-centered patterns emerge.*

The immigrant family, with some mother-centered patterns, was nevertheless for the most part father-centered. In their search for order and cultural continuity the immigrants resorted to a use of rigid controls. These efforts failed and rebellion of the youth ensued, bringing with it much personal deviation and disorganization.

The chaos in the community and in the family, characterized by conflicting values and roles, was internalized by the parents and children. In turn these conditions raised havoc with any attempt to produce stability in the native family or cultural continuity for the immigrant family. Familial relationships were primarily distant, with much aloofness and indifference. Family members were unable emotionally to relate to one another, or to establish a feeling of belonging. Out of such a familial climate the capacity for men to relate to women, or women to relate to men, was hampered. Their relationships were replete with misunderstandings and distortions. For both types of families, the personalities that emerged out of the disorganization carried with them the signs of inner familial turmoil.

CHAPTER 9

PROSPERITY AND DECLINE

IN spite of certain general periods of economic prosperity, mining in Coal Town was tenuous and economically unpredictable. If we turn our attention to the table on page 184 some interesting employment trends come to light.

The period 1904–15 shows no consistency in amount of work available for the individual miner; instead we find fluctuations from good years to bad years. This trend is particularly important because we characteristically think of boom communities as being economically lucrative and we ignore the lean years interspersed between.

The 1914–15 period ushers in the prosperity of World War I which comes to an end in 1919. A miner:

Before World War I we were just like we are today. The coal mines were only working in the wintertime before in 1912–'13–'14. They began to pick up a little bit in 1915 because they were shipping coal to Europe. In 1917 when we entered the war the mines started working every day.

During the period 1904–19 there were actually six years when work for the miner was plentiful, four years when it was moderate, and six years when it was poor. Thus there was no prolonged period of prosperity. There were simply some years that were better than others.

During the early boom years money was plentiful and prices were high. In part high prices were the result of the refusal of the mining company to allow private merchants to purchase or rent property during the period 1904 to 1918. Mining management feared economic competition from private merchants, but the main reason for management's refusal to allow merchants to enter may well have been a desire to eliminate a potential threat to its control of the entire community.

Victor tried to keep out outsiders. I know that the farmers would come in and sell their produce but they couldn't stay.

AVERAGE NUMBER OF DAYS MINE WAS IN OPERATION PER YEAR
BY TWO-YEAR INTERVALS FOR THE TWO [a] COAL TOWN MINES, 1904–51 [b]

Year	90 to 109	110 to 129	130 to 149	150 to 169	170 to 189	190 to 209	210 to 229	230 to 249	250 to 269	270 to 289
1904–5	x									
1906–7										x
1908–9					x					
1910–11	x									
1912–13							x			
1914–15							x			
1916–17									x	
1918–19								x		
1920–21						x				
1922–23					x					
1924–25			x							
1926–27					x					
1928–29						x				
1930–31			x							
1932–33		x								
1934–35				x						
1936–37					x					
1938–39				x						
1940–41				x						
1942–43									x	
1944–45										x
1946–47								x		
1948–49					x					
1950–51				x						

[a] Mine Number One opened in 1904 and closed in 1948. Mine Number Two opened in 1918 and closed in 1956.
[b] Data compiled from official state mining statistics.

After the Victor era control was slowly relinquished by the Swift Mining Company. Nevertheless, private merchants were prohibited from coming into Coal Town until 1918.

It was in 1918 that the first private store was started here. No property was sold to the merchants before this time but what happened was that they sold a piece of property to an immigrant and they forgot to put in the clause about not putting up a store. Well, he decided that he would beat them and put up a store and they tried to run him out but he eventually beat them and really had a good business.

After mining management relinquished its rigid control the pattern of discouraging outsiders was taken over by a few Coal Town merchants who made it difficult for new persons to set up business in Coal Town. The patterns of force and coercion, characteristic of the community by this time, were often employed to accomplish these ends. A merchant:

There was a merchants' organization in Coal Town who did not want other businesses to come in and they let it be known and it was dangerous to set up another business because of the opposition of the private merchants. I remember a man here, for instance, who wanted to set up a feed store in Coal Town. Now there was already one feed store there and the owner of this feed store made it very clear to this person that if he came there to set up his feed store it would mean trouble for him and it would be better for him to stay away.

There were many lucrative activities which the merchants were not eager to share. Miners in their eagerness to spend often drew coupon books on their wages from the Company and for a discount traded them for cash from merchants. This was one of the most profitable business practices merchants had. A miner:

Well, of course, there was a lot of trading. They done trading on coupons. We issued them. They was a lot of work. The books were $2.00, $5.00, and $10.00. You would come up and the fellow who was working at the coupon window would look over your account and see how many tons you had and multiply it by the tonnage rate and see what you had drawn out and withhold so much for union dues and issue coupons up to the hilt. And the fellow sold them to the merchants at 25 percent off. Well, now, as an example, you could buy these books from these fellows for $7.40 for $10.00 and then go to the company store and buy so many cigarettes. You would be surprised at how many merchants here in town did that. They would take one-fourth off.

Slowly, however, the coercion of businessmen diminished and merchants moved in to organize their activities. Mine Number Two was opened in 1918 and by the early twenties the population had grown to about 2,338 persons. Approximately 759 structures erected in Coal Town were already built by this period. This figure may be contrasted with 25 structures built between 1930–39 and 20 built between 1940–53. Estimates of the number of business establishments in the early twenties of all types would run to about 150; about ten of these were managed by professional persons, physicians, dentists, lawyers. Passenger trains numbered fourteen a day and stopped at a large, modern, well-built depot.

The Decline of Mining Operations

The effect of the World War I boom was to obscure the oncoming decline of the amount of work available for the miner. If we return to the table we note that with the exception of a very small increase between 1926 and 1929 the over-all trend between the years 1919 and 1932 is one of gradual decline of number of days the miner worked. This in spite of the opening of Mine Number Two in 1918.

It kept getting worse and worse until '26. These two mines used to alternate after '26. One would work one summer and then it would go down and the other one would work. Just before the Depression things were pretty bad.

The amount of work available for the individual miner improved slightly between 1932 and 1942 and increased markedly during World War II. It was during this period that many believed the coal industry was back on its feet. Once more the feeling of indefinite prosperity became manifest. All of this was short-lived, however, for after the war the more basic trends reappeared and for all practical purposes the end came. The original Mine Number One opened in 1904 and closed in 1948. Mine Number Two opened in 1918 and closed in 1956. A mine employing a relatively small number of persons was opened in 1952 and is still in operation. Many of these miners, however, are not residents of Coal Town but have been drawn from the general area. Today 350 persons are employed by the mining company as compared with 1,176 persons employed during the peak years.

PRIMARY FACTORS IN THE DECLINE OF MINING

The decline of coal mining has been a gradual, nondramatic process which goes back for many years. The factors responsible for the decline are well known and generally include the following.

1. Use of other fuels. The widespread use of cheaper and in some instances more efficient fuels played an important role in the decline of the demand for coal. Using Coal Town as a case in point we learn the following from census data. In 1940, 55 percent of the residents used coal and 45 percent used kerosene or gas for cooking. In 1950, however, coal was used in 25 percent of the homes, 49 percent used gas, and 25 percent had switched to electricity for cooking. The change indicated here is conservative. Changes in other communities not dependent on the mining of coal for a livelihood have been much more drastic and complete.

2. Competition from other mining fields. Competition from mines in other sections of the country raised havoc with the industry in Coal Town. Especially important were the open-shop mines that paid lower wages and could sell coal at lower prices. Coal Town miners, well organized, were able to demand and receive a good wage for their efforts.

These coal mines in this county could not compete with the other mines and particularly they could not compete with the open-shop mines.

3. Mechanization. The most significant over-all factor in the rise of unemployment in the Coal Town mines stems from mechanization. Mechanization, which increased production over the years, also replaced the miner. Such a development is, of course, not unique to mining but has been part of our over-all industrial growth and has been at the very core of labor-management disputes for many years.

Data compiled from official state mining reports indicate the following trends with respect to mechanization and displacement of the miner. Up until 1928 the trend was one of an increase in tonnage mined, along with an increase in the number of employees. During this period, however, mines were becoming gradually mechanized, although the full impact of such mechanization does not appear until the thirties. Thus by 1934 there is an increase in coal production and a decrease in the number of employees. This trend continues even during the most productive years of World War II, during which period the *highest tonnage* in the history of the community was produced with a *relatively small number of employees.*

The effects of mechanization were gradual but the majority of our informants who were miners traced the beginning of the decline to the early 1920s.

I would say that 1922 was the beginning of the decline of the coal mines in this area. Then when they put in the machines, the hand loaders dropped out. From '22 on the mines were dropping off all around. There were twenty-three or twenty-four mines working in this area at one time. Now there are only three.

A number of miners felt that demands for higher wages hastened their replacement by machines.

The machines were coming in and what happened is that any time your wages are increased, the mine is forced to cut corners somewhat and they cut corners by bringing in the machines. Mechanization has been the most important factor in the decline of the large number of persons who are coal miners.

Mechanization not only had a direct effect in reducing the number of miners but brought with it certain indirect effects which ultimately worked to the disadvantage of the miner. Thus once the pattern of mechanization was established mines that could not be profitably mechanized were shut down, resulting in still further unemployment. A mine examiner:

It is too expensive to modernize these mines in our county because when a mine is old it cannot profitably be modernized because the entrance ways are so small that the mine machinery cannot pass through. Some of the mines have such small entrances that only a donkey can get through. Some of this was used in the early mines and there is no attempt now to modernize them.

ADDITIONAL FACTORS IN THE DECLINE OF MINING OPERATIONS

In addition to the major factors of more economical fuels, competing mines, and mechanization there were other factors respon-

sible for the decline of mining in Coal Town. Some of our informants believed that mining management's speculative interest made
it prone to extract as much coal as possible in the shortest period
of time. Thus management was often careless in its mining methods.

Often entire sections of a mine collapsed, making further digging
impossible.

Carelessness lost the mines. They worked them out so rapidly. They never
got to the boundaries. Each mine has a boundary. But when they were
careless a whole side would often collapse and couldn't be mined.

Those down in the mine could see the end approaching. In one
instance the mine was simply "worked out."

I knew what was going to happen before the others did in this area. I saw
that they were reaching the end of their territory down inside the mine. I
heard that they were being worked out. You see, they were getting close
to a line. Now, each coal mine has a line or limit to the territory that
they can work and we were going way under around over to Nobility and
the mine at Nobility was right up against ours and I could hear the
Nobility men down in there shooting the coal on their side. That meant
that we were getting pretty near the end of our line and boundary so I
figured that things were really going to go down. Well, what happens is
that you get a decline in trade and business. Now, you also get a decline
in the number of days that you work.

In addition to the signs of unemployment which increased over
the years there were other indices that suggested that "all was not
well" for the mines in Coal Town. Good Will Tours purportedly
designed to stimulate business were common.

In the twenties the first signs were here that coal was playing out. We
made a Good Will Trip of about 1,500 miles over dirt roads to advertise
Coal Town coal. About twelve or fifteen hundred people went in forty
or fifty cars through the South. I remember that it was in the spring of
the year and we had a complete caravan. We had auto mechanics and
had everything that you needed. We even had our own bootlegger. We
had plenty of bootleg whiskey which we called "Old Cherokee." Why,
we had a carload of "Old Cherokee" that was taken along especially for
the purposes of cheering us up. A car would drive up to this bootleg car
and the driver would hold up one or two fingers which meant one or
two bottles of whiskey. We had a lot of fun. The trip was financed by
the people who went along and it cost about $50 per person. What we

tried to do was to move more Coal Town coal. We did this because the coal orders were slowly decreasing. The factories began to hedge on fuel orders and I guess this was the first sign of the Depression. We believed that it was temporary, however, and it struck home in the 1930s. I remember specifically, it was 1932 after Roosevelt was elected. I went to town one day and I noticed how many loafers there were on the street. They were pitching washers. When the banks closed I had only one silver dollar in my pocket.

A NATURAL HISTORY OF COMMUNITY DECLINE

With time the signs of economic decline became more pronounced and patterned. Out of this appeared a kind of "natural history of community decline" which possesses some predictability and regularity. We cannot tell whether the pattern of events about to be described is applicable to other communities in similar circumstances. Nevertheless, it is our belief that a satisfactory description can be worked out for *one-industry communities*.

The initial rumor. Coal Town appeared to be susceptible to rumors. At the slightest indication of unemployment, rumors about the close of the mines begin to appear.

Sometimes before a mine closes, anywhere from three to four years, the people sort of feel somehow that the mine is going to close. At first they thought that the closing was temporary. They just kept rumoring it till it goes down.

Change in the working patterns. If the rumors are well founded additional economic signs appear. One of these is a decline in the working time of the miner.

You could tell that things were getting bad when the mines began to work less and less. Why, one time we had to work a half-time split for two years. You wouldn't work a whole lot then. Why, I can remember for one month that all I drew was three shifts as far as pay was concerned. Some of the people moved but most of the people stayed. They couldn't spend very much money. They didn't live like they did before and the fellow sort of has to go down, particularly if the fellow does not have too much saved, it really gets hard on him. You see, there's always a let down when things go bad.

You could tell when things were going to get real bad and that was when you used to get very little work at the mine. Finally there would be less and less work as time would go on.

At first there is the belief that the layoffs are temporary. A native miner:

In this period in 1922 these mines started to go down. For example, the mines closed in Hartdale. Gradually these people hoped for better days: There is a sort of false optimism about this. Even today, they hope for better days, even when business dropped off. I told them that they were fools, that they were finished, that coal mining will never be another boom as it was in the past.

Business decline. Hand in hand with the decrease in work goes a decrease in business. A merchant:

When the mines go down, business goes down too. The businesses that operate on a close margin, that is marginal businesses, fall in and are failures. You see, the miners are free spenders and when there is money, they usually spend it. When there is no money, then the miners have nothing to spend and, therefore, the stores go broke. When work was good, business was good. Why, I used to drive up to Coal Town in the downtown section and see plenty of people on Saturday nights. Why, the other day I drove up to town and sat in my car for about an hour, and I'll bet that I didn't see half a dozen people. Everything was closed up tight, even the drug store.

Credit tightens up and merchants become fearful.

The merchants had a long list of people that they carried on credit, and if you went and asked for credit, why it was sort of difficult to get on if you didn't already have credit because they didn't want to add any more new accounts. The people got restless. They were wanting to be on the move. Everything was on the run. They got downhearted.

The lumber business is one of the first to feel the effects. Home construction and repair stop almost immediately.

It has been on a steady decline. This lumber business that I am in really gets hit. For years there were not even a house built in this town. Last year was my worst year since 1924. Usually when a community goes down there are plenty of empty houses that people leave. You can buy a house for little or nothing.

Mobility. Finally executives and office personnel begin to sell their homes and move out. When this occurs top-level mining management has decided to abandon the community.

When the mines began to play out, the supervisory forces would seek better opportunities in other areas. There was a gradual moving out, first of the supervisory personnel. After the Swift Mining people moved their offices to K—— you could begin to notice that things were going down.

Miners and their families commence to leave also, first those without property and children, later the property owners.

When the community begins to decline the people begin to move out. They begin to leave here. They have to look for jobs somewhere else. Those who own property will sort of stay here and look around for jobs in the immediate area. The young people leave here to go to cities, anywhere that there is work, Lake City, Riverview. Many of them would go to these places and get married.

Some of the people pulled out of town. Houses were left, some were rented, they were run down.

Often families are separated during the economic crisis.

Some of them would leave their families here and go to Lake City to work. For instance, down the street there the second house, the man even today is in Lake City and his family is right down here.

The impact of mobility on population figures begins to appear. With respect to our Coal Town data the following population statistics are worthy of note. The population of the community increased from 2,338 to 3,816 between 1920 and 1930. The increase was primarily due to the birth rate rather than to immigration. By 1940, however, the population, largely as a result of emigration of families, dropped to 3,006 and by 1950 it had dropped to 2,516. These were precentage declines of 21.0 for the decade between 1930 and 1940; and 16.38 between 1940 and 1950. After 1950 the population continued to drop. By September, 1953, the population was approximately 2,300, which was a percentage decline of 9.7 in four and one-half years.

Once mobility commences and people start to leave, friendships are terminated. At times those who remain have difficult problems of adjustment. The following excerpt gives the remarks of an upper-class resident who so completely identified himself with his associates that he felt alone and lost when these people left.

You hit the nail right on the head when you say that most of my friends have gone from this community. You see, I used to pal around with all the mine officials and pretty soon when the mines began to close down they left. Now they have left me high and dry here in this community. One man in particular, I still get together with when I go fishing, he was superintendent of the mines here. They came to me just before the mine closed and said, "You'd better get the hell out of the community because we're leaving." I thought about it for a while but then I decided to stay because I have too much here in this community. Oh, I am wealthy and I have enough money that I could start over again but after all, I am not getting any younger so I preferred to stay here. Yes, I am lonely because most of the people here I don't associate with. Most of the people here in town, they don't have any guts. They won't try anything. They won't try anything new. For example, the grocery store, that is, the supermarket across the street, is going out of business. They want to sell. All you would have to do would be to get somebody to buy that store and maybe put in a good supermarket or else buy a lot over there by the bank and put in a supermarket. But no, nobody has the guts. There is no groceryman here that is willing to do this. It would take only about $60,000 to get this thing done but do you think they want to do it? No, they don't.

Consumer habits. Once the decline of the community is underway consumer food habits undergo change. Many of the luxury food items are no longer in demand since the higher salaried personnel leave. The miner, on the other hand, is forced to budget more carefully.

Gradually chain grocery stores catering to a populace of limited means move in. Some of our informants suggested that one could tell a great deal about the state of decline of a community by the kinds of chain stores that were in business.

Homes. The exteriors of homes begin to change.

When things began to go down here houses didn't have fresh paint on them. The houses get run-down and everything else gets run-down. Those that stay here don't take as good care of their property as they used to.

The value of property begins to decline rapidly.

Some of them get a job somewhere else. It causes depreciation in your property. You can't hardly sell a house here. People can't pay the taxes.

Gossip. Once the community enters a period of decline certain personal and social characteristics begin to appear. Destructive gossip directed toward others emerges and becomes an important ingredient in the interaction between people. Gossip, although previously present, now increases and becomes pronounced. Frequently it takes the form of *magnifiying* the extent of another's *misfortune*. A grocer's wife:

Gossip tends to increase. Why, it happens in the store all the time. There has been so much lately, I noticed, and you know when you work in the store you want to close your ears to that but you just can't help overhearing some of it. Rumors start easily and they get bigger and they get bigger. For instance, my husband cut his hand with a knife, and then this rumor began to grow that he had cut his finger off and then that he had cut his arm off and well, that's the way it goes.

The miner who manages to hold his job becomes the subject of gossip. His relatively better economic position is usually explained in the following way. A miner:

The people are envious of the fellow who works. I can remember that I used to work seven days a week. I know that I felt many times that people were talking about me and whispering about me, saying that I did so-and-so in order to get this job. When the mines worked only two days, why I worked full time. I did have some friends and they would say that well, apparently he has joined the Masons in order to get work. Well, they spread this sort of gossip about a person, just sort of run a man down.

Gossip often takes the form of injuring one's personal reputation. Frequently it concerns itself with tales of sexual promiscuity and husband-wife infidelity. During such periods of fear and uncertainty "character assassination" becomes a common occurrence. No one is immune and persons presumably friendly are capable of turning on one another.

In addition to gossip, the community becomes overrun with rumors; almost any story can be peddled no matter how fantastic. Often a rumor, no matter how unfounded, becomes a basis for action. A miner:

The rumors begin to increase when a community goes down. Good rumors and bad rumors increase. There are ups and downs. The people are susceptible to rumors. They call some of these rumors "washhouse rumors." These "washhouse rumors" are rumors that are started in the showers after the miners come up on top and wash before they change into their street clothes.

Psychological effects. Gradually a marked feeling of pessimism and discouragement becomes overtly evident in the people. Hopelessness pervades the members of the community and begins to appear in their attitudes and behavior. The experiences producing this might not be significant were they isolated experiences. Viewing the entire history of the community, however, we note that they constitute one line in the entire chain of events producing cynicism and hopelessness among our informants. A miner:

People get dissatisfied when things begin to go down and they don't know what they are going to do. They can't make it in the city because they don't have enough money. They get worried, they get downhearted. The community spirit goes down. It's enough to make a man get down in the dumps.

Another miner expressed it this way:

They get depressed and blue. You can feel it a long time before it happens. I don't know what it is but no matter where you go there is just a gloom that falls on you. The men stand up on the street corner and talk about how bad things are going to be. You feel this for a long time before it happens and then if it doesn't happen, it will in just a little while, they say. You can't exactly put it into words. They think, well, we are going to have to go away or something like that. In our case, it just seemed like we thought, well, there was someone else that was going to look after us. It seemed like a few more people went to church. You get a beaten-down attitude.

People are afraid to take a chance or venture into a new situation. Out of such fears much inertia comes. A miner's wife:

Then there is a sort of a suppressed feeling in the people. When the drag is gone, everybody sits down. The community feels sort of beaten. People are five years older even in a day when they work their last shift and they know there are no other jobs to be had. There is nothing to keep them alive. You are afraid to take a chance. You are afraid to gamble. People have little money. They want to hang on to it. They don't know when they are going to get another dime and you aren't going to spend what you do have. When the person knows that the mine is going to close, he pulls in his belt and he doesn't know when he will work again. When the community goes down, people get a depressed feeling.

One college graduate adjusted this way:

I have a sort of inertia and it affects me and I sort of rock with the times. You see, I go to my books when business is bad. I'm curious. I've still got my curiosity and I'm aware of many things that I don't know. I realized this when I graduated from college but I know very little. Once you lose your curiosity about things in general, you are lost. You see, you can't afford to lose your curiosity and still exist.

Many talk about moving out but some are even afraid to do this.

There was a feeling of "I've got to go someplace—or else." But you never do. The people get downhearted and think that there isn't much future in the town.

The problems of community decline are particularly acute for middle-aged males who encounter difficulty finding employment in new industries.

People get blue, they are worried. They won't hire any one after you reach the age of forty-five or fifty. This seems to be a rule here and I know many of the old miners who would do much better work than two or three young men but these old persons can't get a job because the mines say that they are too old to work.

Middle-aged people begin to worry—is it better to stay or to leave?

They just began to think about whether they were going to have to move and leave home when the coal plays out. I know back in 1950 my husband was working and they said the mine was going to have to be closed. Right then we started wondering if we was going to have to move. My husband got a job at the ice plant and all the time he was working there he disliked it. It is just a continual worry whether you are going to have to leave your home or not. When people are getting older, that is an awful solution to think about. It is so hard to get employment when you get up to about fifty. Even if you knew the mines weren't going to work very much, it didn't bother you too much. But when it came to the point that you knew it was going to shut down altogether, it was just kinda appalling. I thought that maybe we could go to work for the state. That was the only thing I could think of.

Personal identification. In spite of the disintegrating effects described there are other signs which point to integration, signs which in many instances suggest for the first time a very real feeling which these people have for one another. It seems to be fairly characteristic of these individuals that they are more helpful during periods of stress than at other times. (See material dealing with mining disasters.)

It was reported that some people became friendly during the period of decline.

When the mines began playing out everyone became somewhat closer because we had to share a common tragedy.

Further, it is worthy of note that more civic improvement projects have been undertaken since the decline of the community than during earlier periods. Some of our informants felt that out of the sharing of a common tragedy people came to realize how much their own interests were tied to the interests of their neighbors; from this an identification with each other emerged. A miner:

During the decline in the community the relations between people can be described as brotherly love. You see, we have done more for this city since the mine closed down than we have ever done before. When things get tough community relationships get much friendlier and they get better than they do during the good times. During the good times people are out for what they can get themselves.

THE FUTURE OF COAL TOWN—POSITIVE ATTITUDES

There was a tendency for a number of our informants to feel that the decline of the community was temporary and that at some future period prosperity would reappear. Much of this is in our opinion based on wishful thinking rather than on anything demonstrable. For some informants there was almost a feeling that fate in some curious way had robbed the community of its destiny, a destiny sure to return.

Some businessmen were even reluctant to admit that the town was declining. They interpreted such comments as derogatory and as being detrimental to future business. One outspoken merchant had this to say:

This community is holding its own. There is not many businesses here but we are ahead of things. This community is not going down at all. We are a damn sight better than you are over in D——. This is a false story about the fact that Coal Town is a declining community; this makes me plenty goddamn mad. Take a look at what is going on in Birdtown. The problem here is to get some small factories, they are going to come down to us. It is a logical thing that they will come down to us here. We will not even have to fight for them. Then we will be fixed. Then we will really sock it to them.

Some extolled the virtues of the area and suggested that the following natural attributes would enable prosperity to return.

I have never lost faith in this part of this state. You see, we have everything here. We have water and we have the land to hold the water.

Others reported that the present decline is simply a low point on a cycle. Hope is ever present for these people. A retired miner:

This town was as good as any town. We had our trials and our troubles. We had our booms, we had our ups and downs. We had floater people that would come in and then go out; when they were working, why they could be just as good as any other person in any other town. Any town has a low point and then climbs back up to a high point. I think that the community is declining now, and it will decline until they get something in here to bring it up but I think it's just a matter of time before they do.

A number of informants believe that since coal reserves still exist, mines are bound to reopen.

I think there is a vein of coal about nine or ten feet thick about 900 or 1,000 feet deep and some day some company will go down and get this coal, or I think they will.

I think that something will happen and make this community about as big as it was before. There is lots of coal here and I think that there could be some more coal mines started here. I think that they will sink another mine. It will be a mechanized mine sure, and they won't employ too many men but I think it will be a better mine and at least there will be employment. I think that's what's going to happen.

The coal isn't played out in Coal Town. There is another vein of coal down below this. That is that new vein of coal they are getting around D———. They will get that coal down below when this top seam gets worked out, I believe. They will have to work some vein of coal. There is millions of tons of coal in that old mine, just laying there. A man told me there was about eighty cars of coal loaded at the bottom of that shaft at Mine Number Two and they didn't take time to pull them out. I don't know why the mines closed. There is lots of time to pull them out. Lots of coal down there they didn't get out. These operations was to get this easy coal.

So-called statements from mining management are often quoted.

My boy asked me something about it. I said them high officials study about it and they say from ten to fifteen years the coal is going to come back strong and people are going to come back and use it like it was. He said it might be gonna happen. That is what he was talking about. That is what you hear from them officials about the coal. They claim they got two or three veins of coal in the ground yet.

Some even feel that there are very real agricultural possibilities. One miner presents the case for a farming community:

I don't think that the coal mines will come back though we do have plenty of coal here. It seems that as if the coal has finished in this area and I think the future as I said before lies in the farming community. About the future of this town, I think that this is going to be a good town yet. I think it's going to be a good, clean town, too. It's going to be all right. You see, we are getting to be a good farming region here and I think that this will be a farm area. This will be a trading center for farmers and farm families. I think a farming community is better for people than an industrial community. Those people are depending on the industries, are very unhappy. In the farming community, people care about their homes.

Most of the talk, however, centers around the possibility of attracting new industries to the community. Many believe that Coal Town has the necessary prerequisites for attracting new industry. A miner:

I would say that the future of this town is somewhat encouraging, especially if new factories would come in. We have a good government here and I think that the people will try to do the best that they can. Most of them are property owners and they keep up their homes. Taxes are lower and there is a very good spirit here. Now I think that is primarily responsible to the appearance of Mr. Q—— in the community. He seems to have added something to our town. Those lights, for instance, are a very good example of what he has done for this community.

Some believe that industries are bound to move out of the large communities and that when they do, Coal Town will get them. A merchant:

I think industry is coming to the small community and I feel that we are going to get some of them down here. At that time the young people will come back because they can live here very cheaply. After all this is the best town in this part of the state. I do not think that we will have to put up a fight to get industry here in about five or ten years. I think that is the only logical way in which they can move. They will have to move from the larger cities and the only logical place for them to move is, of course, Coal Town.

Others believe that there will always be a Coal Town. A merchant:

I think there will always be a Coal Town regardless of the coal mine. I think they will just be about as prosperous as they are today. They are going to draw industry. I believe that if they ever get this lake it is going to bring industry maybe bigger than what we think. I believe the coal mines isn't going to hurt anything around here. Property is not depreciating any. A lot of people want to live in a little town like this. Land is a lot cheaper here than it is other places. The kids are not overcrowded here.

THE FUTURE OF COAL TOWN—NEGATIVE ATTITUDES

The majority of our informants were not optimistic, either about their own futures or the future of the community. These people believe, and in the opinion of the writer rightly so, that the coal mines are finished and there is no real incentive for stable industry to move to Coal Town. With a history of high labor costs and a strong tradition of union organization, Coal Town has little to offer industries looking for high profits and a stable labor situation. A miner:

We have been trying for years to get some good industry in here. But they are afraid of our labor situation. I have been on a lot of committees and that is their argument.

Well, it is just what has happened in German Town today [coal ran out]. A bunch of the civic-minded people try to bring other industires to take the place of coal mining. It is going to be hard to do this. You take the coal miner, he has always been used to a good day's wage. I believe that is a detriment. Other people try to get the same wage as the coal miner. That increases the cost of labor.

Many see no hope and accept what appears to be the inevitable. A retired miner:

Well, you asked me about the future. I wish I could see a brighter future for this community. Our mines are gone. It is going to be pretty bad here if we don't get some factories. Oh, I guess people can go back to the farms. They can build up the land and they can have a living. There is nothing here for the younger generation. Young people have to leave here and go to the cities like Lake City and Riverview.

The old and inadequate remain, the young and ambitious leave. An immigrant's son:

There has been a constant exodus of people from the coal fields since 1924. These were people who were very dissatisfied and who wanted to leave and make something of themselves. Most of the people, that is the more intelligent ones, sell out and pull off. The old die-hards hang on.

A retired miner:

I would say that the ambitious and industrious people have left these communities and the community consists of the very young who are unable to leave and the very old who cannot leave. As the population decreases the people want to leave.

A miner's wife:

This town is gone. I think there's just a bunch of flunks around here. They'll never build up this town any more. I think it's lost. It's gone. There is no future here and I don't believe that they will bring any industry in here because there isn't enough water here in the first place. The future here is not promising.

An immigrant:

But that is all past and gone. Coal Town is as good as dead now and nothing can be done about it. I know I won't be here much longer. It is like me. It won't last much longer either. The people are old. We're both just old. [Here W—— gazed long and wistfully at the ruined mine, the weather-beaten, paint-starved, crumbling old houses across the way.] This is a finished town. It has served its purpose. The young have nothing to keep them here and the old will eventually die off.

In this regard it is important to note that emigration of the younger segments of the population has markedly affected the distribution of age groups in Coal Town. In 1930 the percentage of the population over twenty-one was 58.2. By 1940 it had increased to 63.9 percent and by 1950 to 70.1 percent. Approximately 25 percent of the residents of Coal Town are currently sixty-five years old or over.

The exodus to the city continues and while this must be, parents wish it could be otherwise. A father speaks:

What the hell can we do? What kind of future have we got here? What future has this town got? All we can do is hold on to what we've got an' do the best we can. We have to send our kids away. But what the hell, what chance have those kids got here? My girl is going to Lake City to be a nurse. I see no hope for it. I can't see any future for Coal Town. It will inevitably go the way of all mine camps. Agriculture is rather poor here, its coal is gone, and it doesn't have anything to trade on.

Many speak of Coal Town as a place where old people retire on relief, social security, and pensions. A miner:

Well, it looks like this community is going to be an old folks' home. When I came here I was an old person and I was only thirty years of age. We just didn't have any old people here when I came here. The schools are kept in because they brought in the kids from the country. That's why they are working now.

In this connection we would like to point out that while there appears to be little future for the youth, the miner receiving social security and a pension currently has a more secure income than at any previous time in his life.

The economic base of the community is tied to the income brought in largely from relief, social security, and pensions. An immigrant spokesman:

What happens to the community when the coal mines go down. This community has been harder hit than any place, probably than any place in the U.S. The community is so hard hit that I don't know one person in this county that they got a job within the last two years. I am supervisor of general assistance here. What I am telling you is the truth. The only thing that saved this community is in Coal Town we have 15 percent of the homes getting miner's pension. I can name you 107 cases. Most of the people, on the average, they are older. Most of our town is on miner's retirement. A lot of them are over sixty-five and get social security, too. We have quite a few of them get other aids. Most of the thing that is keeping this town up is the miners' welfare. Relief is not too bad in

Coal Town. Two and one-half percent of the people in the city of Coal Town is on relief. Most of the young people we have been trying to encourage to find jobs. There is child aid and old age pensions.

Retired miners reported:

This is just like an individual growing up from birth. They bloom in the twenties and the thirties and then like I am and then like old W—— there. That is how the town is. I will tell you what keeps it going today, what little outside work there is at Birdtown and German Town and around. I guess the biggest factor we have here is the social welfare income. Social security and the miners' welfare and the state old age assistance, family assistance and surplus commodities, those things are all factors in keeping the things rolling along.

It is no noise, quiet. I don't think we will be hurt much. That is what the old folks are looking for—the miners' pensions and social security are not bad income. You have your home paid for. The miners keep up your taxes and insurance. I think most of the future will be mostly retired people. My son said he would rather come here to retire. I can show you a number of people who have already done that.

The old people are predominant here at the present time. The young people are leaving the community. Old people draw their pensions, social security and miners' pensions. A few of them work for the city part time and a few of them work in their garden. Some fish and hunt. Many of these old people are just doing nothing. All they do is just sit on their back porch or front porch and rock and wait for their pension checks to come in. Coal Town is nothing more than a residential area comprised mostly of an older class of people. I don't think that there will ever be another boom here. These mines are pretty well played out.

As previously suggested, the majority of businesses in Coal Town went bankrupt or left the community. A merchant describes the past:

This street used to be full of businesses. There were four or five groceries on that street, a furniture store, and a supply store for the miners. All that's left is the theater, a plumbing shop, and a barber shop. There was a small bar and poolroom there also. Now, in this side of town there was a confectionery and three grocery stores. To the south there were three grocery stores. I would say that less than 25 percent of the businesses are here that were here in the boom period of the town. On the north side of town there are three stores. There are only two of them left. There seems to have always been a grocery store in every other block in this town.

There were also two blacksmith shops and four dealerships in automobiles: Ford, Dodge, Chrysler, and Studebaker. Cars used to come in on the trains. You see, they had big ideas for this town and they figured that the coal would never play out, would just keep on going. This was their one mistake, because they never planned for factories and for diversification.

The agent at the railroad station had this to say:

At the present time there is no passenger train. I haven't sold a ticket in so long that I wouldn't even know how to start. There is no need to sell tickets here because there are no passenger trains. The only thing that we have here now is coal trains. When people want to go, they either go to C—— or German Town or E——. I remember when we had fourteen passenger trains a day and now we have none. They came in from New America and up. One line had two trains a day. They shuffled from here to New America. The miners used to commute on the trains. They had five or six coaches on another line that would be loaded to standing room. A lot of them worked outside. You could stand on the street and listen to the whistle.

One or two merchants who depend on area trade manage to do well. The residents of Coal Town with limited incomes, however, cannot afford to pay the prices asked by the smaller private merchants and prefer to shop at supermarkets in nearby communities. They report that prices tend to be high and choice is limited in Coal Town. A miner's wife:

We shop in German Town because prices are higher here than elsewhere. Sometimes we go down to the grocery down the street and get a few things but only because we run out. You see, you have more of a selection and variety when you shop in German Town or Hartdale like we do. We even buy our groceries over there. The stores don't come in here because the business is bad. Why, you only have one clothing store in town and if you don't like what Mr. L—— has to sell, then you just don't buy anything. I don't know how it has held up as good today as it has but it's not bad here. At least 70 percent of the shopping goes on in Birdtown and German Town.

SUBMARGINAL INDUSTRIES

The tenuous economic balance between a submarginal existence and very real poverty has made these people vulnerable to unsound economic schemes which at times verge on being swindles. Economically destitute with little to offer, they have had to contend with small, unstable industries which expect almost everything but promise nothing. Such industries demand free rent, low taxes, and guarantees of cheap labor. At the slightest indication of community unrest they threaten to leave and to withdraw what little economic support they may have afforded the community. Coal Town has had its experiences with such industries. A husband reports on the present one:

Why, even today there is nothing here for the girls except this damn sweatshop over where they pay 55 cents an hour. It's real bad. Why, I wouldn't even dress up to go out of the house for less than a $1.25 an hour. Now, I tell these girls here that but they go ahead and work down there in that damn sweatshop anyway.

A description of employment difficulties in these industries, well corroborated by others, goes this way:

My wife used to work in the dress factory here. You see, they have a minimum wage scale of 75 cents an hour but there is a way of beating this and they institute a training period of fourteen weeks and for this training period they pay the worker at the rate of from 50 to 65 cents an hour. Now business comes in spurts and if they have a rush order then they advertise for new workers and take them on as learners and then they can pay them from 50 to 65 cents. They can usually catch up with their work in a fourteen weeks' period and by that time they have finished and they let the workers go.

Many feel that these submarginal industries have no real interest in the community, and this they resent.

When these communities go in and raise money in order to build a building to get an industry into the community, that is bad for the simple reason that it means that the company does not have any stake in the community. Whenever there is any trouble or the threat of trouble, the company can always threaten to get up and move out. I know this has happened in many of these small communities.

When a community has to pay an industry to come in it usually gets the poorer ones.

Today I just don't know where the money would come from in order to pay an industry to come into Coal Town. We won't get industry here because we don't have the money to pay them to come in. Now I know that when you have to pay an industry to come in, it doesn't always mean that it is a good industry because the good industry will pay its own way rather than wait for someone to make a payment for it.

An industry with substance would receive the real cooperation of the residents, according to our informants.

I think that we in this community would help an industry without any trouble if we could be assured that this industry was honest and was not a fly-by-night venture. We need a big industry here, not all of these little, small ones that you have to bribe to come into your community. If an industry is worth its salt, it will pay its own way and not wait until a community has to provide a building or make some concessions to it in the form of cheaper taxes.

THE FUTURE OF COAL TOWN: A THEORETICAL ANALYSIS

The economic future of Coal Town and communities of like heritage is, in the opinion of the writer, tenuous indeed; but this is hardly a startling discovery. More pertinent may be an assessment of the factors which have gone into creating things as they are and which are important for the future of Coal Town.

LEADERSHIP

To begin with, Coal Town has never had leadership sufficiently interested in or capable of attracting new, stable economic endeavors. Nor has the leadership been of a type that could orient the community to the social changes which have struck the community since the middle twenties. In our opinion this condition stems from the fact that Coal Town has never developed a group sufficiently interested in the community *as a community* or in its perpetuation as a *cultural identity*. A sharp contrast comes to light when we compare a one-industry community like Coal Town with the declining one-industry mill communities in the eastern part of the United States. In these latter communities some of the aristocracy that emerged over the years felt a sense of identity with the community.[1] The community had been their ancestral home and

---

[1] The writer does not advocate an aristocracy. The term is used to suggest the important role which leadership groups can provide during crisis periods of community life.

there was a paternalistic concern for the populace. In these communities the leadership that was furnished was able to mold sentiments, feelings, and family prestige into constructive programs of reform designed to enable the community to reorganize its economic base. Such a class, with attitudes we have described, was never present in Coal Town. Perhaps in time a group with such attributes might have emerged. Perhaps, too, whatever exploitative attitudes these people formerly had may have become tempered in time with social feeling for the community.

Nevertheless, such a development has not taken place in Coal Town, and regardless of the factors involved there is today no constructive leadership of any stature. Instead there are a few well-meaning persons who engage in street cleaning campaigns and park renovation.

CULTURAL VALUES

A second factor pertinent to Coal Town's future which must be assessed has to do with the cultural values that characterize life in the community. At the start of our study we pointed out that the cultural conflict which occurred between the native and the immigrant was in reality a conflict between the values of a subsistence farming and hunting society and the values of an industrialized society. The Europeans, to be sure, had been reared in peasant societies, but their orientation encompassed working habits consistent with and demanded by an industrial order. We refer specifically to the immigrants' values of thrift, industry, hard work, and ambition. In almost all conflicts between peasant and industrialized societies, the latter have won out and their values have become predominant. We cannot make this claim for the conflict under discussion. For in fact it is quite clear that industrial values have never been able to establish themselves successfully in any part of this cultural area. Furthermore, in the value clash between the native working habits and the immigrant working habits the values of the native have become predominant. The effects of this are seen most clearly in the life orientations of immigrant children who have remained in the area. This condition has become the subject of bitter resentment on the part of the immigrant parents, who are greatly disturbed about this development.

Thus the work habits of native and immigrant children tend to be similar. Both groups have a set of attitudes which make their adjustment to an industrial order difficult. They possess an immature type of conformity and an explosive individualism, without direction. They resent responsibilities, especially those concerned with meeting working schedules and routines. Absenteeism is high and provoked by the slightest dissatisfaction. Hunting and fishing are important values and have always been more attractive than work. Management in the few industries present has in some cases attempted to solve this problem with pep talks and increased benefits. These efforts appear to change attitudes little. For the few industries present there is always the potential danger that an increase in wages may result in an increase in absenteeism. There is a marked tendency for these people to be satisfied with little and to avoid planning for the future; a way of life not easily changed. If one may earn enough for a week by working three days instead of five, three days' work becomes sufficient. Working habits are much like they were in the preindustrial era. The effect of all this has been to entrench a way of life which is basically at odds with industrialization. As presently constituted, the patterns of life and working habits plague any stable industry that attempts to move in. *For any industry there would be the initial problem of what to do about one hundred years of local cultural history.*

PSYCHOLOGICAL ORGANIZATION

A third significant factor to be understood in assessing the future of Coal Town has to do with the personalties of the people and their ability to adapt to a new order of things. Here we are confronted by some very complex problems, for in part we must synthesize some of the effects of life in Coal Town on the personalities that evolved. In spite of the many pitfalls implicated in such an analysis, and of the many problems in generalizing about a population, we believe the following conclusions to have validity.

Superimposed upon the basic cultural values previously discussed are the personally demoralizing experiences of life in the community. When all is said and done, there have been relatively few positive human relationships for the vast majority of these people. They have exploited others and have themselves been victims of exploitation. They have grown up amidst patterns of violence, fear, cynicism, and hopelessness. In this regard it is well to point out that an entire generation has been reared in an environment where they have never known their fathers to have steady work and where unemployment was the rule rather than the exception. Further, they have little faith in the motives of others and lack the capacity to identify consistently, be it with other persons or with things abstract such as community growth. Life in the community has fostered skepticism to the point where their confidence in any new enterprise or scheme can readily be undermined and destroyed; and while such an attitude is understandable in view of their experiences, it constitutes a formidable barrier to their acceptance of new things. The capacity for these people to change, to visualize new alternatives, is limited. For the native population, social change is reminiscent of the introduction of coal mining and brings back memories of the native-immigrant conflict. Equally significant is the notion that *social change for native and immigrant means accepting things that are different. Differences, be they matters of food, language, or work, have now become identified with frustration.* Thus social change and personal disorganization have become linked in the thinking of these people.

Attempts to bring about changes have produced inner conflicts for many already weary of a life of frustration. Many have simply withdrawn from the conflict and remain inert. Thus in spite of all the talk about change, there is fundamentally little concern about changing things as they are. A merchant:

People just talk about bringing in other industries. They never really were too concerned about it. I think that is basically what is behind this lethargy and inability of persons to act in the community. In 1925 the people realized that the one-industry town wasn't so good, so we went on this Good Will Tour that you have probably heard a great deal about. At that time the feeling was that things were not so good here.

Whether changes should or should not consciously be introduced is a question not germane to the present study. Can changes be effected if all that we have said is true? If one wishes to enable the community to survive economically or the youth to earn an adequate livelihood, changes become a necessity. It is apparent that the "academic medicine-man approach" replete with pep talks, street cleaning campaigns, and evangelical speeches can be of little avail. At best such techniques may even be dangerous since they produce no lasting changes and therefore plunge a population such as this into deeper hopelessness and cynicism. Our informants recognize this when they say:

The composition of the population is such that a pep talk at this time would not aid them. There has been so much betrayal and so much mistrust that the people have lost faith. They have lost faith even in their own faction. Both sides have lost faith.

In the immediate future it may be possible with a detailed knowledge of the cultural organization to work with these people within the framework of their own value system. Put another way, we might suggest that one who knew the area could approach these people in a way not antagonistic to their value system; and by so doing organize an effective labor force.

From a long-range point of view we immediately recognize that few industries will want to become involved in these intricate problems of social change. Thus the alternative may involve the uprooting of many segments of the basic value system if one wishes to hasten the process of change. Whether the effects in terms of personal disorganization and conflict which such changes may produce can make the effort worth while remains of course a moot question.

CHAPTER 10

SOCIAL CLASS STRUCTURE IN COAL TOWN

AN understanding of social class in Coal Town is rooted in several factors. Most significant among these is the pattern of these people to think in terms of "class differences." This recognition of differences stems from the division of labor and from the social discriminations they observe. They think in terms of social separations and behave in accordance with them. Thus these phenomena of social class differences are realities.

Likewise they view the behavior within each social class as having marked inconsistencies between what people profess and how people actually live; or between an outer façade and what is believed to go on in personal lives. Such a feeling is especially pronounced among our less privileged groups. All of this, which appears throughout our data, has helped foster in these people an attitude "that things are not really what they seem to be," that people are full of duplicity. These attitudes have been transmitted to their children and have become entrenched in their thinking.

From the sociological point of view it is important to recognize that these inconsistencies which our informants recognize make class typing exceedingly difficult. The members of each class, in spite of the predominant patterns and characteristics that are mentioned, possess in thought as well as behavior certain inconsistencies. In this regard it is important to remember that Coal Town was a frontier-type community for the major part of its history. Thus the community's value orientation permeated the entire class structure and left no class immune from the basic patterns described in previous chapters. Finally, the characteristics of any single class in Coal

Town, for example, the upper class, might well come closer to approximating the characteristics of, let us say, the middle class in another, perhaps larger, community.

SOCIAL CLASS DIFFERENCES

Coal Town was a community sensitive to social divisions from the very first. Differences in social class constituted such a division and they expressed the values and sentiments of the community. These values included control of others through economic power, contempt for differences, envy, resentment of others, and impersonality.

The class structure of Coal Town until the 1920s consisted of a small upper class which included mining executives, physicians, and dentists, an insignificant middle class of office personnel and teachers, and a large undifferentiated lower class consisting of native and immigrant miners. A miner:

During the early days, well, at the top, of course, there were the mine officials, the superintendents, and their families. There was the supervisor's staff who remained apart from the hordes. The mining officials were the big shots in the early days in this town and they tried to run the town. At the bottom were the miners and their families. In between were people who worked in the offices. When Victor hired the people to work, they were all thrown in the same pot. The natives, the immigrants, and all the others.

Since outsiders could not purchase property until 1918 there were no opportunities for private merchants to initiate businesses. It was not until outside capital could be invested in shops and an occupational hierarchy established that a middle class of any real size emerged. By 1925 these developments had occurred and a threefold class system (upper, middle, lower), separate for native and immigrant, was well on its way. This organization is depicted in Figure 2.

There is substantial agreement between native and immigrant with respect to the ranking portrayed in the figure. A male college graduate:

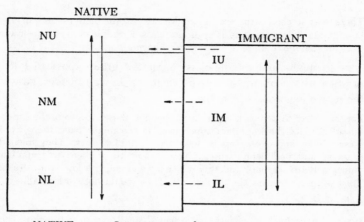

NATIVE

IMMIGRANT

NU

IU

NM

IM

NL

IL

NATIVE: Separate native class structure
IMMIGRANT: Separate immigrant class structure
↑ ↓   Social mobility within the immigrant or the
                       native class structure
◄ — — —   Direction of and extent of social mobility from
                       the immigrant to the native class structure

NU Native upper class composed of mining superintendents, select merchants, bankers, mining engineers.

IU Immigrant upper class composed of English-speaking miners who occupied supervisory positions from England, Scotland, Wales, Ireland.

NM Native middle class composed of teachers, public officials, skilled miners, small merchants, office personnel, store clerks.

IM Immigrant middle class composed of skilled miners from Finland; small merchants from Central and Southern Europe; skilled miners from Austria, Croatia, Lithuania, Poland, Russia, Bulgaria, Italy, Greece; semi-skilled miners, who worked in the pits, from Central and Southern Europe.

NL Native lower class composed of miners with minimum of skill, unskilled workers, workers irregularly employed, poor white trash.

IL Immigrant lower class composed of irregularly employed immigrants from Central and Southern Europe; disorganized immigrants without family or church affiliation.

FIGURE 2. SOCIAL CLASS ORGANIZATION FOR COAL TOWN, 1925–1950

There was a class structure, I would say, of the natives and of the immigrants. There was and is an upper class, a middle class, and a lower class divided into both native and foreign-born groups.

Both upper- and middle-class immigrant groups possessed less prestige than comparable native categories. Lowest in prestige was the native lower class. A native:

For the native there was a supervisory element, those who were the superintendents and the important supervisors in the mine. Then there were these clerks and storekeepers who were middle class. They owned property and had been farmers. Now, below these there was another group, a bottom group, and this was what we call the low white trash. They were even below the immigrants. They would not work at all.

A lumber dealer:

When you go back into class, there was a small group at the top. The mine officials, the bankers, and the two business people, I would say, were in the top group. There was a middle-class group which would also take in about 50 percent of the miners. On the bottom was what we call the scum of the earth. These people worked enough to get along. They were drunks. They were poor white trash.

One miner pointed to these characteristics:

I would say that in the community there were three classes. First, the group that is financially in good standing, and second, a group of moral, decent people, and third, a group on relief. There are no immigrants in the upper native group. What these groups want out of life is a little bit different and many in the lowest classes would not work half the time and they wouldn't work if work was available.

RECOGNITION OF CLASS DIFFERENCES

For the most part our informants recognized the existence of social class differences and displayed little hesitancy in discussing them. A native miner:

There are three groups: mine officals at the top, banking officials and top businessmen; and these on the top mix only with themselves as far as social relations are concerned. There is a second group of smaller business people here and then a lower-class group.

A native merchant's wife:

There are upper and lower groups here in Coal Town and there is also a middle group. There is a lower-class drinking group that go to church on

Sundays. There is also a middle-class bridge club group and these persons in the bridge club group often go to towns outside of Coal Town for their entertainment. Most of the time they are working as miners or else they work for the State on the road. Some of their wives work and in some cases they make as much money or more money than do their husbands. Then there are those damn people underneath. They never work. The kids go unkempt and hungry. They live in houses that are run-down. They don't want much out of life. All they can think of is getting to the store and buying liquor, and once their check comes in through the mail, they go down and blow it all in at the tavern while their children and their wives go hungry.

A middle-class merchant:

There are these three social classes here. There is a high group, that is the church people. I know, though, that among this high group there are some drunkards who are members of that church. They also run around with some different women. I know they owe me grocery bills but they will not pay.

A native lower-class woman observed:

There is also an upper crust here. I think that the bankers' wives and merchants' wives would belong to that. Then there is a lower crust here who hangs around the taverns and just try to get by the best way they can. You see, you have these crusts everywhere.

CLASS AWARENESS AMONG THE YOUTH

Young people were aware of class differences. A native girl pointed this out about her home:

In my family we were taught to be friendly and to be nice to certain boys because they were good boys and because their appearance was good. We also got some nudges too about families who were not up to our moral standards. There were always stories about the rough and tough kids and we were warned to stay away from them.

Students observed distinctions. The daughter of a middle-class family:

I noticed the different social classes when I went to school; there were some here who had more money to spend than others and this was the basis for social classes in schools. Another factor that was important was whether or not they had their own car. Now, quite a few of the students did have their own car. The parents would want their children to keep up with the Joneses, and many of these parents were miners and they wanted their children to be sure and keep up with the Joneses because they thought that that was important.

A middle-class girl pointed to these factors:

In the school there was a group—I would call it a group with high ideals —and then there was a rowdy bunch. The highest class in the school was composed of students like the daughter of the doctor in the community and the children of the operator of the Electric Company. It also included a merchant's daughter. There was not too many of those people there at the time that I went through high school. The kids associated together and were considered high society. Then there was another group in school—the poor kids. The natives as well as the immigrants were mixed in this. They would say, "He doesn't dress as nice as the rest of us." Things like that, you know. Why, you couldn't even talk to these kids they were so backward. You never visited them and you were not even interested in them. They didn't have any cars.

DENIAL OF CLASS DIFFERENCES

A small group of informants denied the existence of social classes.[1] Typical of the informants who denied the existence of class was the tendency to point inadvertently to indices of social class. A miner's wife who denied the existence of social class:

You see, this no-class idea makes it a good place to live. The Company houses are called "Silk Stocking Row" but I would feel as good with the mining superintendent's wife as I would with anybody else. You see, this is a melting pot. Our people, you see, all came from foreign countries. Why, my grandparents came from England. You see, I belong to the D.A.R. I can trace my family tree all the way back through the Revolutionary War into England. I take a great deal of pride in this. Why, I can trace my ancestry back to a captain who was a friend of Washington's in the Revolutionary War.

An upper-class retired male:

You see, we didn't have any classes here. I would say that some of the merchants were members of the upper class. You see, with some of the miners we did mix socially but we were not in the rowdy crowd or, as

[1] Interviewing at this point was exceedingly difficult, not only because the subject was a delicate one, but because informants confused social class with (1) nationality, (2) religion, and (3) fraternal orders. It was necessary for us to convert our terminology into questions which would be meaningful to our informants.

you might say, the drinking crowd. We were interested in education and in the spiritual welfare of the community.

A miner:

I don't see any class. There may be a lower class. What you might call the "Okies." They are so low-down that you wouldn't want to associate with them. There is an upper crust and a silk stocking row here. These are words that are used to refer to people who the people think have money. People think that the Jamisons have a lot of money, but I know it is not true. They don't like him because he used bigger words.

There were no social classes—but . . . A miner:

The people feel that they are nearly all the same. Why, the banker and the ditchdigger would mix together, I would say. There used to be a clique here, and there still is. There is an upper crust, for instance, a doctor, and a banker, and the merchants would belong to this, but you know, I don't believe in that myself. Though some people do. Some people feel that they are a lot better than others. I can't tell any difference, myself. We have here just a few people who think that they are better because they have money, or because they are more educated. Now we do have a lower class, and some of these people are pretty rotten people. They are not considered as anything at all. Some are ornery, they won't work, they are always on relief, they are always laying out at night, and taking up with anyone.

REACTIONS TO SOCIAL CLASS DIFFERENCES

The patterns of envy and resentment which appear throughout our data were manifest in considerable resentment about the existence of class differences on the part of the less privileged classes. Such a resentment is perhaps not unusual in a community where *social differences* have been associated with disprivilege and discrimination for a large section of the population. Below are several middle-class reactions. A middle-class native miner:

There are some here in this community that figure they are better than others. There, for instance, would be the upper crust, the silk stocking people, the banker—and he would feel a lot better than some people. And a lot of coal miners, too, think they are much better than anybody else. There are even a lot of just ordinary coal miners, too, that think that they are better than other people. Of course, there are the bosses' families, and they all think that they are better than the rest of us. You take, for example, the two houses there across the street. Both of them men are bosses and they associate together and carry on together but they don't associate with me and a lot of the other fellows.

A middle-class immigrant miner:

That is natural [social class]. We have people here that don't amount to anything but if he had a chance to get something good in his life, then they think they are the best. That is wrong. I don't like that. I have seen many men like that. They act like big shots but they are not. They are just like me, a poor man. What they have I am glad they have but they should speak to somebody. They should speak back. I am in favor of good friends. If you speak to them and they don't speak back to me I must just tell them, "If you don't want to speak to me just tell me." When they get money or buy automobiles or something like that they don't speak sometimes. It don't make any difference what kind of car I have, I like everybody. I am not against nobody.

Our lower-class people were especially sensitive to the treatment which they felt grew out of differences in class. Some resented these patterns. A lower-class native woman:

It seems that some feel better than others in this community. They don't have too much money here, I would say, but some of the natives act like big Ikes. I think that if the people think that they are better than anybody else, that's where they're mistaken because to me it doesn't make any difference.

Another native woman from the lower class:

We have always had people here who think that they are better than others. They think that because they have a little bit more than you have. The kids think that way, too. It is for this reason that we do not like this place.

People are snobbish. A lower-class native male:

Oh, yes, you run across them every once in a while [people who think they are better]. I call them stuck-ups. I don't know what would be the right name for them. Some of them ain't got any more than I have got. They think they are something. You don't have many in the early days. They have more of that today. You meet people here on the street and they will pass right on the walk and never see you. I don't know why. I know them and I know pretty well that it ain't what they have got that makes them that way. They work a day's work just like the rest of these miners. I can tell you one. Jim Billings, hell, I knowed Jim ever since before I moved up here. His dad and mom lived right down there across the hard road. There wasn't finer people lived I don't reckon. He had a brother the same way. I wasn't acquainted with the girl. She is a little distant-turned that way, too. Jim will pass me on the walk right there and other people that he knowed all his life and never see us. Well, back yonder he never did have nothing. Till he went to work down here at the mine and he got bruised up and then he got a pretty good rake-off off that. Then his woman went to work so I guess they picked up pretty good stakes.

Even the children suffer. A lower-class native miner from the South:

There are a lot of them here that look down on you and a lot of those that look down on you are church people, too. I think they're two-faced. Just because they wear a necktie, they think they are better than you are. It's always been true of the people around here. At least, ever since I've been here. They want to look down on you. It makes it tough on the kids. They look down on the kids and the kids don't treat each other as they should. It was certainly hard, I know, for me to have my kids growing up, but now they all have good paying jobs and they're away from here. I'm sure glad that they are, too.

A case of bitter resentment. A lower-class native from the South:

We do have some people who think they are better than others. Some don't even have a pot to piss in but nevertheless they think that they are a lot better than you are. I worked in the mines for a long time and I don't have anything to show for it except my furniture. Why, I don't even own my house. I don't understand why some people have all that they do and some of these foreigners have everything. They have a new car and I don't even have a car. I don't have a damn thing. I know that one person, for example, has a lot more things than I do and he's no better off than I am. Why, they own their own homes and big cars and they get ahead but I can't get ahead. The other person thinks he's better than you are if he has a little bit more money. Sometimes they don't even speak to me and other times they do. It makes me mad and I've known this friend for a long time; and he passes me on the street and sometimes he speaks and sometimes he don't. Well, that sort of thing, I don't like it.

Some felt that they were better off. A lower-class woman:

The upper crust across the town here, I don't think are really upper crust. They think they are but I know that in some instances I am better than they are. For instance, we are going to own our home in another three years, and I know some of the members of the upper crust that don't even own their own home. Of course, they are Company homes and they have to rent, but if they lost their jobs with the Company then they wouldn't have any place to live. Now, I think that I am better than they are.

In spite of the resentments which our less privileged informants had, there is no evidence to suggest that a change in class position was not possible for native and immigrant. Such changes involved conscious striving and the assimilation of the necessary prerequisites, especially for the non-English-speaking immigrant.

THE BASIS OF THE NATIVE SOCIAL CLASS ORGANIZATION

The significant factors determining the native social classes in Coal Town have been occupation, economic power and control, habits, manners, wealth, and education. Of all these criteria, economic power and control are perhaps the most significant. Economic power in a one-industry community places those in control in a most advantageous position, since they have control over the social and personal lives of community members. A particular position in the mine or a business became important in so far as it gave one control over others. In a culture where power to control is an important value one observes ramifications throughout the society. Such power permeated the whole pattern of social relationships in the community; persons were evaluated with respect to their ability to manipulate and control others economically and personally.

Having said this we must recognize that economic power was not in itself a sufficient attribute for upper-class status. There were, for example, native union leaders who had a great deal of economic power. They lacked other attributes for upper-class status, perhaps wealth and education, but in all probability personal manners and customs. There were many with wealth and power who could not become members of the upper classes. An upper-class male:

Wealth did not mean anything as far as social classes were concerned because you had some bootleggers who were very wealthy, but they were not in the upper class. I can remember that many of them used to make a great deal of money, particularly one bootlegger who ran a whorehouse in connection with his establishment.

A merchant:

The distinctions were not based on economic factors here because boot-leggers really made the money during the 1920s. One fellow here made copper pipe, and that was his trade in the Old Country, and he came here and became almost a millionaire. Why, he made a lot of money, I can remember, but he was not in the upper-class group, merely because he did not conduct himself with the proper manners or behavior. Social distinction would be based a lot on personal conduct and habits.

Personal conduct was more important than wealth. An upper-class male:

It was how one conducted himself, personally, that was the important thing in this community, that is, the manners and customs were even more important than wealth. As far as that is concerned, there is not too much wealth differential here in this community. For many years the average businessmen made about $1,500 a year. Now the coal miner made on the average from $900 to $1,100 a year. Well, you can see that that is not too much difference in terms of money. Now a good businessman may have sometimes made $3,000 or $4,000 a year but that is about all. Now the face boss did earn $1,400 a year. So you see, as far as wealth is concerned, there was not too much difference.

Thus upper-class status was based primarily on a favorable combination of occupation, economic power, personal habits, and etiquette in social situations. Social classes were broken up in accordance with the relative distribution of these criteria.

THE NATIVE CLASS STRUCTURE

THE UPPER CLASS

The native upper class consisted of mining engineers, superintendents, bankers, and select merchants with economic power and control. Coal Town had only one physician and one dentist for many years; they were also part of the upper class.

I was one of the first merchants here. My friends were the mine bosses and the superintendents. The engineers were college-trained people and they were extremely nice people. We associated with such people as Company officials. These immigrants, however, would not form part of our own social circle.

Social interaction among the native upper classes. Members of the native upper class in general mixed with each other; with those performing the same skill the interaction was on a more intimate basis. This was especially true for those in mining. A mine supervisor:

Most of my friends were mine supervisors and we used to associate together. Every month or two the officials would have a sort of get-to-gether meeting, like a big supper, over to the Country Club or at one of the hotels here in the county. We would have a nice, big feed and talk things over. Everybody would say a few words. That was a sort of good thing, I thought. The Company men would be on more intimate friend-ships with each other than they could be with union men, though there would be sometimes some pretty close friendships between Company and union men. They would not mix as much.

The associates of an upper-class native woman:

Well, I would mix socially with that bridge playing group. The one that owns that variety store, the wife of the owner of the lumber company, the wife of the vice president of the bank; those are the bridge players. There would be a few women whose husbands are bosses at the mine. The leading class in the community, I would say, would represent those persons.

A lumber dealer:

We always associated with the officials in the mine, and as far as social contacts were concerned, we associated with them more than with the other merchants in town. You see, the town was pretty well isolated and our family couldn't go to the saloons or to the whorehouses, so there was no place to go and nothing to do except to associate with others like us. Our family was hard put to find such people in this community.

An upper-class view of the present:

These families who are the leaders are those who have been here for a long time. I would say about twenty years. They would be business peo-ple, professional people, people like us here in this room. In fact, we are the leaders.

Interaction between class levels was limited and confined to par-ticular social situations. A middle-class miner:

The men would mix, for instance, at a bowling alley in which a banker would bowl next to a coal miner but they would not mix at home nor would their wives associate with each other, nor would they entertain each other in their homes. You see, all of these other groups would sort of stay together and they didn't mix much with us. I think that those who were at the top were friends of most of the people of the community, but I think they wouldn't have just anyone over for dinner to eat with them, but just some special friends of their own.

When members of the upper class mixed, they engaged in the same activities. An upper-class male:

There were many bridge parties here and the Company and management organized a bridge club. We used to play cards, go to church together, have clubs and lodges in which the people would associate, and there would be calling back and forth, and visiting. I would say that the members of the upper class used to play bridge together instead of going to the pool hall. They used to throw drinking parties at home rather than in the local pub. They would go for a weekend somewhere, such as a hotel, and they used to have many guests in their homes.

One merchant in the upper class, who was particularly status conscious, preferred mining executives to other merchants. In this regard it is well to remember that a merchant's affiliation with mining management invariably brought "checkoff" privileges with it. The "checkoff" was a system whereby the mining company withheld some of the miner's pay each week which the miner owed to a merchant.

Native upper-class male organizations. Membership in social clubs and fraternal orders was symbolic of class membership. The most preferred native upper-class organization was the Rotary Club. Our informants reported that membership in the Rotary Club was restricted to certain persons in prestige occupations. Membership was desirable if one wished to get ahead.

There were many social cliques in the community and if a man wanted to get ahead, I think it would have been best for him to join the Rotary Club. That was the top group.

Members were selected carefully.

The Rotary Club was limited. Sometimes there was a big hassle in the clubs when tavern keepers wanted to get in, and there was a great deal of discussion and argument. Some of the people wanted to bring the tavern keepers in since they were a business.

One native with aspirations said:

I could work my way in with this top group, I feel. I could join them in
the Rotary Club. In fact, I have had not just one invitation to join the
Rotary Club but several to join. I could drink with them. Some of them
are heavy drinkers, not all of them. They have their social activities
together and I think that if I really worked at it, I could work up into
this group. Now, not everyone can do this but I think that I personally
could.

Native upper-class female organizations. The most preferred
group for the upper-class native women was the sorority. Persons
were selected on the basis of the occupation of one's husband and
the prospective member's personal reputation. Personal reputation
included: absence of heavy drinking, attendance at church, and
"proper" relationships with the opposite sex. In this latter respect,
upper-class female behavior approximates the conventional, middle-
class female behavior usually expected in larger communities. It is
especially interesting to note that in this community, within recent
years, both upper- and middle-class women, in an attempt to dissociate themselves from some of the past community history, have
identified themselves with conventional middle-class standards of
sexual morality.

We do not let women of low moral character into these organizations. I
think that heavy drinking would keep a person out of these women's
clubs. We know just about who to ask to join the clubs, but we are very
careful in the persons we ask. I don't know how to explain this but a
person sort of feels, or he sort of knows, who to ask and who not to ask.

Membership in the sorority was restricted.

We had a young woman here who was the wife of a very young mining
engineer, who was a member of the club, and she made the remark one
time at the club that she certainly didn't want any dirty miner's wife in
this club. Well, that got out, you know how it is here in a small community.

Membership could also be controlled this way:

Now, in these organizations it takes only one vote to blackball a member
from getting in. Now, some people who are already in the organization
may vote against someone else, that is, blackball them, just because of a

personal resentment or jealousy. This is one way in which the women get revenge on other women in the community.

THE NATIVE MIDDLE CLASS

The native middle class in Coal Town consisted of teachers, public officials, small merchants, office personnel, clerks, and skilled, regularly employed workers. Our informants described them as upright, honest, law-abiding citizens *concerned with their families* and with a great deal of interest in the church. Although there were many patterns of inconsistency with respect to these virtues, our data suggest that at least certain sections of the middle class were concerned with the development of a stable community. Middle-class informants were more likely to describe themselves in terms of *behavior* (ethics and morality) rather than in terms of *occupation* or *personal power*. A middle-class informant sees his class this way:

The middle class, I would say, is composed of some pretty nice people. They mingle together in order to play cards. Some are in business and some work in the mines. I think that the deciding factor here is whether or not you are honest and whether or not you treat people right. I think this is more important than what your occupation is. There are persons here that tried to make it a better community. These are the ones I mean.

Miners were members of the middle class as well as of the lower class. In addition to occupational skill, the essential difference between the middle- and the lower-class miner was given as follows:

Now a miner in the middle class and a miner in the lower class would be different. The difference would be in how they felt about their families. There would be different habits that the men would have; and I would say that the miners in the lower class just did not care about their families.

The "strivers" were in this middle class. A merchant:

There is a tremendous striving among some of these people to get ahead. In other words, the attitude is expressed often in this store here when customers come in and say, "Well, can I get a refrigerator or stove that is bigger than the one the Joneses got here last week?" And they already know what he got and they want something that is bigger or better.

Native middle-class male organizations. Middle- and lower-middle-class male organizations in Coal Town included the Masons, the Elks, the Moose, the Eagles, the American Legion, and several smaller organizations. None was so important as the upper-class Rotary Club for affording prestige to its members. One middle-class informant made this observation:

Anyone can get into the Eagles or the Moose if they want to join. To get ahead you have to join the Rotary Club, and you can go to the Eagles for your beer. There is a different kind of people in the Eagles Club.

Middle-class male recreation consisted of hunting and fishing trips. The main recreational outlets for middle-class women were the church and lodge. A middle-class male:

I would say that the recreation and the leisure time of the middle class would be that the fellows fish. They buy boats and trailers and do some hunting. The women stay at home and are active in church work. I would say that the middle class is also active in Eastern Star activities.

Native middle-class female organizations. The social organizations in which the majority of middle-class women in Coal Town participate are described by a middle-class woman:

There is another level of clubs, the middle level, and these I would say would be composed of the Rebeccas, the Eastern Stars, the Junior Women's Club, and the Royal Neighbors. I used to belong to the Maccabees and the Pythian Sisters but I dropped out of those and now I belong to the Rebecca Lodge. My close friends in the lodges are wives of miners who worked on the top, not who worked in the bottom.

For the younger women, the Junior Women's Club affords the greatest prestige.

I'm a member of the Junior Women's Club. I'm satisfied with that. That is my level in keeping with my finances. It costs much more money to get into the sorority. I could get in with the sorority, though, if I wanted to or if I was willing to spend that money, but I don't want to spend that much money. Now, my husband has been asked to join the Rotary Club but he figures that he cannot afford it as yet.

Some feel that membership in the Junior Women's Club is more selective than in the upper-class sorority.

We are kind of select in the Junior Women's Club. You see, most of us are girls who were raised here. We never went in for running around or for bad things like that, but we were pretty nice girls when we grew up. A newcomer is usually invited to join these clubs when she comes into the community and when we have time to look her over. The Junior Women's Club is a little bit more selective than the sorority. The women who belong to the sorority think that they are on top, but we have some women here that the sororities take that we wouldn't take in our Junior Women's Club organization.

THE NATIVE LOWER CLASS

The native lower-class people were on the lowest rung of the social ladder, even in comparison with the immigrant lower class. The native lower class was singled out by our informants to be those who worked irregularly and those who appeared to be indifferent to the needs of their families. Many were miners with a minimum of skill. Others were without any regular occupation. Informants from other social classes identified them as lazy, shiftless drunkards, who were dirty and unkempt and who mistreated their wives and children. A middle-class male:

There was a lower class who didn't care about owning anything and who were always on relief. They didn't care about going to church, and they spent most of their time going to taverns. We have about fifty families here that I would not care to make a loan to. I think there are about that many families in this community that are worthless.

An upper-class male:

We also have some here who are in the lower crust, that is, the lower grade of people. They're sloppy and their homes are sloppy, and around their house. Some of them neglect their kids and they're drinkers and they're filthy, immoral characters. We don't care about them at all and they don't seem to care about their family.

The members of the native lower class were drawn from those natives of the area who failed to make an adequate adjustment to mining; and also from the Southern migrant miner. The Southern migrant miner constituted the largest section of the lower class. The Southerners were intensely disliked by the native from the area, as well as by the immigrant. For the more privileged classes, there

was the resentment about the Southerner's personal habits. For the
native from the area, the Southerners were outsiders with whom
they were in economic competition. For the immigrant, there was
the resentment about the Southerner's prejudice against immigrants.
A merchant:

I would say there was another group of persons in the community from
the Deep South. This was the illiterate group who was very biased in
many areas, particularly in religion. Their attitude toward work was not
good. They were not very good workers. There was a great amount of
absenteeism and these people would take off whenever they felt like it;
they just wanted to get by.

The son of an immigrant:

There were a bunch of native Alabamans who came up here. There was a
big conflict between them and the foreigners. We called them the "shoeless ones" because they didn't wear shoes and they were always filthy and
dirty.

There were no social clubs or lodges for the native lower class,
either male or female. There were no recreational patterns for lower-
class females.

For recreation, the lower-class male liked to drink in taverns.
Like the native middle-class male, the lower-class male hunted and
fished. The lower-class male put greater value on hunting and fishing than the middle-class male. However, the lower-class male
hunted locally and with little equipment; he fished in streams
stocked with carp, buffalo fish, and bullheads. These species of
fish were low prestige foods to the other native classes.

THE IMMIGRANT CLASS STRUCTURE

The values of the natives' system of social class were incorporated into the social class orientations of the immigrants. In spite
of the immigrants' overt resentment of natives, there was an identification with their values. Occupation and economic power were
most significant in the immigrant class structure, followed closely
by nationality, personal habits and customs, the ability to speak
English, wealth, and education. Especially important was the tend-

ency for the immigrants to take over the significance of personal habits (for example, cleanliness) in the evaluation of their own group.

THE IMMIGRANT UPPER CLASS

Although disliked by the non-English-speaking immigrants, the English, Irish, and Welsh miners occupied an upper-class position owing to several factors. These included their economic power in supervisory mining positions, as well as their positions as union leaders. The fact that they spoke the English language facilitated greatly their ability to maintain their favorable class position. All of these factors made it possible for them to control mining jobs in Coal Town.

The Scotch, the English, and the Welsh came over here as top management and top union officials. They were the bosses and they had a lot to say about who got the jobs.

Some of the English-speaking immigrant miners could have moved to the native upper class without great difficulty. They seldom did this, however, preferring to maintain their powerful position in the immigrant group. A native upper-class resident:

There is some difficulty about placing the English on this scale because the English could cross the line, either on one side or the other, but not the immigrant [non-English-speaking]. If the English were placed on the immigrant side, he would be at the top, but he was just as apt to be placed on the native side and in that case he would be near the top, but not on the top.

The English-speaking immigrant miner tended to give an overly favorable view of life in the community. Our opinion, that he had a status to protect, was confirmed by this tendency. An upper-class native:

I would say this, why they would give an overly favorable picture is that the English in the Old Country were just plain nothing when they came over here. Over here, they were treated with some respect. They have fared very well, comparatively speaking. Their position in the community has been tremendous compared to what they had in England. That is their big point.

THE IMMIGRANT MIDDLE CLASS

The immigrant middle class was composed of small merchants and skilled miners who came from non-English-speaking countries in different sections of Europe. The few from Finland ranked high in the middle class. A merchant:

After the English came the few Finlanders. The Italians and Slavic elements were somewhat together. The Serbians and Croatians were next. Then Lithuanians, Polacks, and Russians.

THE IMMIGRANT LOWER CLASS

The immigrant lower class consisted of Central and Southern Europeans defined as unkempt and irresponsible by their own groups as well as by middle- and upper-class natives. Here especially we see the values of the native middle class becoming manifest. The son of an immigrant:

Why, the lowest group among the immigrants would be the Russians and the Lithuanians because they were personally dirty. Why, they would go to the toilet even under the house despite the fact that they had a place to go to the toilet in the back of the house.

Many of the immigrants who became members of the lower class lost identification with their own groups and were never integrated with the native group. These were downwardly mobile people who usually had suffered a great personal tragedy in the loss of family members; others were immersed in culture conflict. In these cases demoralization was often the end result. An immigrant's son:

There were some European immigrants in that class, too; those who became distant. That is, they pulled away from the church and the lodge; and this happened to men especially when their wives died, that the men lost their tie with the church and with religion and usually when that happened they really slipped. I can recall that some of the immigrants fell from their higher places to a much lower place in the community.

The son of an immigrant:

There was in this country a tendency for the immigrant to abandon the church. The natives pulled us away from the church. They were interested in doing this. In addition, there was some disillusionment with the church because the dollar displaced the church. I can remember when I was a boy, we ran around in packs or gangs; we were away from religion.

IMMIGRANT MOBILITY INTO THE NATIVE CLASS STRUCTURE

Although the English-speaking immigrant could move with the native upper class with relative ease, the non-English-speaking immigrant encountered much more difficulty in moving into the social classes of the native. He could, however, change his position more easily within his own class structure. Acceptance into the native social classes was possible when the immigrant mastered the language and was able to assimilate. An upper-class native male:

Ordinarily the immigrants could not mix with the upper- or middle-class natives for the simple reason that they would not have been accepted. If he did, it would be because of manners.

An immigrant miner indicates the importance of language:

The immigrant could get a better job if he had an education; but the immigrant did not know how to use the language and so he could not get an education; and since he could not get an education he would have to remain working underneath the ground in the mines.

The immigrant could move into a native social class through intermarriage with a native. The native parent, however, usually disapproved of daughters and sons marrying the "furriner." A native woman:

The native parents thought it was a step down if their children married immigrants and they usually said, "We couldn't do anything about it." They indicated that they didn't particularly like it. Some foreigners thought intermarriage was good and some thought that it was not so good.

Immigrant parents generally did not look with favor upon such marriages. Often the immigrant who became involved in intermarriage encountered the resentment of both groups. An immigrant's son:

Now, in the case of a person that tries to get from one class to another, take the immigrant for example, he might be tolerated by the upper group but he would earn the resentment of his own group when he tries to pull out of it. He lost his place with his own group. He was never at home in the upper group. You see, if a fellow just had an immigrant name, it would go hard for him. That was all you needed.

Residential patterning according to class was somewhat haphazard. There were, however, two areas which were distinctly recognizable to our informants as belonging to particular groups. These were the upper-class area and a segregated area where the immigrants lived. An early settler noted this:

Most of the immigrants came here as single individuals. Most of them were not married. These fellows were set up in six-room apartments. Usually a married couple would take charge of an apartment and take in as many as a dozen boarders. They lived in one part of town. All the company officials lived in the wooded section on the north side of town there. They lived entirely apart from the rest of us.

A middle-class native describes the neighborhood of the upper class:

I can remember that Central Street was owned by the mining company and all the people who lived there were company people. They had more money and more recognition than anybody else in the community. There is an upper crust group, or a silk stocking group, that lives over there on South Central Street.

An upper-class native:

I would say that the upper-class families are those that live on Central Street. They are, however, sort of mixed in with some of the middle class on these streets.

A lower-class native observed this:

Well, you know, there is a different class of people, yeah. There wasn't over ten or fifteen at the time. I know they had the saucers and stuff like that. They sort of stuck together; I believe they are that way yet. All their homes are right there on Central Street.

The immigrant lived elsewhere. An immigrant presents his reaction to assimilation:

They are all the same to me. We got some in our nationality and they wouldn't even live in this neighborhood because they think this is the old foreign neighborhood. They want to move into where, they say, a better class of people live. I tried to talk to some of them in Croatian and they wouldn't talk to me, they wanted to talk American. The next time they had some trouble then they would talk to me.

Religion and the Class Structure [2]

The development of organized religion and certain dimensions of social class were intimately related. It is pertinent, therefore, to examine in detail the nature of this relationship. During the early history of the community, social class as a factor in religious organization had minimum importance. Those with economic power and prestige had no consistent affiliation with any particular church. As well-defined classes emerged, however, church groups with social classes having power relations developed.

The Upper-Class Native Church

The majority of upper-class native people belonged to the Southern Evangelical Church, which in Coal Town has always possessed a strong fundamentalist orientation. Some changes in doctrine have occurred, but these stemmed from the initiative of a particular minister rather than from the congregation. The Southern Evangelical Church was, from the very first, the most powerful religious organization in the community.

Right after the 1920s the Evangelicals began to grow and now the most prominent church is the Evangelical Church.

As the years progressed the church grew in prestige and attracted members from other churches.

At the present time the Southern Evangelical Church is the largest and the most active church in the community. It has a total of 517 members and enjoys the highest prestige of any church in the community. The banker, the leading merchants, and the mine superintendent are active members of the church.

A Methodist:

I would say that the upper-class part of them went to the Southern Evangelical Church.

An informant, not a member of the Evangelical Church:

The best class in town—that is, the teachers, the bankers, and the merchants—were attending the Evangelical Church then; and today there

[2] See Appendix E concerned with religion in the early, coal camp days.

would be those same people, I guess, and a lot more. I can't recall what
the church has done here for the community, but there are a lot of individuals in it that stand out.

An Evangelical:

Most high-class people attend the Evangelical Church. We have, for example, the leading merchant, the mine superintendent, the mine surveyor.
These men live up in those big houses on Central Street. All of these people belong.

The members of the Southern Evangelical Church in Coal Town
have always actively tried to attract certain persons. An upper-class
resident who did not belong reported this:

I had a lot of pressure put on me to join the Evangelical Church but I did
not. The Evangelical Church asked me many times and I told them that
I have my own religion and though I do not attend church I belong to the
church in H———. I go up there once or twice a year. I think they have
respect for me since I did not give in and join the church. I remember one
time that they had a church census here a few years ago and the Evangelicals wanted to find out who were members and who were not and
then they started to work on the people who were not church members.
The Evangelical Church is the strongest now.

In proselyting lower-class people the assumption of converting
those who were morally inferior was pronounced. A member of the
Evangelical Church:

There are three or four of us girls who go out and visit these lower-class
women and try to get them interested to coming to the church. Whenever
we can think of such a person, we usually put her name down on a list
and then when we have time we go out and visit her. Sometimes we go
twice or three times a month on such visits. You see, we feel that it would
be on our conscience if we didn't try to lift these people up from their low
level.

Whether lower-class people would have been acceptable as members in this church remains a question.

THE SOUTHERN EVANGELICAL CHURCH AND ECONOMIC POWER

Our data suggest that during the major part of this community's
history the organized religious bodies, owing to their nonworldly
orientation, had little to do with actively promoting beneficial social

changes in the community. Their approach was one of imposing restraints on conduct considered unacceptable. Further, there is some evidence for the belief that Southern Evangelical members received economic and social benefits not extended to members of other churches. Such a development was possible since mining and business leaders were affiliated with the Southern Evangelical Church.

The mine officials belong to our church, the mine superintendent is a very active member. I would say that the strongest church in the community is the Evangelical Church. The Evangelicals are the big power and this is particularly true in Coal Town today.

It was also the opinion of our informants that it was possible for the economic leaders who were members of the Southern Evangelical Church to control not only internal church organization but the jobs of members in the community, as well as the direction of community change. With respect to the internal church organization, one former church member pointed this out:

You take, for example, the case of Smith, the mine superintendent. He moved in here and took over. The church consults with him before they do anything. Then he got into the Rotary Club and he took that over. He is always the head man in everything.

A woman who was formerly a member:

Why, you should see how they do when Mr. Smith comes into the church —about half of the members move over and sit by him. Why, it's a disgrace. The minister has to take orders from him. There is a big turnover here because some of the ministers feel not too good about this situation and when they say something they are forced to leave.

Our informants reported economic coercion, especially during the declining years of the mining industry. In speaking of one economic leader, an informant said:

In order to get ahead the people should belong to his church. He asks them to come to church and if they did not come, he would take their jobs away from them. That is why most of the mine officials belong to the Evangelical Church. He controls all the labor in this town and can hire and fire anybody.

Many of our informants indicated that it was possible for the Evangelical Church to control an election. We were unable to ascertain the truth of such an assertion.

You see, there is a group here that works behind the scene. The membership in the Evangelical Church can win any election they want to.

THE CHURCHES OF THE NATIVE MIDDLE CLASS

The Methodist Church and the Christian Church were churches of the middle class. Their power in the community was never great, and at present both are in a state of rapid decline. The minister of the Methodist Church, speaking of the membership, said:

I would say the bulk of the membership is the working people. I would say the largest group are the coal miners. We have one man who operates a garage. We have the undertaker, and we also have a school principal and his family and some teachers. The middle-class people go to the Christian Church and the Methodist Church.

THE CHURCHES OF THE NATIVE LOWER CLASS: THE NAZARENE; THE APOSTOLIC

For many years the lower socioeconomic groups of Coal Town were extremely dissatisfied with the churches that were controlled by the middle and upper classes. In part their dissatisfaction stemmed from what seemed to them to be deviations from scriptural teachings. Many reported that sermons deviated greatly from the Bible. Others felt that the churches tolerated conduct which was not in keeping with religious teachings. Still others believed that these churches were making too many accommodations to worldly pleasures. Finally, and most significant in view of our data, was the feeling on the part of the lower social class people that their presence in these middle- and upper-class churches was not really welcomed. They believed they were shunned because of their dress, personal habits, and inadequate speech. This rejection they intensely resented.

We attempted to analyze the stated motivations for the dissatisfaction of these lower socioeconomic people. Since the native Protestant churches in Coal Town were all fundamentalist in orientation, the assertion on the part of our informants that their dissatisfaction stemmed from the deviations in scriptural teachings turned out to be superficial.[3]

Although the upper- and middle-class churches made some modifications, we were informed that changes in *basic religious doctrine* were minimal. All of this led us to the conclusion that these lower social class people were part of the old native group, who had never really accepted industrialization and the changes with which it was associated. Further, these people felt essentially inadequate in social groups which were economically and socially more secure. The basic factor in their withdrawl from the upper-class churches of Coal Town stemmed from these class differences rather than from a basic difference in religious doctrine.[4]

In 1938 the Nazarene Church was organized, followed by the Apostolic Church in 1945. A merchant:

The Nazarene and Apostolic churches grew from the old-time residents and from membership in the other churches. They tend to be very poor economically and I would say that the members are much poorer than those in the Methodist and Christian churches. They are very small churches. I myself do not see how these groups get along.

A Methodist:

I don't know much about these little churches. It's all right, I guess, if you want to go to these churches, if you live right. They have a woman minister in the Apostolic Church. They are doing some good down there. You see, there are always some people that feel more comfortable down there than they do in our churches. Somehow or other they don't feel too well when they come into church and see the other people. Now, of course, they are just as good as anybody else but this makes them feel uneasy. Well, these little churches, like that, take these people in. The poor element go down there. We don't have this attitude, though, toward these people. We don't feel that they are low-down. It's their own self-consciousness. You see, they feel they are lower down.

[3] Cf. William W. Sweet, *Religion in Colonial America* (New York, Charles Scribner's Sons, 1942), Chapter 9.
[4] Cf. William W. Sweet, *The Story of Religion in America* (New York, Harper and Brothers, 1950), Chapter 21.

How the Nazarenes started; one version:

I belong to the Church of the Nazarene. There wasn't many belonged to this church to start with. It closed down for two or three years. Well, I will tell you that I heard a fellow say one time that there was two neighbors lived together and one of them had a wheelbarrow. He threw it away piece by piece as it wore out. This neighbor would pick it up. Finally, he had it all throwed away and his neighbor made a good one out of it. That's the way the Nazarenes started.

How the Nazarene minister came:

The Nazarene Church has been here for about ten years but the doors were closed for about seven of those ten years. Brother W——, we call him Brother rather than Reverend, works part time and is the pastor of the church. You see, there are only a few paying members and they give him groceries and money but that isn't enough to keep him and his family so he has to work. We have the best attendance on Sundays; we don't have no trouble getting members. The church has geen knocked so much that many people are afraid to become members. They figure once they got it, they figure it might close up again and they wouldn't have any place to go. The pastor what we have came in from —— one day. It was very interesting how it happened. He came by Coal Town and he saw the church and he noticed that it was closed; so he went down the road but he didn't get very far because he said he just couldn't get that church out of his mind. So he came back here and looked at it again and the Lord opened his heart and he said that he was supposed to be the pastor of this church. That was the way it happened.

The members of the Nazarene and Apostolic churches, to be sure, focused on differences in religious doctrine. A Methodist:

I do know that if you are a member of that church, you have to be very strict. I think that it is too strict for most people, that Nazarene Church. You see, you can believe in other religions and not be so strict but you have to be strict in the Nazarene religion. For example, there is no smoking. The true Nazarene will not show their arms or their legs. They will wear no jewelry, not even a wedding ring, unless it serves a purpose. You cannot wear any jewelry. Now, you can wear a watch because it tells you what time of day it is. You can never cut your hair, that is for the women, and I think the membership is very limited because of this. You see, you have to completely change your ways if you belong to that church and not many people are willing to do that.

Some Nazarenes pointed to this:

The Nazarene is a lot closer to the Bible than most of the other churches and this don't suit most of the people because they had rather have their pleasures and belong to a church that don't make much difference. I can remember my daughter one time was collecting money for the church and she went to a filling station and there was a good Evangelical and he said, "Well, how much did I give you last year?" She said, "You gave me a dime." He said, "Well, I'll give you two dimes this year." She said, "Well, I don't think that's a very Christian thing for you to be doing to be playing checkers, you see."

Other Nazarenes remarked on these inconsistencies:

We have had some good Christians here in this community and we have had some good bootleggers. You see, so many of the people wanted to be both—that is, they wanted to be Christians and they wanted to be bootleggers. Now, as quick as they leave the church, you see, they smoke. Why, I can remember going by one day that you couldn't hardly see the people for the smoke outside the church. Why, if they got religion they would be cleaned up and they wouldn't do things like that.

Proper living was stressed.

A lot of people think that they are going to heaven and they are going to miss it by a country block. Now, I live right and I don't believe in backbiting other people. We live according to the Bible.

In our opinion, however, these religious differences between the members of the Nazarene and Apostolic churches and other native Protestant churches were employed by the former group as compensations for the inadequacies they felt. By pointing to their religions and themselves as being *morally superior* and different, they were able to construct a feeling of superiority over those who were economically and socially secure. Nevertheless, in spite of their alleged moral superiority, the Nazarene and Apostolic members were no more tolerant toward other churches than the other churches were toward them. In turning our attention to what appeared to us to be the more basic reasons for the rejection of the middle- and upper-class Protestant churches we note the references to social rejection which were voiced by lower-class people. One informant commented on the matter of dress:

The Evangelical Church used to be friendly here but now the people would snarl up their nose at you if you got to the church in overalls. They make all sorts of comments about you and about your clothes if you are not well dressed. I call them "mutts" up there. It's been that way in the Evangelical Church for a long time. You see, the minister up there has certain picks, certain ones that he goes to see. I know that many of the people who change from the Evangelical to the Nazarene Church are often people who are afraid that they do not dress well enough to attend the Evangelical Church.

Another informant mentioned the element of unfriendliness:

We used to go to this Evangelical Church but it was just like walking in an icehouse. It was so cold and nobody paid any attention to you. Our church is friendly and the people down there don't think that they are better than anyone else. Up in the Evangelical Church they show off their clothes.

A member of the Evangelical Church:

Many say that the Evangelical Church is an upper-class church and they would not like to come because they would not feel comfortable. Well, I think that after you get to the church building, there is no class. Now some may feel out of place. I guess that would be true because our members are big dressers.

A Nazarene points out the friendlier air of his church:

We have got the name of not being so snotty in the Nazarene Church. We visit longer after services. We stop and talk longer. Seems like to me we are a little closer to one another. Well, that is just a fellow's personality. A fellow in a Nazarene Church could dress any way he pleases on Sunday. I heard one remark made by an evangelist that he was told to never unbutton his coat in one of those other churches. He is in the Church of the Nazarene now. He didn't like that idea. I am like that, too.

One Nazarene anticipates the future:

I don't know what these Evangelicals are going to do in heaven because there are going to be some Nazarenes up there and somehow or other they are all going to get together. It will really be a lot of fun to see how they act up there when those things take place.

ATTITUDES TOWARD THE LOWER-CLASS CHURCHES

The majority of our informants, from the middle and upper classes, looked upon the churches of the lower class with a mixture of humor and contempt. The people were identified as emotional and unstable. Some of our informants responded this way:

We don't go for these small churches here in Coal Town and there are not many people that are members of them. I don't know why they aren't too popular here, though, they don't have too many people going. I guess this is a different method of religion altogether. They get excited and they shout and things like that. It's not too dignified. The poor people don't have good clothes and they feel that they don't have to dress up when they go to those kinds of churches. They say that if you go to the other churches here, you have to get all fixed up, and if you don't get fixed up, then the people don't know you at all. I guess they would be afraid to come to our church or to the Methodist or to the Christian Church.

A near disaster:

This Nazarene Church down here is just like a show. We call them Holy Rollers and they put on some pretty good shows. They get up and confess. I remember when one old woman down here, some time ago, she was the town whore, joined the church. Well, she got up there and started confessing and she began to point out some of the men that visited her and she got to calling names and pointing to the men, and they were sitting right there in the congregation. Well, you should have seen them go. Some of the men got down on their all fours and sneaked out from the church. They stopped her before she could call the minister's name, which I am pretty sure that he had been over to see her. That was the funniest thing I can remember.

Another description:

They felt that there was a class of people here in Coal Town that wanted these services. We call them Holy Rollers. I can remember one incident and that was a man who worked for me down at the lumber company by the name of N——. This man said that he had been to a meeting at what we call the Bugtussle Church in 1921 or '22 and he described them as having a wonderful meeting; and the people were all speaking in strange tongues. Three or four people were rolling on the floor at once and men and women would fling themselves around. They had no control over their bodies. He thought it was a wonderful thing. He said that it made you feel close to God. Well, I was interested in what he had to say and I mumbled some mumbo jumbo and I said, "Well, how is that, N——?" He said, "Well, I didn't know that you could speak in strange tongues." Well, I just gave you that as an example to show you how ignorant that people were here and what nonsense could be put over on them any time anybody wanted to.

The Church of the Immigrant Upper Class

Most of the upper-class immigrants were members of the Episcopal Church, established in 1927. Membership was confined to a small number of English immigrants who established for themselves a favorable economic position in Coal Town. Nevertheless, the church itself never appeared to occupy a position of economic power in the community. It served largely as an integrating force in the life of the English miner. The establishment of the Episcopal Church is described:

When we first come here the English people didn't have a church to go to and they was trying to start a little Episcopal Church and they held their meetings in the basement of the Methodist Church on Sunday afternoons. They held their meetings in the City Hall, too. Then they built this little church. It was a portable building and it was shipped down from up East, piece by piece. A bishop from the Eastern states started it. The men of the church built it themselves.

The Episcopal Church has been closed since 1954. The members now drive to the county seat for Sunday religious services. Its most active years were from 1930 to 1945 and its peak membership was composed of fifty-two families. One of its charter members describes the present situation as follows:

As you know, the church still stands and could be used, but there are so few members that we cannot operate. After 1945 it was a losing battle. Most all of the members left and there are only nine of the original families still here and we are all old folks. We have to drive to the county seat for services. There were just us English families who belonged and we didn't get any new members.

The Church of the Middle- and Lower-Class Immigrant

With the exception of some Irish who were part of the upper class, the immigrant middle and lower class belonged to the Catholic Church. Some of our informants indicated that the Catholic Church exercised control over community affairs, but the writer was unable to verify this assertion. This church exhibited from the first a greater concern for community affairs than any of the Protestant churches.

Many Protestant informants, in spite of their prejudices, reported that the Catholic priests were known for their broad interests in the community and the personal problems of the people. The Catholic Church appeared to be more aware of the recreational needs of youth and more lenient toward the cultural pattern of drinking, which was pronounced among large sections of the populace. Such acceptance of worldly pleasure was a source of resentment on the part of the native Protestant churches. A Catholic informant:

The Catholic Church started in 1919. It was the most liberal church in the community and is even so today. It was very powerful with the immigrant group. The reason for this was that the priest was a very unusual person. He saw good in everyone. He opened up his basement in the church to young people for entertainment, and this meant for young people from other churches as well. He did not say that only the Catholic boys could use the church. The church basement was used for such things as games, parties, dances, playing cards, meetings of clubs for boys and girls, religious clubs, sports, and the tennis courts were open near the church for everyone. The Father furnished equipment for everyone and he expected all of the kids to work and help take care of their share of the work that needed to be done around the church or in the basement. This tore down a lot of prejudiced feelings of persons toward each other. The Father set a very fine example by helping anyone in distress. I can remember that people from other churches would come to him with their problems which they could not take to their own ministers.

THE PRESENT

The existence of social classes is still a reality in Coal Town. Class differences, perpetuated over the years, brought resentments which are not easily forgotten and which have been transmitted to the youth. Thus, interaction between members of different class levels is still limited to certain civic and public affairs rather than encompassing intimate personal interaction. However, some change is noted in the fact that at least one Southern European immigrant has become a member of the upper class. In the past, upper-class affiliation was associated with definite economic benefits. Today what remains is the enjoyment derived from the possession of power and prestige.

There is no money to be gained here if you are a leader in the community. It is only prestige and power.

What was once a struggle for power between mining management and labor no longer exists. This has now been replaced by another struggle—a personal fight for power among the remaining elements of the upper class. Our upper-class informants were critical of others in their class:

I think, though, that Mr. Smith tries to publicize himself too much. All the time he wants to get his picture in the paper. Sometimes George, the leading merchant, and Smith get along and other times they do not. You see, George used to be the real leader in the community and he associated with the mine officials. When they pulled out, he was left high and dry and does not like this new position. He also drinks quite a bit. He drinks more now than he used to. I think that being left alone bothers him a great deal.

Another upper-class informant has this view of the members of his class:

There are a lot of mixed feelings here about this man Smith. Some think he's good, some think he's bad. Well, you see, we still aren't working with him. He is stepping overboard a bit, I think. Others think that he is doing wonderful. Smith is considered pretty good too, by some, but by me, no. You see, he is not a very good type of person. He's too conceited. He has no mercy on his employees, or his children, or his wife. He drinks much more than is tolerated in this community. Now, on the other hand, his wife is a very wonderful person. I think if she were running the store, it would be an entirely different picture. Anthony is considered as a leader, but he is not too well liked. He is too conservative. They say here that if you want to borrow a nickel from him, you have to have five dollars for security. He did not get as far as he should have, somehow or other, he doesn't mix well. You see, he has been at the bank so long that he sits back, and many other people go forward. I think it's just his personality, though, he is a member of the Evangelical Church. There were so many here of the upper class who left and there are very few, if any, left of what I would really call the upper class.

SUMMARY

Social class divisions are recognized as phenomena of the small, as well as the large, community. In this small community, social differences were apparent from the first and they manifested themselves in a well-defined system of social classes. The ingredients of this system of social classes included basic values which arose out of the way of life which characterized the community. Thus, in effect social classes became a means of entrenching the value order which was already present. We observe, for example, that where one belonged with respect to *ethnic background* became a factor in the stratification of these people. We note, also, that people are ranked according to their ability to control and exert economic power, as well as their differences based on personal habits, occupation, wealth, and education. These community values likewise affect church membership; they played an important role in determining which church people were affiliated with, as well as the power of a particular church in the community.

Underlying the entire system of social classes were certain basic community feelings. There were the envy and resentment of the underprivileged groups toward the upper classes and the contempt on the part of the more privileged classes toward the lower classes. Although we have concerned ourselves with questions of social differences, both here and elsewhere, we shall in the chapter to follow synthesize the similarities which characterized the community as we deal with the questions of themes and values.

CHAPTER **11**

LIFE IN COAL TOWN: THEMES AND VALUES

IN preceding chapters we have analyzed the general patterns of social life as they evolved in Coal Town. At this point we turn our attention to the effects of such patterns on persons living in these surroundings. We therefore raise what is, from our point of view, one of the central questions of the entire analysis, "What occurs to the human personality when it is nurtured in a social climate of the character we have described?" Is there a common orientation to life, a core of themes and values present in those who have lived in Coal Town? We believe that a common orientation does exist and it becomes manifest in these themes and values:[1] *impersonality, self-effacement, isolation* and *separation, conformity, anti-intellectualism, resignation, cynicism,* and *suspicion.*

Our data suggest that in spite of *cultural differences,* certain basic life views characterize native and immigrant, and these are also to be found in the personalities of their children. Such a statement may seem contradictory in view of the time spent in stressing differences between native and immigrant. Nevertheless, we wish to point out that the differences between these broad cultural groups were apparent only in particular phases of cultural life. The native and immigrant, for example, differed in attitudes toward work, food, and religion. At deeper levels, however, both the native and immigrant held certain values in common. Each possessed tendencies toward *impersonality, self-effacement, superstition, separation* from others, and a pronounced belief in *conformity* to their respective

[1] We have included a discussion of those themes and values which are pronounced at this time. Others, such as violence, are unimportant now but could presumably become important in the future.

group. Each group tended to resist change, to be *suspicious,* and each manifested marked *anti-intellectual* tendencies.[2] The most significant factor which created a similar core of themes and values was the ongoing interpersonal experiences between native and immigrant. Patterns that were partially rooted in both groups prior to their experiences in Coal Town were accentuated by interpersonal life. Here we note that many facets of the native-immigrant conflict, the economic deprivation, and other community phenomena contributed significantly to patterns of suspiciousness, fear, and rumor. These phenomena tended to nurture and accent similar themes and values in both groups. Natives and immigrants each had different perceptions of the other group. Each saw the other as being alien and therefore peculiar. They became mutually antagonistic because of these differences, and yet out of the sum total of human relationships between the two groups profound similarities appear.

Thus we note that *certain basic similarities, historically present in both native and immigrant,* as well as *the interpersonal life of the community,* contributed to a set of life views which characterized these people in the past and persists today.

THE MAJOR ORIENTATIONS OF COAL TOWN PEOPLE

IMPERSONALITY

When summarizing life in Coal Town, we note that for the vast majority of residents life has been characterized by a quality of marked impersonality. We employ the term "impersonality" in the more general sense of identifying human relationships which are devoid of warmth, empathy, or respect and where human personalities are viewed as commodities to be used or manipulated. These qualities of human interaction which clearly have been pervasive in the life of the total community are reflected in our data.

In conversations with our informants we noted *constant refer-*

---

[2] The reader is reminded at this point that both groups were traumatized prior to industrialization. Both native and immigrant groups came out of economically impoverished circumstances and both had traditionally been unsuccessful in changing their social status.

ences to things rather than to people. One of the few intellectuals we encountered identified his orientation by saying:

Books to me are important. People are not.

Much greater interest was shown in physical structures in the community than in people and their problems. When members of the community were discussed the context was usually derogatory.

The quality of interpersonal life. Human relationships in Coal Town were and are characterized by a flagrant disregard for the feelings of others. One forty-eight-year-old informant reported this from the past:

There were a lot of strong emotions in those days. No one worried about making friends or influencing people. I was downright plain rude and I ignored a lot of people. It made them mad at me and some of them have never forgotten it.

There was little empathy for the person who encountered misfortune. A merchant recalled:

You see, if you got hurt or something happened in the community, say you were down in the tavern and you got killed or hurt, then the community would say this, that you had not any business in that bad place in the first place. You ought to have minded your own business and have got the hell out of there, very first. I can remember that my parents drilled this into me from the very first, they told me that there were rough places and bad companions and that if I wanted to associate with them, why don't ask for any help from them. These bad places and bad companions were pointed out to me as being bad and I was supposed to stay away from them, but you see places like this, such as houses of prostitution and taverns and forbidden places, held a fascination for the kids. That's natural, there was so much of it around.

A businessman reports this attitude among people in Coal Town:

Another attitude in this community is if someone has a lot more money than you have, then you can fleece him and you are right in doing it because he has so much money that he won't miss it. If you don't take this attitude, you are really not in the swing of things here in this community at the present time nor in the early days.

A sixty-year-old miner expresses the current disinterest in people as he experiences it:

I think that this is one of the important things about this community and that is that the people they don't have any belief in anything that is worth while as far as people are concerned. It's a strange sort of feeling and I have often puzzled about it and thought about it a great deal.

Nicknames. One of the most interesting dimensions of impersonality appears in relation to nicknames, which are very common in the community. The lack of feeling for others is manifest in the selection of names that are generally derisive; frequently the real name of the individual is completely unknown.

They have people in this community that hardly anybody would know them by their names. That is how they do here. There are some funny nicknames around here such as Skinny Sam and Kid Andy, and well like next door to me is a Croatian who is a good neighbor but he is crazy. They call him Crazy Steve. He talks to his chickens all the time. He is quite a character. He doesn't bother anybody. He is a bachelor and he never married. I don't know what his real name is. We just call him Crazy Steve here. You see, the people here would call you anything that came to their mind.

SELF-EFFACEMENT

A second major theme which appears is concerned with the attitudes of Coal Town people which border on self-depreciation. Such attitudes arise, we believe, from the quality of life which characterized the area prior to industrialization and were accentuated by the development of mining. The native from the area felt inadequate to cope with the ordinary demands of life. His existence was submarginal, and taboos on change and development accentuated by industrialization were ever present. There were, to put it simply, marked feelings of inferiority.

For the immigrants, feelings of rejection and insecurity emerged based in part on their inadequacies in understanding the new environment and in part on the hostility of the natives. Much of this rejection was internalized by the immigrants, who in fact learned to hate themselves for being immigrants. Thus attitudes of self-depreciation emerged out of a fundamental lack of respect and understanding which both natives and immigrants had for themselves. The kind of social climate necessary for the development of a healthy self-image in which basic self-esteem can emerge was almost never present in Coal Town. These people were and are immersed in self-effacement, and they *project this onto others* with the ever-present tendency to belittle and berate friends and neighbors. This practice is so pervasive that it extends to several phases of social interaction. One informant described it this way:

There are always people that are ready to kick on a man. After all, no one is perfect, you see, and I would say that we have a lot of people here that like to jump on somebody and belittle him and make fun of him and do him a lot of harm if they can; or if they don't happen to agree with him. Resentment is underneath this. At times it is covered up but at some times it erupted into violence. There is a tendency here to belittle the community and for persons to belittle themselves.

Humor and the projection of self-effacement. The use of humor as a means of showing one's contempt for others is well recognized in Coal Town and is accepted as a pattern of interaction. Humor is employed to humiliate, embarrass, and control the behavior of others. At times these practices verge on being sadistic. The content of the humor is focused on other's misfortunes. For example, to acquire a venereal disease was considered humorous.

During World War II this area had one of the highest rejection rates due to venereal disease than in any other section of the country. Why, the boys used to tease one another about venereal disease and if anyone contacted venereal disease, this was a big joke. This is what I would call running around with your brain in your pants.

One informant distinguishes between the outer appearances and the more subtle functions of expressing hostility through humor.

The humor here is most unusual. There is a lot of egging on in the humor around here and sometimes it is very cruel to a sensitive person. There is a great deal of personal satisfaction for an individual doing this to a victim. Personal prejudice will also creep in and you will really work over your enemy or your victim. You see, the outward appearance is friendship. Much goes on underneath though that is not friendship, but it is done under disguise of friendship.

There was a tremendous undertone of resentment always coming out at the slightest provocation. You see, those who kidded you the hardest were the ones who really resented you and disliked you. There was a residue of that here because the people had to stay in this community. They felt that they were stuck here and I think the kids were really bad about it. They got this from their parents because they had to stay here in this dirty place.

The sensitive person found such patterns difficult to endure. Herein lies one of the very subtle characteristics of this community— there has been no place for the individual with his personal sensitivities and differences.

The people around here kid each other a lot. You see, the fellows that couldn't take it, they left. The people that this type of kidding bothered were driven out of the community. They just couldn't stand it here and today there are not many of them left. You sorta have to take it if you want to stay here very long.

Rumors and gossip. Another dimension of the contempt which these people feel for others is the destructive need to spread rumors and gossip. This tendency, historically present in the community, is very much alive today and flourishes at the slightest provocation.

Rumors and gossip for these people are related to the intense hostility which they feel; reality is frequently distorted. To have unreal ideas about next-door neighbors and the community is common. In one instance, concerned with a seventy-five-year-old man who had worked for almost sixty-five years of his life, a neighbor remarked, "That old bastard never worked a day in his life." Rumors and gossip are freely manufactured.

There is a lot of gossip around here. There is talk about neighbors, particularly. That is, people you know. It's sort of like old hens among the women. One of them starts it and the others make it worse. There are plenty of rumors around here. Why, I can go downtown now and say that I saw a panther in the woods across. Well, I get to talking about it and sure enough three or four other people would say that they saw the same thing. Well, that's how it goes. You find out a lot about people, you see, from the talk that goes on.

Rumors and gossip have always been an avocation in Coal Town. A twenty-five-year-old male:

There has always been a lot of gossip here in this community. If you thought about the gossip it would be sort of a problem and would get you down. Actually, it seems to be a form of relaxation. They seem to thrive on it because there is nothing else better to do. There were always plenty of rumors that would get built up and in a town this small everyone knows your own business. These rumors tend to grow and as they pass from person to person they become exaggerated. Why, this town is so small that everyone knows when you go to the outside toilet and they usually watch you as you go out.

Although the basis of destructive gossip is ever present, its particular form varies. For some, a strange man entering a home could initiate the rumor that an illicit sexual affair was in progress. A miner:

There is a lot of personal gossip. For instance, you'll see a man over in the neighbor's yard maybe talking to his neighbor's wife and they'll say, "What's that man doing over there?" Things like that. You can find out all about people at the F—— Club. It seems like they know what is going on all over town.

For others, a promotion means that somebody has been bribed. In some instances, one who reads and questions is accused of being a subversive, a communist. People expect the worst and enjoy finding incidents embarrassing to others. A twenty-two-year-old woman:

You see these gossipers, and especially the women, are always looking for skeletons in everyone's closet. Well, the old expression, you know, that "an apple don't roll far from the tree," is really applicable here. I would call this being two-faced myself. All of the people here seem to be two-faced. All ages engage in this gossip and it's not just the old people that do.

A retired miner said this:

We've got a lot of gossip around here. People will talk good to your face and then when they leave you, they will talk behind your back about somebody else. You can tell some people not to say anything and it will be all over town before dark. You just talk about your next-door neighbor and then that story that you say will not only circulate but it will get worse and worse. These rumors and gossips have always been here but it seems to have gotten worse. It runs through the town like wildfire. These lies particularly, and these lies keep building up all the time.

ISOLATION AND SEPARATION

Such contempt and hostility toward themselves and one another, coupled with the difficulties in accepting differences, developed into a third major theme: feelings of isolation, of separation, and of not belonging. We refer here not only to separation from people but alienation from any consistent set of life goals or purposes. Our Coal Town residents are like a people without direction or a knowable destiny, suspended in time and space. One informant said this:

There is feelings of being apart from other people which I don't know exactly how to describe but you sort of feel it here in this community. There is no place to meet and just talk. They keep pretty much to themselves. They leave you alone and they expect you to leave them alone. Everybody seems to stay by themselves.

One miner, typical of a group who failed to marry, expressed his separation from others by adding:

I have never had a happy period. All of my life has been unhappy. You ask me as I look back over life what things were the hardest for me to bear. Well, that is not easy to answer. I guess, how to make a living. That has always been the hardest thing for me to bear. Friends do not mean much. I never had a girl friend.

Although characteristic of all age groups, separation and isolation are especially felt by the older people. A miner's wife:

You know the thing that upsets me is that the people who used to know you, well, they don't speak to you any more now when you get old. We call it "getting up in the gee." You see, this means that people maybe have a little bit more money and they think that they are better than somebody else. You see, it's this way when you get old, they just don't recognize you. They say, "Well, she is just an old woman and we won't visit her. We'd rather visit with some other people."

Many of our informants were keenly aware of these pronounced themes of isolation and separation. Various reasons were offered as an explanation for such a development. Many believed the social structure demanded such separation. Some, for example, felt that social class affiliation dictated separation between groups.

One example of a powerful man in the community that does not mix socially is that of L——. He does not mix very well. He doesn't visit much. His wife belongs to a club and they sort of keep to their own kind. They always have in the past and even up at the present time.

Others feel that separation and isolation are necessitated by business factors. A grocer reported:

We go out of town very often when we want to engage in social activities, or to do a little visiting. We go to the city. You see, you have to keep a barrier between yourself and other people here, especially when you are in business. When you cater to too many classes, you can't do too many things with each class. For instance, if someone invites you to a party and you can't go and then somebody else invites you to a party and you go, then the first person says, "Well, he and his wife would not come to this party of mine but he went over here to the other party." I don't have too many intimate friends here because of the nature of my business. I'm always away from social pleasure and friends around here and I stick strictly to my own business affairs. That's the way it goes.

Some blamed the isolation on family responsibilities. A housewife reports as follows:

I never mixed much with the people here in this town. I have always had a family to care for and I have always stayed at home. I visit and I go up-town everyday to buy my groceries but I don't associate very much with the people here. I never visited over twelve people here around this local neighborhood. I never run out, you see, of the house but I'm always here. I can remember one time that some of my children came in from D——— and they couldn't find me and they got very worried because they had knew that I had never visited much and that I never got out of the house, and they left me a note and told me to always be sure and tell them even when I went out.

To be sure, particular factors in the Coal Town social structure were conducive to separation. Nevertheless, much of the separation and isolation which characterized the life of these people was at the deeper levels of personal organization. Regardless of initial cause, basic feelings of impersonality, contempt, and hostility have been internalized at the psychological level and are expressed in the various patterns of human interaction.

The role of religion in isolation and separation. The majority of native Protestant religions in Coal Town, irrespective of denomination or social class, have been characterized by an adherence to fundamentalism and a pervasive nonworldly orientation. Such a view has contributed to the separation and isolation which these people feel. The predominant Protestant orientation emphasized the need to abstain from worldly pleasures. A native female:

We could not do anything at high school because the churches would oppose it. We had a Teen Town here but it folded up because some of the kids were absent from Sunday School after one of our big parties on Saturday night. Everybody thinks that everybody else is going to hell in this community.

The native Protestant churches with their religious orientations were generally aloof from the real problems of the community and they did very little to bring about constructive changes.[3] For the vast majority of church-going Protestants, what may have been a counteracting influence to unfavorable conditions in the community never really materialized. During the periods of community growth and turmoil, religious activities dealt exclusively with the questions of life in the world to come and with faith in divine providence; this contributed to a rejection of this life and subsequent indifference toward life in the 'community. The native Coal Town Protestants resent any tendency to remove this nonworldly character of their religion. A native woman:

We like to hear the Bible preached here as far as sermons go; and we don't like for the preacher to get off on things that are not in the Bible. There are many members in the church who don't like to hear preaching from the Bible; and they don't like to hear it because they are not living right. This sort of hits them when the minister begins to talk about the Bible.

Deviations are resented:

I would like to hear a good, gospel sermon. I like a minister who sticks to the Bible. We have gotten off, I think, into the world a great deal and some of the preachers that we have had here used to get off into the world and do all sorts of things that they weren't supposed to do.

I like to have them tell you about your meanness. That's what I like about sermons. I think the preacher should really get down and if it really hits you I think you should be man enough to tell him about it. If the sermon hits me, I think it's a good one. I don't like all these flowery sermons; both my wife and I like to have him stick to the Bible. Now, some of them can't stick to the Bible and when they can't do that I don't think they help their members very much.

[3] This attitude of aloofness from the community was less pronounced for the Catholic Church.

For some the sermon constitutes a form of therapy.

Now, I like to hear good short sermons, something good. I like to hear something that hits you just right where it would do you the most good. Sometimes you have heard these sermons over and over again and they don't do much to inspire you. Oh, they will start with the Bible but they don't really preach it like they used to but wander off and then some of them usually end up with the Bible. They use too many modern illustrations of some of the meanings of the Bible. I think that most of the people in my church would want the pastor to stick to the Bible. You sort of feel better when you come back from church. I know that I do.

Well, I'll tell you what kind of sermon I like. I like a good Bible sermon. Not those that get away from the Bible. I think all the members of the church feel as I do about this type of sermon. You know, you come away feeling better from this type of sermon. It sort of raises your spirits and makes you feel better. It sort of gives you hope.

Mobility—physical and psychological. People who feel psychologically alienated lack roots. Thus many of our Coal Town people move from place to place in search of economic as well as personal stability. Such behavior represents another dimension of their feelings of not belonging.

Always the search was away from an examination of themselves; always there was the hope of finding stability in another cultural situation. They have thus become perpetually marginal, misfits moving here and there but belonging nowhere.

The majority of those who moved away went to urban communities, but adjustment in these new areas was marginal and difficult. Urban life for these people has been frustrating and dissappointing. Economic adjustments were difficult and any search for more meaningful relationships did not prove fruitful in the urban setting. A father:

They definitely are not happy in the cities. Every year in Lake City all the group from Coal Town, I don't know how many we do have there, but they get together once a year for a reunion. They come back during vacation, all of them.

Thus a specific cycle of events emerges whereby those who leave, when once confronted by the city, begin to glorify life in Coal Town and seek to return.

I think the fellow that goes away to the city forgets the past and the past to him seems very favorable. I think this clings to you and makes you want to come back to this community.

After a while disappointment sets in. Thus back and forth the movement continues; each time there is the anticipation of finding something new, something worth while. Whenever the pace becomes too difficult in the city there is a return to Coal Town. A merchant:

Many people here came back to this country community because life is easy here. There is a hunting and fishing interest and the people can let the world go by. There are old friends here and living costs are cheaper than in other places. Past acquaintances and the old times bring the people back. Drinking friends are still here too, and that enables a person to have a draw back to this community. There is a big contrast with the city. The city was hell for the people who left here and tried to settle there. There was a tremendous amount of hustle and bustle. The costs were terrific and they were extremely cost conscious. The people were lonely up there. I know that. The parents would brag on their children and how good they would do up there but these kids would want to come back home here, too. At least there is some contact here with people.

Return to Coal Town is often followed by more disappointment. A female college graduate:

There seems to be a pull to come back. These people flock back here on weekends and holidays but when they come they are blue and disappointed. They are seeking something that they have lost here. They want some place to call home. They are not satisfied when they get here. There seems to be a peace of mind here and yet they are not happy. They can't make a living here, yet they like it here and they can't stay here. I can remember one example, a girl friend of mine, her father worked in the city for twenty-five years. He has moved back here to this community six times. He's been in love with this place but he cannot stand it here. He's not able to change to urban ways either. He feels secure here but he cannot earn a living here. He does not fit in the rural area nor in the urban area either. This is the pattern of coming back to this community. It's somewhat of a family pull or of an individual pull.

Even those who are satisfied with their economic plight feel personally inadequate in the urban community and are emotionally tied to Coal Town. A miner talks about his son:

He would like to come back. He was raised here. It is home to him. They don't any of them like to leave here. They have spent a lot of money coming back here on weekends. My boy comes home every weekend. He told me he may stay over two weeks this time. There is a lot of boys like him from Coal Town that works away. I know you will see them here on weekends quite often. They just like the southern part of this state, that is all I know.

Others who did not move lived with an air of suspension and a pronounced feeling of not belonging. This developed into one of the most interesting characteristics of the community: "the nomad spirit" reported by so many of our informants. This attitude has been sufficiently immobilizing to result in a lack of identification with the community and a failure to support its growth. The feeling of not belonging helped foster an attitude of being a stranger with no vested interest in the community's future. The "nomad spirit" was described this way by one of our informants:

This nomad spirit, which was here in this community during the early days, really makes up the atmosphere that the stranger feels when he comes to this community. Those who stay here resent the attitude of the nomad spirit. As you get older you don't resent it as much as you did when you were younger and able to fight back. Many people, you see, resent their being here. They don't like to be here. They only wanted to be here for a very short time. But somehow or other they are stuck in this community. They tend to disregard the community, too. In other words the attitude is: Let's don't build anything that would be too permanent because we don't want to be here and we don't want to be associated with it.

Some described the feeling as a "camp scent" with characteristic impermanence.

There was a sort of camp scent about this community. That is, it was not permanent, you see. The people always had the feeling that they would stay here for a while and then move on. There was nothing permanent about it. I can give you one example of a man who came into the community and decided to rent a house since he was not sure that he would be here very long. Well, I told him after five years that why didn't he go ahead and purchase the house. He could have been paying for it for the same price that he had rented it, but he said no, that he couldn't do that because he thought that he might leave any day. Well, he had finally rented that house for twenty-two years and he could have bought it in ten years. But that's how it is here. You see, there is a sense of not much real value. What was valuable in this community was the cash, though. That is, the money, and they didn't put money in land or in permanent improvements. They put money into things that they could derive pleasure from or else in automobiles which they could move from one place to the next.

The mobility which characterizes these people is, in one important sense, related to the manner in which they tried to achieve a sense of personal order and stability. They have sought personal order and stability by changing their occupation and the cultural situation. These changes are all to their credit. Nevertheless, they have neglected perhaps an even more significant facet, namely, their social-psychological orientation, their basic world views, their concepts of living. From our point of view their failure to come to terms with themselves at the level of self-understanding is understandable in view of all the complexities involved in such an undertaking. And yet because of their failure to do so their endless search is almost doomed to result in continued disappointment.

CONFORMITY

One wonders how a people possessing such facets of open rebellion and violence can also be conformists. Yet at certain basic levels these people do possess very pronounced tendencies toward conformity. Our Coal Town people, with intense feelings of separateness, have very real needs to belong, and these needs to belong are expressed through conformity and a fear of nonconformity. Such conformity is a blind, indiscriminate conformity to the values of the majority. These people, without real roots in themselves, are easily intimidated and tend to give up their differences in order to gain acceptance. For example, many felt that if they were affiliated with the union or the mining industry they could be accepted. To be affiliated with mining and with the union was considered by many to be of greater value than upper-class status. So important was this value that persons from the more privileged classes would frequently reject their own class, choosing instead to make some union affiliation in order to have a feeling of being like the majority. The son of an upper-class businessman reports this:

When I was fourteen years old I joined a hod carriers' union and I considered myself a grown man. I didn't have to do this because my family was quite prominent in the community. I know that I was the happiest man alive when I joined that hod carriers' union because at last I was a union man. As I mentioned to you before, if you were not a union man in this community, you were actually nothing.

Another son of a merchant claimed:

Whether you were like others or not was mostly based on whether you were union or non-union and this included merchants and their children. You see, they did not belong to the union and if you did not belong to the union, you were out. You could tell about the feelings. I know that I wished many times that my father was a miner because I was on the outside.

One upper-class informant was ashamed of his mother because she was different from the mothers in the homes of miners.

I know that my mother was very attractive until she was forty years old and when I was growing up I felt ashamed of her because she was so attractive and did not wear long dresses and black hose like the miners' wives did. Isn't that something? Now this was the pattern here. You see, the miners' kids were proud of their families and if your family didn't fit the pattern they really let you know about it. The kids would draw off in their own group to say something about the mines or else the union and this was considered a secret and not for the ears of us other children. This was the pattern here in this community and don't let anyone tell you that it wasn't. I know because I was on the outside.

The son of a lumber dealer tells us:

You see, we never felt that we were on the inside. I can remember that I was forced to stay out of things. I definitely had the feeling that I was an outsider. It's a terrible feeling because it makes you feel inferior and I have never forgotten that feeling. It was just a sort of resentment against us and we couldn't help it. Many of the times I wished that my father was a miner so that I could be included in these little play groups.

To be different from the group in matters of dress invited trouble. An upper-class male:

I can remember that I was the first boy here to wear bell-bottom pants and I really took an awful ribbing on that. You see, if you had some difference, particularly in dress, why, you were really ridden hard by the people here in the community. I was also the first here in this community to wear knickers. Boy, what a ribbing I got for wearing those.

There was considerable pressure on those who did not drink.

There were no outside clubs here and you usually had to drink in the saloons or else in the home of the people. For instance, if you ever went to a home the first thing that they would give you would be a drink of corn liquor. Well, it would be bad if you refused, so you would have to go ahead and drink. If you didn't drink you were really given the needle here by the people.

Violence as a way of life was highly valued by the group. Conformity brought acceptance. A merchant:

The group considered the most violent person the best. This is what the group believed. If the differences is a great amount of violence, they will be held up by the group. If not, they are held in contempt. The most preferred companion was one who could give and take violence. If he could give and take he was held in esteem and with less contempt regardless of what position they were supposed to maintain in the community. That was both in action and words. If attacked, he had to fight. If he would not resist, he might as well forget about it. He would fit alright if he defended himself with violence. If he would not reply or wouldn't pay any attention to it, then he was held in contempt. Even though his ideas were held in contempt, if he was man enough to get up and defend himself, he was respected.

New members in the community were quick to conform to the patterns of violence.

They [the immigrants] soon found out that one of the quickest ways to get respect was through violence. A man was judged by his ability to go along with violence. Just being a decent person was not enough.

Respect and faith in the law as a tool for justice was traditionally discouraged and resorting to law was a sign of weakness. These attitudes still have certain residues. One miner had this to say:

In this community each person had to care for himself. You would have to stand up for your own rights because no one else would. You had to beat the other person over the head and take care of your own problems rather than having the police take care of them. That was one of the common unwritten codes in the community. It was a sort of sign of weakness if you called the police because you were supposed to settle your own problems.

Another said this:

A man usually took care of things himself. That is, there was either individual violence or mob violence and it was a sign of weakness to call the police or to take care of your troubles in court. This was viewed as the weak way out.

One individual who wanted to deviate from the group stated that he consciously tried to become an "eccentric." By so doing he felt that he would be immune to the criticism of others and he could be himself.

In other words, if I could acquire a reputation here for being eccentric I thought that then I could do just about what I wanted to and wouldn't be bothered and the people would say, "Oh, well, you know him, he's eccentric and he's liable to do anything." In that I think lies a great measure of personal freedom in a community such as this.

The same informant, who possessed certain intellectual interests, had need to discuss the teachings of the great philosophers. In order that he not be humiliated by the group, he cloaked the identity of the philosopher and presented the philosopher's beliefs in modern colloquial terms. For example, in conversations with a semiliterate friend he would speak of Plato as a man named Joe, whom he once met and who had a particular belief. He would then turn to his friend and suggest that they talk about the idea. By interacting in this manner he would communicate with others and yet not alienate himself. In his own words our informant stated it thus:

As far as recreation is concerned, I guess I engage in sleeping and reading, reading economic books, and particularly ancient history. The people here resent the idea that I do all of this reading and I can never mention it to them. If I do mention it to them, I usually relate some incident from Plato as being due to the fellow that I met at the café a week ago and so forth and so on. In other words, I would translate it into common language so that these people would know the story as though it happened only a few days ago. That is the way in which I communicate with them. There are not many people here in this community like I am. I think that it is a good policy of social insurance for one to be eccentric because if you are eccentric then you can do as you please. You see, you have to communicate with people in a certain way and I'm eccentric alright but I'm not a rigid eccentric.

ANTI-INTELLECTUALISM

Much of the stress on conformity was an outgrowth of a general anti-intellectual orientation which is pervasive for a large section of the Coal Town population. This suggests a fifth cultural theme which is characteristic of our population. We use the term "anti-intellectual" to suggest the ever-present tendency to view social change with suspicion and to reject alternative patterns of conduct as untenable. Formal education is viewed with favor when it is tradelike in character and contributes to earning a living. But educational programs were resisted from the very first. Natives reported the following:

They had some trouble getting the high school because the country people did not want it because they thought it would mean higher taxes. They voted it down three times. They had more votes, you see, than we did here in town. The immigrants wanted the school and we finally got it the fourth time. That was in 1921 and 1922.

Well, when we took a vote to create the high school district here, we failed because of the opposition of the farmers. These farmers did not want schools and they were very strong and had a very strong vote. Well, we took another chance at it and my wife even went out and worked for the votes. She used to stay home and mind the children for some of the women who would then be given a ride to vote.

Education in the broader sense of equipment to understand the universe and its problems meant very little. The desire to learn new and different methods of thinking or believing was opposed as an attack on social values. People who read, who think, who question, are viewed with suspicion. Intellectual curiosity and political subversion are synonymous. That universities consist largely of Communist sympathizers is a widely accepted belief.

To display intellectual ability and interest meant almost certain humiliation, and many persons who grew up in this climate learned to reject themselves because of intellectual interests and aspirations. The son of an immigrant said this:

If you showed any intellectual ability, you were a misfit. Any ability that you might have was played down. These I refer to as environmental cripples in this area. These are the persons who had the ability but who were forced to forget or were not encouraged to go on and develop their intellectual capacities.

To display musical interests was to ask for group censure. A father:

You see, I remember when I had my boy here and I wanted him to take music lessons because I like music a great deal. Well, when I suggested this to him everybody laughed at the idea. You see, if you did anything like this, if you wanted to improve yourself or wanted to take piano lessons, you were a sissy.

RESIGNATION

Much of what the Coal Town resident longs for in his escape from his community and the city relates to a wish for the simple life, devoid of conflict and anxiety. The native historically lived in a cultural climate in which he wished for little and valued a life without pressure to engage in hard labor. These values now characterize the child of both native and immigrant. Further, many natives and immigrants, immersed as they were in conflicts, stresses, strains, and general demoralization, have withdrawn from actively trying to make things better and have resorted to taking it easy. Thus we have a sixth cultural theme, the resignation which characterizes the people of Coal Town. A fifty-five-year-old miner said:

There was the tendency here for them to become somewhat confused about the communities in which they lived and many of them would try to solve this confusion by taking things easy.

Much of what these people hope for today is revealed in their levels of aspiration, the shallow living they pursue, and the quality of interaction. A college graduate had this to say:

Some people live here for forty years and they are not too receptive as to what goes on in the community. Some actually have no awareness of their community and they also have this attitude of not giving a goddamn about things. They're concerned with their own personal interests and pleasures. You see, this is one form of the inertia that you have. It is a closing of one's life and interests. You see, all that they really seem to think about is sex and a little money. That's about all. There was pleasure that the people often found in that, and I view that as a sort of escape from the world.

A number of informants reported life this way:

There is a lot of talk about fishing and hunting. I quit hunting and fishing but I worked with several boys who fish all the time and that's all they want to talk about. We don't visit much except on the streets, but none of this visiting from house to house. We have never done that in Coal Town since we have been here and the people just don't come over and see us either.

A widower stated:

What I like to do with my spare time is fish and hunt and keep a garden but I haven't been able to do that last thing for some time. What I like to talk about is baseball, hunting, and fishing. I take my meals out, don't fool around with cooking here. I take such magazines as the *Country Gentleman,* the *Legion Magazine,* and *U.S. and News Report.* I talk about politics and I hang out around the filling station most of the time. I think you have seen me when you drive to the station. I also hang around where it's nice and cool; what we do is to follow the sun. We find a little breeze and then we keep moving with it and keep getting back out of the sun. We just stand there, talk, and look at the people when they go by. When they play ball over here at the ball diamond I usually go over and watch. I get a big kick out of watching the ball games. I am very contented with my life here. The favorite topic of conversation is fishing and hunting.

A college graduate who operates a marginal business described his motivations this way:

I did not always have a single purpose in life and I didn't try too hard. I was always looking for the easy way out. Most of the people here just sit back and wait. You see, this is a town that has been owned by a coal company. There has never been any big surge of "big city" attitudes here. The miners would work hard during the winter and save up enough to last out the summer, during which time unemployment was quite heavy. We had a large group of mobile people here who didn't want anything out of life. They got an advance in wages, I remember, up to $5.00 a day for working in the mines and they seemed contented.

A miner made this observation about people in his own occupation:

You know, when I think of it, it seems to me that the miner tends to give up. Even when they are in their fifties, they tend to give up and not expect too much out of the future. You see, he has to give up because there is nothing else that he can do except mine coal. He can't turn to anything else at that late stage and because of his age. He has no other trade. It's kind of rough. Most of the miners own their own houses there in Coal Town and they have no other place to go. If you were over forty-five years of age, you see, there's just no goal in these communities where the coal has played out.

A former resident of Coal Town made this observation:

Say, what the hell's wrong with people down here anyway, they act like they're beat, like they don't give a damn about anybody, or something? The other guys up in Lake City notice too when they come down. Some of 'em don't even come down any more.

A successful, industrious merchant reacted this way to the people of Coal Town:

You know, I do not have any respect for the people here because they are willing to sit back and do nothing. I think that they are lazy and that they are not ambitious. They don't want much out of life. I can't understand it myself. I am always willing to go ahead and to do new things but do you think these damn people here work? No, they don't do a goddamn thing. All they want to do is to sit around and do nothing.

The youth especially seem to typify the pattern of resignation, according to our informants. Many of our informants felt that long periods of mining unemployment had affected the outlook of youth. In this regard it is important to note that a large section of one generation grew up in an environment where they could never recall a steady job for an adult member of their families. The son of a miner:

The mining industry was never a too-secure industry. There was always unemployment and as the young people grew up at home where there was unemployment he could not remember periods of economic security. He could not remember a period in which there was steady work for his father. This, I think, would tend to make one very lost, confused, demoralized, and prejudiced. It robbed the person of his ambition. It would have a very demoralizing effect on the person.

Some felt the attitudes that young people have are the result of military service.

I think sending them to the Army hurts them a lot because when they come back they don't want to work. They don't do anything in the Army there except a lot of goldbricking and they just don't give a darn whether they work or not when they come back home. I've watched some of these boys who, I guess, used to be pretty good as far as work was concerned. They would go into the service, stay a few years and come back, and they weren't worth killing. I know quite a few of them here now.

Most apparent among the youth is the tendency to have limited horizons and goals, to settle for less than they might normally be able to achieve. Many of these youths are unaware of their own basic wishes and abilities. Having grown up in a social climate where abilities are neglected and associated with disappointment, they find it easier to let things alone. They are both *ignorant of what they are* and *afraid to discover their inner resources.* A college student points this out very clearly in the following remarks:

I know many kids with talent that just didn't do anything with that talent because they couldn't cope with the outside. They did not feel a part of things on the outside. They were afraid to adjust there or to stay on the campus. I remember when we went to college, why, we used to come running home because we had a little world all of our own. We wanted to break out but the welcome mat was not out for us. We never felt that the people on the outside of this community were part of our social world. I can remember that we used to try to arrange our classes in the morning so that we could run home and eat our dinner and then we would stay home all day.

One student with considerable ability felt inadequate to venture permanently out of Coal Town.

I guess you wonder why I came back to Coal Town after I left college. Well, I really don't know myself. When I was in college I never really made the break from home. You see, I used to take the paper from home and I used to fool around a lot and somehow or other I never really did break the tie from home. It's a funny sort of relationship and I don't understand it myself.

A college graduate made this observation about her friends:

The kids that grew up here when I did don't expect much from life. Well, in my class in high school there were many who could make upper grades but they didn't want to. Out of my class, fifteen to twenty started to Lake City University but couldn't take it. They chickened out and came home. Some people are still trying to find themselves.

Many of these students lack any orientation with respect to goals or social expectations. They are fundamentally unequipped to cope with the outside world and its demands.

No one told us what to do in high school. When we got out, you didn't know what to expect and you didn't know why you were going to college. The only alternatives were college, going into the Army, or for the girls maybe some secretarial work or nursing. We didn't know anything about it and the groups that I went to school with had never been to a large town. They didn't know what to expect and they didn't know how to get along in a large town or a city.

There is little understanding of the restriction of one's interests and of life as a problem. What we have termed resignation is viewed

by our informants as laziness or lack of ambition. A miner had this
to say:

A lot of the fellows just layed around town and wouldn't do anything after
they graduated from high school. They loafed until the Army got them
and some of them are still loafing at N——. Most of them were sons of
coal miners and it didn't take too much to satisfy them. If you take a
young kid just out of school, all he wanted was a pair of overalls, a blue
shirt, and some shoes and that is everything that he wanted. He was just
satisfied to do nothin' and to loaf. Why, across the street from where I
live they used to loaf from dark till midnight. They would sit on the bench,
talk, and do nothing. They had no purpose in life. This was a young
bunch that the war got but they continued this after they came back from
the war. I would say that the parents gave it to them. It's beginning to
quit now because we don't have any fellows left. They are very lazy and it
doesn't bother them to do nothing at all. They have, I think, grown up in
homes where the folks don't work. Many just give in and don't do anything
about the children.

Another middle-aged miner reports this:

Most of the young people here are just bums. They don't want to do anything. They don't want to make anything out of themselves. Why, you take
G——'s boy. He is a louse, first class. All he does is live off his old man.
That is not a good thing to do. We don't have many young people in this
community who are willing to make something of themselves.

A lumberman:

All some of these young fellows look for is the end of the shift and payday.
Young people here don't have too much ambition. I don't know why, I
guess they need to get away from home. If they got away from home
they would have to work but down here they would rather sit and draw
that rocking-chair money until it runs out and then get on relief. I have
never been up against anything like that and I have always had to hustle.

Many of our informants felt that the values among the youth
indicate an unwillingness to assume responsibilities. On the question of debts, a merchant said this:

The kids just don't seem to have a whole lot of ambition here. What they
want is a car and a television set and they can't afford the payments on
their car. You see, they are living beyond their means. What they do is
love luxury and keep up with the Joneses. I think that is what's responsible for most of this. They lay around here and do nothin'.

A male, aged twenty-two, reported this:

It seems to me that the young people here don't care. Most of them have cars, stay out, and the girls stay out later, too. We have an 8:30 curfew but that's not in force. Nobody ever pays any attention to it. The reason that we have delinquency and that so many are in trouble is that they are left alone to run wild and to run loose. A lot of the young kids run around and drink and go to the taverns. The boys come down here from the other communities to flip the girls and things like that. Many of the girls get flipped here at an early age.

CYNICISM

A seventh theme which emerges in our analysis relates to the deep and penetrating cynicism present among people of Coal Town; a cynicism based on the life they have witnessed and experienced, a life in which there is little to hope for and little to expect. People are viewed as being essentially destructive and the predominant philosophy is "to get the other guy before he gets you."

The cynicism of which we speak has been nurtured in an environment where the influences for constructive human growth were few; where hope was crushed by the circumstances of life itself and by the impoverished human relationships. Cynicism appears in several areas of community interaction. One observes it, for example, in relation to political attitudes. According to the views expressed by our informants, there is little that they expect from elected officials, and the question of voting is a challenge where one tries to select the person least likely to fleece the public. As one person put it:

You see, I believe that all politicians are crooks and it's not just here but everywhere that they are crooks. It's the same thing. People have no faith about politics because of local and international wars and conflicts and disturbances. There was no interest in the types of political leaders that we have. In fact, there was a great indifference in this community.

The quality of interpersonal life which has characterized this community is replete with associations that have always been tenuous, associations that have contributed to the cynical attitudes which these people possess. A merchant:

You couldn't depend on anyone staying with you long enough in order to do anything. It was sort of very temporary relationships here. I can remember a justice of the peace who ran on a sort of ticket of this sort. He would tell things about other people and then he would go to the persons he had talked about and say that you had said something about them. This was how he operated. You see, all of this makes you wonder about people and you would sort of have to laugh it off because a person would always be on your side when he was talking to you but you couldn't trust him, and if he was talking to someone else, let's say your enemy, then he would be on his side. So you see, we never learned to trust other people.

Friendships could never be counted on. A merchant:

Why, all social relationships here were uncertain. The relationship between husband and wife was very uncertain and as far as business was concerned, you could never trust another person. That has always been true in this small community, though many persons don't believe it. This I have observed many times and I have wondered about it. They talk about the city being cold. Well, this was one of the coldest places I have ever lived.

One could never feel free in discussions even with friends.

Relationships were sort of touch and go. These types of associations and relationships would sort of make you leary about what you said to other people. You see, you couldn't trust them. You would tell something to a friend and then he would go to the other person and tell something about you. In the meantime this other person would tell him something about you and the two would get together.

A businessman who extended considerable credit to people during periods of unemployment explained his cynicism this way:

You don't expect much principle from these people. For instance, I can give you one example of a man who came to me during the union trouble. He said that his kids were hungry and they were dying for food. He wanted to know if I would give him credit. Sure, I gave him credit, and then things went on and he began to get more and more money and today he is a very upstanding citizen, and I asked him one time if he would pay a little on his grocery bill and he said, no, he did not intend to pay the grocery bill. He said to me, "It's your own fault that you gave me credit. You were a fool for giving me credit because I'm not going to pay that bill." Well, now this person is accepted today as a member of the upper class. This is a terrible thing. You see, they have no principles.

Marked cynicism is manifest in distrust of others and negates the possibility of community identification or growth. An immigrant's son reports his views:

Do you wonder that you can't get anybody together in this town any more, even today? When an old man like T—— got clubbed on the head by sheriff's deputies just because he happened to be standing on the street corner uptown. Why, we expected any minute those nights during the bad union trouble to have our places blowed up. My brother, livin' upstairs then, expected to have his hardware store blowed out from under him any night. It used to be back when we played ball, it was our town, our team, our schools, our this an' that. Hell, these people have been shown the hard way that it wasn't. Do you wonder that the only thing they consider ours today is what's inside their own fences, their own property? I believe they woulda took that away from 'em too if they hadn't layed out in the bushes an' grape arbors every night with their guns cocked. It's no wonder you can't get any cooperation. Even those damned outlaws don't trust each other any more.

SUSPICION

The prevalent attitudes of suspicion and distrust constitute an eighth major theme which characterizes these people. They have learned to anticipate the worst and to suspect the motives of family and friends. They expect little friendliness from others. Further, it is difficult for these people to support community goals since in their experience so-called community goals have become avenues for private gain and exploitation. One informant who has actively engaged in civic projects reported as follows:

There is so much jealousy around here. Things do not get done except by a few who do. Even in the club, the one which is the most active group in the community, the people always say that you are getting something out of anything that is done. The people are very suspicious and they had a reason to be because there were people here who were not honest. In the past people were very suspicious and even today there is the suspiciousness in the community.

Marked suspicion produces groups working at cross purposes, as a merchant observes:

The people in Coal Town are very suspicious people. So many of them are jealous of one another that they can hardly stand it. There is always a faction that is working against other factions. They have never worked together in that community and you always find most of the people knocking something that has been proposed. There is no cooperation. I don't know why except maybe that the people are always envious of something that somebody else has and they don't have.

Many legitimate, necessary activities are never completed because of these attitudes. A grocer:

They are suspicious. They feel that if anything is done that somebody will get something out of it. They have often accused me of being on the School Board in order to get something out of all of it. I have never gotten a nickel from the School Board and I do not intend to. That is not the way that I look at it. You see, some of the people here are too tight. They don't want to be taxed. They want education but they don't want to pay for it. Many of them don't care, they are just not interested at all. There is no real community interest here at the present nor has there been in the past. Even in the club, there are only a few of us that ever do any work. The others just hang on, it seems like. People feel that if someone has got something in this community that is good, that he has acquired it illegally. This attitude is very prevalent here.

SUMMARY

These then are some of the effects of life in Coal Town. They are the various ways of looking at the world which have been internalized in the personalities of Coal Town people. While the events in Coal Town history have had their many dramatic aspects, the most significant and lasting remnant is the way of life which now characterizes its population. The casual visitor who comes to Coal Town would not necessarily be aware of the kinds of values we have analyzed in this study. Since our analysis has tried to capture human interaction at the deeper levels of organization, the visitor who is unwilling to go through the process of inquiry as the investigators have can easily be misled in assuming that a deeper inner life and ethos is not present. On the other hand, the reader should note that although we have focused on certain malignant trends, we recognize the existence of constructive forces among our Coal Town people. Many are warm, empathic human beings who represent counter trends to the values emphasized in the present study. But their way of life is, in our opinion, an exception to the broader undercurrents which pervade life in the community.

It is also our belief, and we recognize the controversial nature of the statement, that inquiries such as ours lead not only to an understanding of a single American community but provide certain leads which offer insights for the understanding of other sections of contemporary American life. This possibility is especially present when efforts are made to discern the implications of sociological phenomena at the local level for processes which characterize social organization in the broader setting. The writer has considered the inevitable dangers in generalizing about life in the small community as compared to life in the larger setting. Nevertheless, if we synthesize the basic themes which emerge in Coal Town, we note that a number of these are synonymous with cultural themes present in other contemporary American communities. Indeed, upon further inspection we observe that none of the basic views presented are unique to Coal Town or any single American community.

Usually the social scientist concerned with the themes of *impersonality, self-effacement, humor, rumors, separation* and *isolation, conformity, resignation,* and *anti-intellectualism* tends to restrict the prevalence of some of these themes to particular locales in our society. For example, we have described our Coal Town people as impersonal, and if one thinks of the large urban community as characterizing impersonality, our statement appears confusing. Nevertheless, it is our belief that the basic patterns of impersonality are seen only in their grossest forms in the urban setting. At the deeper levels of social interaction they pervade our time and much of our society.[4]

With respect to our discussion of the patterns of self-effacement, we note that tendencies toward feelings of inadequacy and the berating of others are commonplace today. The high incidence of mental illness, the tensions and striving in our social order, clearly suggest the magnitude of this problem. Furthermore, that many of us are a lonely, often isolated people, mobile and marginal, without roots or belonging, is a crisis not only for our own society but a crisis for modern civilization in its predicament of moral dilemma and turmoil. In the analysis of tendencies toward crime and corrup-

[4] The writer acknowledges the Redfield formulation of the industrialized small community as being differentiated from nonindustrialized small communities.

tion in places of public office in America, we recognize patterns which currently plague local communities as well as the national government.

Finally, we note that the present trends toward anti-intellectualism, conformity, and the inability to accept differences have been subjects of much concern for American social scientists. The last trend is especially significant for modern social organization since the survival of democratic society may well depend on our ability not only to accept differences at several levels but equally on our capacity to integrate differences in ways which enrich our way of life. The difficulties which Coal Town people have had in accepting differences (both native and immigrant) are not peculiar to any single community. It is our belief that this theme, along with other themes discussed in this chapter, is part and parcel of life in many American communities at this moment in our history. Nurtured at the community level out of the fabric which creates social organization, these themes represent certain segments of human culture. As such they must be reckoned with as realities, along with all their implications for the democratic social process. This is especially a necessity if we as a people are to shape our destiny in accordance with the principles of human dignity we espouse.

ASPECTS OF METHODOLOGY

Appendix A contains the following sections: Frames of Reference, Newspaper Analysis, Public Records, the Sample, and Informant Typology.

FRAMES OF REFERENCE

The listing below is illustrative of some of the ways the various disciplines were utilized and integrated.

ANALYSIS OF COAL TOWN DATA: UTILIZATION OF METHOD AND FRAME OF REFERENCE

History

Method of Collecting Data
1. Collection of data through historical sources, newspapers, census materials, public records, and personal diaries

Analytical Frame of Reference
1. Analysis of antecedents, consequents, and time perspective

Sociology

Method of Collecting Data
1. Schedules
2. Sampling procedures
3. Social survey

Analytical Frame of Reference
1. Analysis of social interaction, institutional development, social structure, group and value differences, cultural heritage

Social Psychology

Method of Collecting Data
1. Depth interview
2. Observation of small-group interaction in unstructured milieu

Analytical Frame of Reference
1. Analysis of socialization process, interaction of individual and group, emergence of personality

ANALYSIS OF COAL TOWN DATA: UTILIZATION OF
METHOD AND FRAME OF REFERENCE (*continued*)

Psychology

Method of Collecting Data
1. None distinctly psychological

Analytical Frame of Reference
1. Analysis of internal organization of learning

Anthropology

Method of Collecting Data
1. None distinctly anthropological

Analytical Frame of Reference
1. Analysis of community life holistically, in light of interrelationships of culture patterns and institutions

NEWSPAPER ANALYSIS

Community analysis which involves a time sequence must rely on whatever historical accounts are available for examination. The writer in this instance was particularly fortunate in securing from the surviving editor a copy of almost every Coal Town *Weekly* from 1919 to the end of publication in 1953. Coal Town *Weekly* was, with the exception of one three-year period, the only newspaper published in the community. Two other newspapers started but failed within a two-year period. Newspapers were systematically analyzed and abstracted by initially inspecting the contents; then a schedule was set up to abstract the contents. We recorded our findings on I.B.M. cards and these were analyzed and evaluated. Below is a list of the items covered in the schedule.

NEWSPAPER SCHEDULE ANALYSIS
Date Issues Missing

I. DEATHS
Murders in Coal Town community: Number
Name type of persons reported involved: Native American Foreign
Indictments per month: Number returned Number not returned
Convictions per month: Convicted Not convicted
Missing persons: Number

II. FIGHTING AND DISORDERLY CONDUCT
Fighting and drunkenness
Name type of persons reported involved: Native American   For-
eign
Convictions per month: Convicted   Not convicted

III. PROSTITUTION
Number of persons reported involved
Name type: Native American   Foreign

IV. THEFT AND ROBBERY
Business   Home   Person
Name type of persons reported involved: Native American
Foreign

V. RAPE
Number

VI. CORRUPTION
Bribing public officials
Evidence of illegal sale or manufacture of liquor: Number
Labor unions

VII. FRAUD
Business   Banking   Local government   Election   Personal

VII. POLITICAL PLATFORMS
Types of statements

IX. MARRIAGE ANNOUNCEMENTS AND MARRIAGES
Number of marriages of persons from Coal Town: Conventional   Intermarriage

X. DIVORCE
Number of divorces: Conventional   Intercultural
Grounds: Mental cruelty   Desertion   Alcoholism   Miscella-
neous

XI. NEWS COVERAGE
Percent of news space devoted to: Coal Town community   Regional   National   International

XII. TYPES OF NEWS COVERAGE OUTSIDE OF COAL TOWN COMMUNITY
Percent of space devoted to: Violence   Politics   War   Other

XIII. MENTAL ILLNESS
Indications of hospitalization: Number
Hospitalization: Male   Female
Occupation: Professional and business   Worker   Housewife
Clerical   Other

XIV. SUICIDE
Number:Male   Female
Method of suicide: Firearms   Poison   Hanging   Other
(what?)
Occupation: Professional and business   Worker   Housewife
Clerical   Other

XV. CHURCH NEWS AND NUMBER OF ANNOUNCEMENTS
Northern Evangelicals   Southern Evangelicals   Methodist
Catholic   Christian   Episcopal   Nazarene   Other
(what?)
Type of announcements: Number   Service announcements
Emotional, back-to-God announcements   Social announce-
ments

XVI. INDEX OF REFORM MOVEMENTS
Organized groups   Individual pronouncements   Political platforms

XVII. EXPRESSIONS OF COMMUNITY FAITH
Newspaper statements and editorials

XVIII. ECONOMIC
Prosperity: Business pronouncements   Employment statements
Bank statements   Other
Decline: Business pronouncements   Employment statements
Delinquent tax announcements   Other

XIX. MINING DISPUTES
Conflict regarding: Pay   Hours of work   Working conditions
Unionization   Technological unemployment   Other
Intra-union conflict—conflict regarding:Struggle   for   power
Other
Inter-union conflict: Struggle for power

XX. ADVERTISEMENTS
Number: Cosmetics   Patent medicine   Clothing   Coal
Town news   Household appliances   Female difficulty
Other
Basis of appeal: Sex or romance   Security   Imitation   Com-
forts of living   Curiosity   Mastery over others   Physical
comforts   Personal hygiene   Other

XXI. SOCIAL EVENTS
Number of announcements: Women's club meetings   Fraternal orders (Nonethnic)   Ethnic fraternal orders   Civic club
activities

Visiting: Out-of-town visitors   Coal Town residents visiting
Social entertaining

XXII. NUMBER OF ARTICLES CONCERNED WITH ETHNIC PEOPLE
Italian   Greek   Bulgarian   Yugoslavian   Polish   Other
(what?)

XXIII. OUTSIDE ENTERTAINMENT
Number of articles: Speakers on topics of national political-
economic concern   Musical, dramatic, artistic events   Information and enlightenment

XXIV. MOVIES
Type of film: Western   Gangster   Love-romance   Comedy

XXV. KU KLUX KLAN
Number of articles
Type of article: Anti-Negro   Anti-foreign   Anti-liquor   Anti-
Catholic

XXVI. EVIDENCES OF PHYSICAL COMMUNITY DEVELOPMENT
Roads and streets   Railroads   Utilities   Construction of
businesses and houses

XXVII. THE AGED (SIXTY-FIVE AND OVER)
Number of articles dealing with aged
Content: Church   Politics   Social (clubs and organizations)
Other (list)

Commentary on Coal Town Weekly as a Source of Data.[1] Coal
Town *Weekly* was sensitive to selected segments of life in the community. It described:

1. Social events, celebrations
2. Criminal activity, fraud, corruption
3. Bootlegging
4. Current fads in clothing, buying, selling
5. Church activities and services
6. Social clubs
7. Economic difficulties
8. Union activities
9. Politics
10. Marriages, divorces, births, deaths

[1] Certain portions of the material in this section have been published in Herman R. Lantz and J. S. McCrary, "Use of Local Press in Historical Research,"
Mid-America (July, 1956), pp. 173–79.

Nevertheless, Coal Town *Weekly* was completely unreliable as a record of the extent of any of the above activities. Thus it afforded us a limited, superficial view of life in the community. As we proceeded in our analysis we became increasingly convinced that the newspaper was never able to penetrate the basic fabric of community life, the feelings and the struggles of the people. It operated always at the periphery of social life and possessed no systematic procedure for the gathering of news items. Whether this is usually the case with a small-town weekly or whether this was unique to Coal Town we cannot say with certainty. Nevertheless, it raised many questions for us with respect to the usefulness of the newspaper as a research tool.

With respect to Coal Town *Weekly* we acquired the following information which gave us some perspective on the nature and character of the news. The newspaper never possessed a secure economic base. Its circulation was limited and tenuous. Presentation of issues or taking sides on issues could mean a drop in circulation. As one resident of Coal Town stated:

See, if you get too many people mad at you in this small community, they won't take your paper, and when they won't take your paper, you can't make a living.

Physical reprisal for the expression of differences of opinion was a frequent occurrence and this intimidated many citizens of Coal Town, including its newspaper editor. All of this meant that many significant items of news were consciously or inadvertently omitted. Much of the space was devoted to "filler columns," sometimes called "canned news." A good deal of the daily news about occurrences in the community and surrounding areas was derived from newspapers outside the community. Much of the news was obviously biased to picture the community as being better than it was and to remove responsibility from local citizens for community difficulties. Perhaps the most fantastic illustration of the former was an effort to picture Coal Town as a health resort for ill people. This when the physical environment was hot and humid, water and sewerage of questionable health standards, and the social climate replete with hostility and violence. The following excerpt was taken from Coal Town *Weekly,* Friday, September 22, 1922:

A HEALTH RESORT

Few people realize that this city is making a record as a health resort that is equalled by few cities of its size. According to the reports reaching the *Coal Town Weekly* there has been only two deaths in this city within the past eighty days. One of these Saturday night was caused by a shooting following the love of two men for one woman, leaving only one death from sickness and this an infant.

There are few cities of over 5,000 population that can boast of a record of this kind.

The city being new in its growth is mostly made up of people of middle age or under who have come here to live within the past four years. It has the flower of manhood and womanhood in this part of the state.

The city administration assisted by *Coal Town Weekly* organized the annual cleanup day which has met with hearty co-operation on the part of the public. Rubbish and tin cans have been removed from the city. The breeding places of flies and filth have been destroyed and causes for disease have been removed. While the city needs considerable more cleaning up, the condition is much better than it was a short time ago.

Another movement to lower the death rate of the city was when the mayor, the City Council and legal department of the city put a ban on the carrying of guns within the city. The arrests became so frequent and the fines so heavy that the carrying of a gun became unpopular. No more pernicious firing of guns and killings as the result of minor quarrels have occurred for months. While there have been three shootings one of which was fatal within the past three months neither of these was caused by drunken brawls, and death from this cause has emphatically been eliminated.

An examination of records suggested that the statistics regarding deaths were completely unreliable and that efforts to remove unsanitary conditions were exaggerated.

Our interviews revealed that many of the citizens of Coal Town were displeased with the quality and editorship of Coal Town *Weekly*. One feels that they might have responded to a better newspaper had it been available. Their comments ranged from mild amusement to deep hostility. An employed coal miner stated:

I can't say that I read the Coal Town newspaper. There wasn't much to it. You see, we have never had a very good newspaper here, and you could never tell whether or not there was any truth in the paper or not.

A barber of Coal Town made the following comment:

The paper here doesn't give a true picture of the community. The trouble was that you couldn't read the damn paper. There wasn't any truth in the paper. You see, the editor worked for his own interest. It wasn't a good newspaper at all. You see, people don't tell the newspaper reporter everything because it wouldn't be too good.

The most outspoken, aggressively hostile statement regarding the Coal Town *Weekly* was made by a leading merchant who had this to say:

You dare to sit there and ask me what type of newspaper and what type of editor we have here. We have never had an editor and we have never had a newspaper. I do not spend any money advertising in a newspaper. Why, I spent about a hundred or a hundred fifty dollars a week advertising over the radio. That is the advanced thing to do. Bah, we have never had a newspaper. That editor was so lazy that he sat on his fat ass and got the news from the other newspapers in the county. That makes me mad.

PUBLIC RECORDS

In addition to newspaper analysis, public records dealing with marriage, divorce, crime, births, death (including cause), and mental illness were gathered and analyzed.[2]

Although it is at best difficult to assess the accuracy of public records, we can in this instance report that the records revealed only the grossest trends. As the description of Coal Town has undoubtedly made clear to the reader, the orderly processes of government and the collection, as well as the maintenance, of public records were not of immediate concern or interest to the citizens of Coal Town. Characteristic of the entire area was the tendency for records to become subject to the personal and political whims of those in control. Such indifference to records, most apparent in statistics dealing with crime, was present in regard to other trends. For considerable periods of time arrests were conducted in a haphazard fashion. At one stage in the history of Coal Town it was necessary for court costs to be paid before an arrest could be made. This condition was dictated by the behavior of citizens who were reluctant to follow through on complaints and by police officials

[2] *Ibid.*

who were somewhat ambivalent about law enforcement. One informant had this to say by way of explanation:

This notion about plunking down court costs, I think, can be explained very easily. It was a policy merely because neighbors would become angry with each other and would call up the police and say, "Come and arrest my neighbor because he is bothering me." The police would come up and charge the neighbor and then you had in the meantime lost interest or had ducked out or ran away and you wouldn't prefer any charges against your neighbor so that left the police holding the bag. They finally had to be sure that you were serious about bringing charges against someone before they would act. In other words, you had to put down the money and this indicated that you were serious enough about bringing charges.

THE SAMPLE

Our sample consisted of 250 Coal Town residents, representing about 110 families, ranging in age from sixteen to ninety-one, although the majority of persons came from the upper age brackets. Since we were interested in obtaining a developmental account of Coal Town it was necessary to construct our sample from those persons who had lived during the crucial developmental stages. We therefore derived our sample from persons who had moved to Coal Town during the following periods:

Period I   (1904–16)   Community Origins
Period II   (1916–29)   The Prosperous Period
Period III (1929–Present)   The Period of Decline

We were able to interview successfully the following sample from these periods:

Period I   (1904–16)   40 (90 percent of residents still living in
                               community)
Period II   (1916–29)   115 (60 percent of residents still living in
                               community)
Period III (1929–Present)   70 (50 percent of residents still living in
                               community)
                            25 (Old-time residents from surrounding
                               area)

Total 250

Our sample was 70 percent male and 30 percent female. The majority of men interviewed were coal miners employed in all phases of the industry. The women interviewed were housewives. All businessmen and ministers were contacted and interviewed. The sample was evenly divided between native and immigrant informants.

Detailed information regarding this sample may be obtained by writing the author. Representativeness regarding categories of religion, economic position, cultural background, and age were considered in the construction of the sample.

INFORMANT TYPOLOGY

On the basis of our interviewing experience a typology emerged into which informants could be placed. Although overlappings between categories were found, over 80 percent of our informants could be placed in the categories listed below.

A. Intellectually honest and insightful. Here we have a category of persons who appeared to report events as they witnessed them. There was an absence of hedging and evasion with respect to the questions asked. Further, their observations suggested considerable awareness and sensitivity to community processes.

The following statement reveals the awareness of the informant to the value placed on violence and its subsequent incorporation into personality organization:

Growing up in this community, some kids would get all warped. They lost all sense of good manners. They got some cynical attitudes. They would see people do violence, and in the schools we used to have the roughest school systems in any part of the state. Discipline was bad. I can remember that one time we had a woman principal and the kids grabbed her and threw her against a wall. Well, there was a principal, a man, who came in here. He used to bodily throw the boys down the stairs. I know that I was very afraid of him personally. I think all of this violence was merely a reflection of what was going on in the over-all community.

We were struck by the presence of inertia during our research activities. One informant had this to say:

There is a great deal of inertia in this area. The fellow runs up against this time after time and he tries to do something and he doesn't succeed and he just gives up. It becomes inertia. I can give you one example in which a revivalist came into the community here and he tried to get fifteen members to come to the church and he went around and saw quite a few people and finally got the promises of the people to show up at the meeting, and then when the time for the meeting came, two persons showed up and he was one of them. He was quite amazed at this and I told him that I was not amazed at all but that what I was amazed about was that he himself had returned. Well, you can see here what's involved.

B. Intellectually honest and uninsightful. Here we have a category of persons much like the above, but they revealed a lack of sensitivity and awareness regarding the deeper levels of community life. They appeared to live at the periphery of life with considerable isolation and insulation from others. These people "went through the paces," yet were not part of community life. There was no apparent effort to evade questions but their responses indicated a lack of sensitivity to life around them.

Mr. B. was asked whether he believed the mining company was interested in the community and the miner. In the following excerpt the informant reveals an amazing lack of awareness of objective criteria which one might employ in answering such a question. Instead of referring to the possible efforts of the employers to improve wages, working conditions, and community conditions, he states:

I think that the Company is concerned about the community today and that it has always been concerned. Why, for example, Basil used to give big picnics free for the miners. I can remember the second Fourth of July that I was here. We had a big picnic down at the cemetery and everything was free, free eats and free drinks. I think that that shows that the Company was really interested in the miner.

C. Intellectually dishonest and insightful. Persons in this category appeared consciously to distort, deny, and at times cover up significant facts regarding life in the community. At times distortion would take the form of exaggerating events, at other times it would become manifest in attempts to minimize. They generally demonstrated an uncanny ability to deny the most obvious developments of community life whenever they felt that such disclosure might reflect on them or the community. These informants could quickly recognize significant community processes, but were able to minimize their significance. The pattern was so characteristic that we could detect almost immediately when we were dealing with this type of informant. For example, these informants never pursued a question and were satisfied to give brief noncommittal answers. Often they kept defensively referring the researcher to other informants who might be more helpful. In conversation we could expect the following remarks:

1. "I'm sure I couldn't tell you anything you haven't already heard."

2. "This community is no different from any other."

3. In answer to a specific question, for example, "Do people visit much around here?" the reply, "Just like any other town."

In some instances informants in this category would never answer the question, but would instead move directly to material which was unrelated and diversionary. The following informant illustrates this tendency. In answer to specific questions about foreigners and natives, Mrs. T., of foreign parentage, stated:

I don't know much about these foreigners and the natives. I think that people have quit neighboring now more than they used to. Many of the women here work at the present time. It has been like this, I guess, for about ten years. I don't think that a woman has to stay in the home and I guess working is all right. You see, all of my girls have worked. The woman is going to step out whether she works or not and I don't think it makes any difference as to whether or not she works. You see, if a woman is at home and wanted to step out, she could too.

In answer to a question concerned with family rule, the same informant stated:

I don't know in my own family whether the man or the woman is the boss. I know that there is not any boss now. It seems as if the young people can get along without a boss. It's not like it used to be. I think that the kids are much smarter now and are able to work out their problems much better than we did when my husband and I were married.

THE EARLY UPPER-CLASS RESIDENTS
OF THE AREA

IN addition to the majority of migrants described in Chapter
2, there was a small group of educated, well-informed persons who
were socially and economically secure. Many of these persons possessed some wealth and migrated because of an interest in changing their class position. They believed that this might be accomplished by moving to a frontier settlement.

The following autobiographical statement suggests that ownership of property among these people took precedence over monetary possessions in their prestige hierarchy:

My father craved land because that was what had given the better
families of the South their standing. In his boyhood, it was an honor to
own plantations and the old-established places gave social prestige that
mere money did not. He wanted this to pass on to his children.

This small group spearheaded the changes which occurred in the
county and they were responsible for what little enlightment the
county possessed. They were instrumental in fostering an educational
system and for organizing a denominational college in 1874. The
expressions and opinions of this group were manifest in the Hartdale
Standard, a newspaper which was in existence for over one hundred
years. The writer inspected a random number of copies from the
1850s and the 1860s and was impressed by the grammatical style,
vocabulary, and general presentation of issues. It was apparant that
such a paper was written for a highly literate population. Typical
of the editions we inspected was a "Poet's Corner" with published
poems on page one. Page two generally included informative discussions dealing with the national issues of the period, page three

with area news, and page four with advertisements. In view of the high rate of illiteracy and general diffidence on the part of the frontier populace, the existence of such a newspaper constituted a bulwark against perpetuated ignorance.

In the excerpt below, concerned with the death of members of a well-known family, the reader will note the literary quality of the Hartdale *Standard;* the selection is from the issue of April 3, 1855.

Whereas it has pleased Almighty God to call to himself within the last few weeks, both the infant son and wife of our worthy brother ———, both of whom died at the residence in Hartdale. The latter on Tuesday, the 13th of March last and the twenty-third year of her age. The former on the 24th of February first last, thus adding additional shades to the dark gloom with which the busy Hand of Death has already enshrouded our town. Resolve, that these melancholy events, demand of us a pause for our own sake and not for our own sake merely but that we may do what we can amidst these afflictive dispensations, pay respectful tokens of sympathy.

An attempt to interest the more literate individual in a book on courtship, sex, and marriage is described below, from the Hartdale *Standard* of May 2, 1856.

It teaches how to make love, it teaches every eye to form a beauty of its own, it teaches how to act when fascinated by a lady, a lecture on love for a private advice to married ladies and gentlemen. This is the most fascinating, interesting and rather useful and practical work in courtship, matrimony, and the duties and delights of married life.

Members of this social class followed in so far as possible their own cultural practices with respect to their personal and familial lives. The primitiveness of the frontier, however, tended to reduce the life of the elite to the life of the masses.

APPENDIX C

ATTITUDES OF NATIVE FARMERS TOWARD
COAL MINING

THE native farmers of the Coal Town region had mixed feelings about the mining of coal and the growth of the community.
They welcomed the economic opportunities which mining brought
with it. The wage scale for unskilled mining work was far superior
to anything available in the agricultural economy of the day.
Furthermore, the increased demand for food, clothing, and the material essentials of living had its effects in all branches of business
and gave the impression that "good times" would last forever. Such
conditions had considerable appeal for persons who had been reared
in an impoverished agricultural economy. Our native informants put
it this way:

We settlers, I think, felt that it was going to be a good thing that coal
was discovered here in our community, because we thought that we
would get something out of it. There was nothing here but worn-out land.
You couldn't raise any crops on it and we thought that the coal meant a
boom, and this meant work and employment.

Coal mining helped things out a lot. That is what brought most of the
people to this here area. We were glad to have the coal because we were
glad to have the money that was coming from it. It let many of us
farmers get a job at the mines and farm too. In fact, practically all the
small farmers worked at the mines at some time.

In spite of the improved economic opportunities, many natives
were fearful about working underground in coal pits. The nature
of the work and the physical surroundings were different, strange,
and frightening. Many of the natives so employed reported nervous-
ness and apprehension about working underground. There were

those who eventually adjusted to the occupation, but many others either left mining completely or obtained positions which enabled them to work aboveground.

The natives were not really attracted to the coal mines. The farmers were afraid to go underground so the Company was forced to import laborers. My father hated working in them mines. He used to say, "I never lost nothing in them mines and I ain't goin' down to find it." Many farmers resented Coal Town and became envious of its prosperity. They hated them foreigners making that money but they were afraid to get into coal mining.

I worked in the coal mines for a while but I never did like it. I always got scared so I quit. I never did like the idea of working under the ground. You could get all rolled up and mashed to pieces. I got rolled up but there was no bones broke. I got out and stayed out.

My folks wouldn't work in the mines. I wouldn't want them to. We had a neighbor boy who was killed there. I said I didn't raise my boy to go into them mines.

APPENDIX **D**

AUTOBIOGRAPHY

MUCH of what has already been described is rather well summarized in the following brief autobiography written for use in this study by a self-educated miner, himself the son of an immigrant miner. We have decided to present his views without interruption and wish, at this point, simply to make a few brief comments regarding certain phases of the writing to follow. We believe that this autobiography is sensitive to the following important areas: the personal reactions of a child to the physical environment, the experience of discrimination and prejudice, and the reactions of the son of an immigrant to other immigrants and natives.

MY LIFE IN COAL TOWN

(Written by the Son of an Immigrant Miner)

My earliest recollection of forty-odd years in this coal field goes back to about the age of three. It was with a mixed feeling of terror and fascination that I stood clutching my eldest sister's hand and watched a steam-powered threshing machine shuddering and clattering along the black, dusty roadway that traversed the coal camp. Its shrieking whistle and the cries of the motley escorting caravan of urchins gathered enroute had heralded its approach. "Trash machine! Trash machine!" was the excited cry.

This event was something quite symbolic. This was in the age of steam, boom time in the coal fields, where hordes of workmen were needed. The trash machine was symbolic of the grimy, black, mysterious mine on the hill, which I could see and hear and whose terrors our elders defied daily to win our bread. It was the biggest thing in my early life and I developed a peculiar fascination for it and came to idolize the men who braved its mysterious depths. In this, I am sure I was not alone. It represented a high adventure to which we hoped to attain. The clatter and roar of the shakers, the chuffing of the hoisting engine, the deep-throated steam whistle were native sounds.

The trash machine was also symbolic of the rural surroundings of the cosmopolitan camp, which I also grew fond of and which strongly affected my ideals in those formative years. What remained of the farm which the camp had usurped lay just across the road. There was the old well under the elms in the pasture, the apple orchard behind the house, the broad farmhouse veranda, the oak-shaded lawn, the bright array of summer flowers. It was a dream-like contrast to our barren, treeless yards and drab houses, in what would rightly be termed "Company Row." But coal miners boarded at the farmhouse then; strange, native-speaking men that I knew in only the most vague and distant way.

My sister's presence in that first recollection was characteristic, too. It was part of the pattern of life in the large families for the older children to take charge of the youngest ones. But my older brothers roamed too far afield for me to follow them, yet.

The caravan of urchins bespoke the heterogeneous nature of the camp's populace. Their cry of "Trash machine," I suspect, may have been a pidgin English term, born among children of immigrants, who had not yet fully mastered the native language.

I am not a native of this coal field, but native to coal mining, in an area where Slavic immigrants were not newcomers, but rather commonplace and accepted. My early environment was my own back yard and those of my Slavic neighbors on either side and beyond, who also spoke our language. Though the children of those large families spoke English, except with the parents, Slavic custom, habit, and association predominated.

Most of the men who visited my father spoke his native language. I remember them as big, powerful, coarse men, handsome and mustached, and early associated the smell of tobacco and liquor with their presence. Their opposite feminine numbers invariably talked over coffee, volubly, expressively, with animated gestures.

I remember a festive occasion when many of these men gathered in our back yard on a summer evening, to celebrate. The occasion, I learned later, was the establishment of a lodge in the town, of which our camp was a sort of suburban appendage. Beer drinking and singing went on far into the night.

Following that, lodge picnics and other affairs uptown, to which my father took me and a younger brother, were a beautiful adventure. Here too, the Slavic atmosphere completely surrounded us.

I remember with what solicitous concern all the older boys accompanied a neighbor to the train when he was called into war service. I also remember with what concern his mother sheltered me and a brother and sister the cold frosty morning my beshawled and anxious mother hurried up the frozen road toward the mine, to look for my father, after the mine whistle's frantic cry of disaster had struck terror into every heart in the camp. Such event bespoke the clannishness of these immigrants as well as the comradeship the hazards of their jobs bred into all the miners.

I pushed out of my narrow Slavic environment at an early age. I explored the farm across the road, searched the orchard for windfalls, and pilfered gooseberries from the farm garden without incurring the wrath of the owners. I ventured out to play with the Polish boys who lived in the "back row," where I usually wasn't permitted to stray, because the shiftless, drinking, brawling Tennesseans were always moving in and out there.

But some of the Tennessee boys did become my early part-time playmates; particularly the storekeeper's sons. I was enticed there by goodies they pilfered from the store. I found little in common with them. They spoke a language almost alien to the jargon of the camp. Terms like "drekly, mightnigh, hit air," were strange to me then. Despite the barren circumstances of my own home, I was surprised at their unclean habits and surroundings. I was cautioned to shun these people, by my elders, because of that and their obstreperous ways.

I learned that the boarders across the road were quite friendly and liked to tease me, especially about my foreign background, language, and name and, no less, about my natural curiosity about everything.

I remember I liked the fat, red-faced native mule driver who let me ride with him on the "dump wagon" that surfaced the camp road with mine refuse. Then there was the affable native brother of the landlord, who on occasion used to load his small truck full of camp children and haul them to school uptown.

As a child I remember the almost untouchable natives uptown and the landlord, I didn't like at that time. He came to collect the rent, smelling of whiskey, and seemed overly loud, overbearing, and oversolicitous of my father's goodwill, but the latter in a superior, master-to-servant manner, like a man talking to a child. He just didn't ring true.

The first clean break away from the home circle was my first day at school. It was with a heavy heart and heavier feet that I trudged that first mile, clutching my sister's hand. At the end of the journey stood the huge two-story brick building, its grounds swarming with strange children. I didn't like it, but I was trained to obey and took my assigned place without any undue urging. After that it was only a matter of days until I again felt master of the situation and was eager to go it alone.

My first teacher discovered that I not only could read my entire first reader, but recite it verbatim. She seemed as proud of the discovery as I was to please her and she put me on exhibition before older classes. But this was the last bit of favor I was to savour for five more years. Although I maintained the family's reputation for scholastic excellence, as well as the boys' for deviltry, I was seldom permitted to forget for very long that I was from the wrong side of the tracks. This bred an affinity for like personalities from the camps and I began to act the part. School curriculum became increasingly boring, except in the subjects which I had a natural liking for. These I took in stride. I feel certain that like reactions to similar circumstances sent many of my brilliant fellow students to the mines at an early age, instead of on to better things.

Prejudice was unmasked to me in the third grade. I'd worn my

Sunday coat on Monday and lost a prayer book from it. The teacher held it up before the class for all to see and called for the owner; a little mockingly, it seemed to me. I stepped bashfully forward to claim it. Somewhere I had already had it impressed upon me that Catholics didn't exactly belong. A girl snickered at me as I passed back to my seat. Just outside the school door, a native boy from uptown had the temerity to call me a Catlikker. I threw him to the ground and fairly stomped him for it. I was soundly paddled by the school principal for this act of brutality and strongly resented the seeming injustice of it. Mostly because my tormentor went scot-free.

On a similar incident in my fifth year at school, a teacher endeared herself to me by taking my tormentor to task. But another teacher, that same year, whom I tried hard to please, held me in ill-concealed contempt. He accused me of copying a map, in the face of an eyewitness's denial, because, "You can't draw that good."

In the camp and in town and around, my older brothers first led me afield, protected me, and showed me the ropes, as it were. They were tough and respected by the toughest. I quickly slipped into the pattern and as quickly learned to go it on my own. I learned to smoke and chew and do other things that supposedly tough characters did to prove themselves; not so much for that reason as to be one of the gang.

My youngest brother and I were very much together. As our horizons grew, the camp, the mine yard, the slag dump, the mine pond and its wooded shore became our playground. Before our teens we were taken in tow by older boys, became leaders of a sort ourselves among the younger members of the heterogeneous pack.

There were few chores at home, other than garden work. Our chief responsibility was to keep the household in salvage coal and kindling gathered from the mine dumps, the yards, and the empty coal cars. There were berries to pick in summer and nuts in the fall. The mine pond abounded in mudcats. But it was not all play. Some of it was hard work. Pulling home tons of coal sporadically the year around in a little hand-drawn wagon, was the most tiring and boresome task.

The hoot of a switch engine in the mine switchyard was the signal to "go walk the empties" in search of salvage. One such trip we jogged barefooted along the dusty road, capping our bald heads enroute.[1] A flying rock kicked up the dust at our feet and a voice shouted, "Ichi doma, you danged hunkies!" The answer was another rock directed at the two faces grinning from behind a corner of the nearest house.

Even the natives and Tennesseans tried to master a few foreign phrases, as did the immigrant children with each other's languages; mainly curses and epithets. The above quoted phrase was a pidgin form of the Slavic term meaning "Go home."

Our boyhood companions included the gamut of the camp's populace, racially. But Italians and Croats predominated. We were nowise selective, except to the extent that immigrants' boys naturally had most in common and a companion of one's own race was closer yet. But even that was not a hard and fast rule.

The various styles and kinds of food enjoyed or favored by the different groups was the subject of much criticism and even contempt. The Italian was labeled a "garlic snapper" by the natives, whose weakness for sweets, pastries, and biscuits was made contemptible in return. Slavs and Italians had much in common, especially "palenta," a soggy corn meal creation which the natives called "johnnycake" when they saw it. Although I never knew one to partake of the delicacy, we Slavs used to rib the Italians about eating cats and were ribbed in turn for our fondness for kraut.

The French and Belgians, though not alone in it, may have been dubbed "frogs" as much for their fondness for that delicacy as their "bullfrog" way of talking.

I found most Italian dishes too highly seasoned. Our fare was coarser and plainer. I had no liking for native-baked corn bread and never tasted a native-style biscuit until after I married. I've since come to appreciate both.

[1] Being cut bald-headed, a common practice among immigrants, was a precaution against dirt and especially lice and other vermin, as well as the quickest and cheapest way of getting a haircut. The presence of lice meant a full-strength kerosene treatment followed by a lye soap shampoo—to be repeated as often as necessary.

The English, Scottish, and Irish—the latter were rare, except as crosses of one of the other two—seemed most sociable, both youths and adults. But the English seemed most compromising. They seemed boastful and were the butt of many jokes and jibes. "Johnny-bulls" we called them and my father, if he betrayed any real prejudice, it was against these and the Tennesseans. But even so, he held certain individuals among them in high regard. At the mine and in the union they, the English, were pushers and connivers for offices and supervisory jobs and easier berths. Yet I never felt unkindly disposed toward any of them that I knew. I even liked their accent, which was made much sport of and aped in jest.

The French I knew seemed the least prejudiced people of all and perhaps the most socially minded. They seemed conservative to a fault, but seemed most generous toward anyone in distress, even strangers, without regard to nationality.

Despite close associations with Italians boys and familiarity with Italians in general, I seldom experienced any feeling of belonging when in their homes, or isolated among them. I felt certain they regarded Slavs generally as inferior, referring to all of us as "some kind of Polacks," without distinction. For this and other reasons some seemed to us to be a little stupid, but in the main mutual respect was the rule, especially as regards my father, who spoke their language fluently.

We were cognizant of their sedulousness, integrity, and general competence, but also of their adept patronizing and disregard of some scruples, which may account for many of them having fared so much better than the average Slav. Their families were usually smaller too. Most of them were not particularly religious-minded. The same applied to perhaps a majority of the camp people. The Slavs were probably the most naive and gullible and, perhaps as a consequence, the most exploited.

I early learned to like or dislike people as individuals and to make allowances for their seeming shortcomings, perhaps in apology for my own. In any group I found some I liked and others I did not and could never seem to be able to fit any of my prejudices or preferences to any one entire group. Even among the farthest removed, the Tennesseans, I found some very interesting and very likeable. I also found myself the butt of jibes from nonreligious Italians as well as others and observed that we were, as a group, as prejudiced against Protestants as they were against us. We attended brush harbor and tent revivals for sport and "Let's go watch the Holy Rollers," was often a common rallying call.

On the school grounds, uptown and in other towns, as we grew older and pushed farther afield, with increased family income and the advent of autos, the same patterns applied generally in a broader sense. Our most intimate friendships were usually with our own kind. The same rule applied equally to serious boy-girl relationships. But by this time old racial barriers were already crumbling and the society generally becoming more homogeneous.

Sex was taboo at home. Sex education came from the older boys, picked up around the playgrounds, shows, pool halls, and not a little from the inscriptions on the walls of public toilets. It was learned more practically wherever boys and girls got together. It was made sordid and the butt of many jokes and pranks. Promiscuity was a sort of sport with young men in their late teens.

Most of us went to the mines at about age sixteen and intimate sex experience began, or sharply broadened, shortly after. But even the most promiscuous usually clung to some taboos. Boys who indulged in promiscuity themselves were often quick to defend the honor of a sister or other close female. Girls of good reputation were usually sought out for marriage, no matter the male's past experience and behavior, and those were condoned by the brothers-in-law. Marriage was serious business, usually within the nationality, or at least immigrant for immigrant, and usually for keeps; especially among immigrants.

There were no hard and fast rules, however, and here too barriers weakened and fell away. Mixed marriages became more common, but often less stable and almost certainly encountered difficulty and misunderstanding to some degree. Three of my brothers and I married across the racial barrier.

I encountered prejudice now and then all through my school days, although this was at a minimum during high school. There I found that the more enlightened teachers respected intelligence more than background and I had the added advantage of older brothers having built a good reputation ahead of me. I feel certain, however, that there was discrimination in the hiring of teachers at that time.

At the mines, where I was a late arrival, being among the youngest of my generation, there was no racial discrimination where actual mining jobs underground were concerned at the time. Any favoritism or patronage practiced crossed those lines. It did, however, appear to apply to supervisory posts. Before 1930, names of Slavic or Italian origin on the supervisory roster were few. In the miners' union those names were coming into ever-increasing prominence.

As jobs grew scarce and hardship increased, it became readily apparent that the frugal immigrants and their sons fared better than the natives of their own economic level and jealousy and prejudice increased proportionately. The common terms of dago and hunky, so long used here mainly in jest, or as a common descriptive term employed by virtually all English-speaking people at one time or another, began to take on strong invective.

When this jealousy and prejudice finally erupted into violence, as part of the bitter factional strife among the miners, which was basically a struggle for jobs, they were evidently employed as a device by the instigators and perpetrators. The old Ku Klux Klan term of "one hundred per cent American" was dusted off and given a stronger meaning than before and racial differences, which had shown every evidence of dying out if given enough time, were re-kindled. Men were compelled to carry arms to protect themselves from former school chums and mine buddies. The bitterness stirred up invaded churches and classrooms and even severed family ties in some instances. My brothers and I were held aloof from all the controversy, mainly by my father's wise counsel, but we were made victims of this bigotry and jealousy to some extent anyway. For a time I was obliged to sneak across town at night, each time by a different route, while courting a girl who was accepted as one hundred percent American though of English-Irish parentage.

The normal processes of integration were disrupted and retarded for a time and demoralization and mistrust were widespread. They are prevalent to some extent to this day.

I am often bemused by my past experiences and observations, which I have attempted to briefly outline here. I can only deplore the folly and stupidity of what I have witnessed and conclude with the observation that people are funny.

APPENDIX **E**

THE ESTABLISHMENT OF ORGANIZED
RELIGION

DURING the coal camp era (1904–14) there was little organized religious activity. The mobile population without roots, the concern with production of coal, and the tenor of life mitigated against the development of organized religious groups. Occasionally revival meetings, of interest to natives from the area, occurred. As some of the natives recalled:

This place ran for years without a church or Sunday School of any sort. The people just weren't interested in it. They were just concerned about making money.

You see, Coal Town had the name of being a rough town. There were not many people interested in religion at that time. We had a hard struggle interesting the people in religion, but we did it.

The earliest church effort to provide religious services to the community was a nondenominational church organized by a few interested Protestant natives.

The first denomination to provide organized religious services to the residents of Coal Town was the Southern Evangelical in July, 1918.[1] That this denomination should be the first is consistent with

[1] An understanding of the nature of early religious expression in the area can be obtained by reference to the following general works on the nature of Southern and Southeastern Protestant religion during the nineteenth and twentieth centuries: William W. Sweet, *The Story of Religion in America,* revised edition (New York, Harper and Brothers, 1939); William W. Sweet, *Revivalism In America* (New York, Charles Scribner's Sons, 1944); Liston Pope, *Millhands and Preachers* (New Haven, Yale University Press, 1942); Charles H. Hopkins, *The Rise of the Social Gospel in American Protestantism, 1865–1915* (New Haven, Yale University Press, 1940); George Seldes, *The*

the fact that large numbers of natives from the preindustrial era came from families reared in this tradition.

I can remember the Evangelical Church was the first church here in Coal Town. You see, when they started to mine down here you had a lot of Kentuckians came in and they were Southern Evangelicals. They were the ones that organized the Southern Evangelical. They were like the English, I guess, when one come in, he sent for the others.

The Methodist Church was also established in November, 1918, and was followed by the Catholic Church in 1919, the Christian Church in 1923, the Northern Evangelical Church in 1926, and the Episcopal Church in 1927. The Nazarene Church was established in 1938, and the Apostolic Church opened its doors to fifteen members in 1945.[2] All churches, except the Episcopal, are still providing services each week.

Stammering Century (New York, John Day Company, 1928); Elizabeth K. Nottingham, *Methodism and the Frontier* (New York, Columbia University Press, 1941).

[2] The Greek Orthodox Church is located in a neighboring community four miles from Coal Town. The Coal Town members attend services two times a year, Easter and Christmas. The members of the Greek Orthodox Church were immigrant miners from Greece and their children. There are no members of the Jewish religion in Coal Town.

INDEX